COMMUNICATION

A **SCIENTIFIC** *Book*
AMERICAN

COMMUNICATION

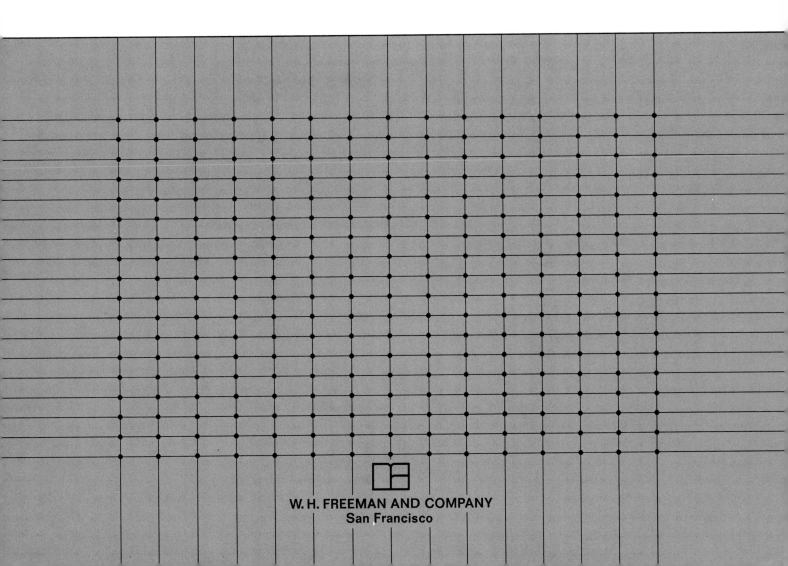

W. H. FREEMAN AND COMPANY
San Francisco

Library of Congress Cataloging in Publication Data
Main entry under title:

Communication.

    "A Scientific American book."
    "Originally appeared as articles in the September
1972 issue of Scientific American."
    Includes bibliographies.
    1. Communication.   I.   Scientific American.
P90.C627   1972   001.5   72–10100
ISBN 0–7167–0866–3
ISBN 0–7167–0865–5 (pbk)

The eleven chapters in this book originally appeared
as articles in the September 1972 issue of *Scientific
American*. Chapters 1–5 and 9–11 are available as separate
Offprints from W. H. Freeman and Company,
660 Market Street, San Francisco, California 94104.

International Standard Book Number:
0–7167–0866–3 (cloth)
0–7167–0865–5 (paper)

Printed in the United States of America

9 8 7 6 5 4 3 2 1

CONTENTS

FOREWORD

The occasion for this book—first published as a single-topic issue of *Scientific American* in September 1972—is the present crescendo in the advance of communication technology. With advances in its "software" as important as in its hardware, this technology is working profound changes in our civilization—in the way we conduct business and politics, in education, entertainment, interpersonal relations, and in the very organization of society. Increase in the sheer volume and velocity of communication is transforming the experience of life in our time. This is one of those occasions when accumulated changes in quantity add up suddenly to change in quality.

Communication is a vital function. It appeared in nature with the advent of the big molecules of life. These molecules recorded the first, chemical, events of solution. The living cell that assembled itself from these molecules raced the communication process to new levels of speed and complexity—evidenced, for example, in the elegant feedback system that switches the genes on and off in the orchestration of the biochemistry of the cell. Through the master molecules of the genes the living cell conducts the long-term information transfer, from generation to generation, of the accumulative experience of evolution.

Communication from cell to cell—by hormones and by the nerve impulse—made possible the appearance of multicelled organisms. Communication from organism to organism hastened evolution onward to the elaboration of ever higher forms of life. It facilitated the organization of organisms in social behavior that gave rise, at last, to the purposive behavior of man. That ultimate step in the evolution of life brought with it the ultimate step in the evolution of communication: the symbolic communication of language. "The first machine tool," in the words of Roman Jakobson, language is the tool that made all others.

From this background in natural history, the technology of communication itself emerges as "natural" and as the central, primary organizing technology of high civilization. That technology may be considered conveniently under three headings. There are the "channels" of communication; within the present decade the carrying capacity of the familiar person-to-person voice and picture channels will be duplicated by channels carrying data from machine to machine. At each end of a channel there is a "terminal." Symbols of the impending new epoch in our culture are the keyboard-CRT console, the videotape cassette, and the hard-copy facsimile transmitter and receiver. Between the terminals is the "network," most conveniently pictured as a computer. In the not too distant future, we will see the computer serving as a public utility—a real-time community adding machine, filing system, library, and switchboard.

The most interesting and portentous question of all is that of control. Only a few people in a few nations have had the luck to live for a little while in history in the "system of freedom of expression." The technology of communication can help extend that system to the world at large or can be the instrumentality of its extinction. It is not in the nature of the technology but in the behavior of men and institutions that the decision lies.

The editors of *Scientific American* herewith express appreciation to their colleagues at W. H. Freeman and Company, the book-publishing affiliate of the magazine, for the enterprise that has made the contents of our annual one-subject issue so speedily available in book form.

THE EDITORS*

September, 1972

*BOARD OF EDITORS: Gerard Piel (Publisher), Dennis Flanagan (Editor), Francis Bello (Associate Editor), Philip Morrison (Book Editor), Trudy E. Bell, Jonathan B. Piel, David Popoff, John Purcell, James T. Rogers, Armand Schwab, Jr., C. L. Stong, Joseph Wisnovsky

COMMUNICATION

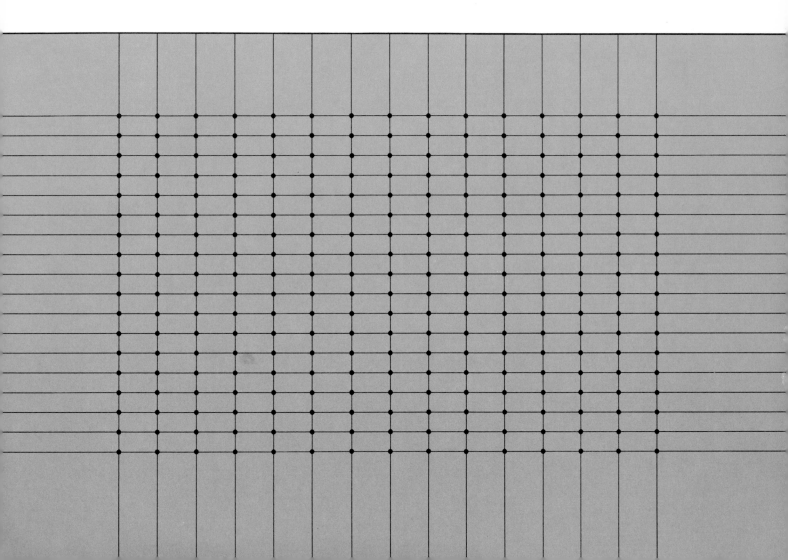

SCIENTIFIC AMERICAN

Communication

it is not only the essence of being human but also a vital
property of life. Technological advances in communication
shape society and make its members more interdependent

by John R. Pierce

Communication

JOHN R. PIERCE

*It is not the only essence of being human but also
a vital property of life. Technological advances
in communication shape society and make its
members more interdependent.*

Our existence depends on communication in more ways than one can easily enumerate. Without our initial backlog of genetic messages we would not be who we are, and without our internal communication system we could not continue to live and function as we do. Our internal communications are handled by a network with nervous and metabolic subsystems [see "Cellular Communication," by Gunther S. Stent, page 17]. Nerve impulses are like telephone calls that are switched to a particular recipient and heard nowhere else. Hormones are like messages addressed to individuals or groups but sent out broadcast; only those concerned need respond. Furthermore, certain cells in the body behave with seeming autonomy, seeking out invaders and destroying them. Indeed, the failure of these cells to destroy cancer cells has been attributed to a blockage of the mode of communication by which foreign or abnormal cells are recognized.

When we think of communication,

however, we usually think of external communication, of those processes by which we communicate with others. Without external communication we might live, but we would be ignorant, lonely individuals. We would have neither the inspiration of accumulated skill and knowledge nor the support of a society. That society, which communication makes possible, supplies us with necessities we would otherwise have to obtain for ourselves. Moreover, communication with others conveys rewards far beyond the basic necessities of life.

Animals live without knowing how they live, and they communicate without knowing how they communicate. By and large, so do we. Unlike animals, however, we speculate about how we live and how we communicate. Our better brains and our unique means of communication—language—make such speculation possible. Occasionally we learn something incontrovertible, and such knowledge can be very powerful in our lives.

Our clearest and most fruitful knowledge is not knowledge of ourselves or of how we communicate. Rather it is knowledge of various physical and chemical processes. That knowledge has enabled us to make powerful tools that have changed our lives greatly. We understand these tools far better than we understand ourselves.

In part that is because the tools are simpler than we are. A television set, a computer or even a national communication network such as the telephone system is simpler than a human being. We also understand our tools better because those tools have been built according to our understanding. It is easier to understand a computer than it is to understand art or the weather because the man who built the computer wanted to build something that would work. In order to build something that would work he had to build something he could understand.

No one man understands all the devices in a big airplane, a tall building or a telephone system, but some men have at least a working knowledge of each. That is not true of man and his means of communication. We have learned some remarkable things, but chiefly we live and communicate not through our understanding of these processes but in spite of our ignorance concerning them.

In our puzzlement about man and his communication it is natural to turn for enlightenment to the sure knowledge and deep insight that we have concern-

ONE KIND OF COMMUNICATION is print. The photograph on the facing page shows the type "form" from which the first page of text of the September 1972 issue of *Scientific American* was reproduced. The columns of type (and this caption) are set by Linotype. The headline ("Communication") is a copper photoengraving, and the subheading is type set by hand. These items and the incidental type at the top of the page are locked into position by a rectangular set of "bearers," which are beyond the margins of the picture. The complete form is used to make a nylon replica that is mounted on one cylinder of a high-speed rotary press and does the actual printing. Running at full speed, the press delivers 20,000 copies of *Scientific American* per hour. Photograph was made at The Lakeside Press. R. R. Donnelly & Sons Company in Chicago.

4

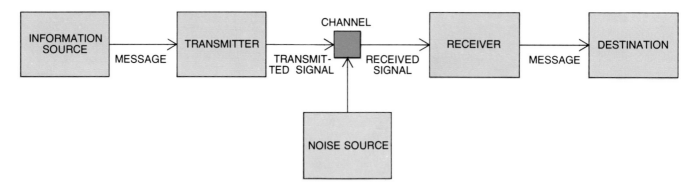

CHANNEL

INFORMATION SOURCE → MESSAGE → TRANSMITTER → TRANSMITTED SIGNAL → RECEIVED SIGNAL → RECEIVER → MESSAGE → DESTINATION

NOISE SOURCE

UNIVERSAL COMMUNICATION SYSTEM symbolically represented in this block diagram was originally proposed by Claude E. Shannon in his influential 1948 paper "The Mathematical Theory of Communication." The usefulness of Shannon's theory to the communication engineer is based in the broadest sense on the fact that it reduces any communication system, however complex, to a few essential elements. Modern communication theory is derived in large part from the ideas outlined by Shannon in his paper.

ing the nature, behavior and limitations of some of man's machines. Frequently it seems that what we have learned about machines should apply in some way to ourselves and our activities. We feel on occasion that the scales have fallen from our eyes and that the means for understanding are in our hands. At last we shall know.

In 1948 two publications created an intellectual stir about communication that has not yet subsided. These works were a paper titled "The Mathematical Theory of Communication," which Claude E. Shannon published in the July and October issues of the *Bell System Technical Journal,* and Norbert Wiener's book *Cybernetics: Control and Communication in the Animal and the Machine.* For the purposes of this discussion I should like to add to these two works a third: *Syntactic Structures,* published by Noam Chomsky in 1957.

Shannon's communication theory (also known as information theory) and Wiener's cybernetics created a broad and lasting interest and enthusiasm. In 1949 Shannon's paper was reprinted in book form together with exposition and comment by Warren Weaver. Weaver's contribution was based in part on an article by him in the July 1949 issue of *Scientific American.* These books alerted the scientific world. Conferences were held here and abroad. Scientists, shallow and profound, tried to extend the ideas of Shannon and Wiener to all aspects of life and art. I remember Shannon's telling me how he sat in a conference watching a man who spoke with his eyes turned toward the heavens, as if he were receiving divine revelation. Shannon was disappointed that he could not make any sense out of what the man was saying. Cybernetics and communication theory have been with us for nearly a quarter of a century. What have they

taught us? I looked through the books to find out.

Shannon's "The Mathematical Theory of Communication" summarizes and clarifies the task of the communication engineer in a remarkable way. The system Shannon studied is a truly universal communication system. As shown in the first figure of his paper [*see illustration above*], it consists of an information source, a transmitter, a communication channel, a noise source, a receiver and a message destination.

In such a communication system the information source and the message destination are usually human beings. As an example, a human being may type a message consisting of the letters and spaces on the keyboard of a teletypewriter. The teletypewriter serves as a transmitter that encodes each character as a sequence of electrical pulses, which may be "on" or "off," "current" or "no current." These electrical pulses are transmitted by a pair of wires to another teletypewriter that acts as a receiver and prints out the letters and spaces, which are in turn read by the human being serving as the message destination.

As the pulses travel from the teletypewriter that serves as the transmitter to the teletypewriter that serves as the receiver, an intermittent connection or an extraneous current may alter or mutilate them so that the receiver teletypewriter prints out some wrong characters. Shannon sums up such alterations or mutilations of the signal by including a noise source in his diagram of the communication system. Ordinarily the signal is an electrical signal, and the noise is an unpredictable interfering signal that is added to the desired signal.

The noise can cause the received message to differ from the message the source wished to transmit. The greater the ratio of the power of the signal to the power of the noise is, that is, the

greater the signal-to-noise ratio, the less effect the noise will have on the operation of the communication system.

This example of a communication system based on the use of teletypewriters is a very simple one. In contrast let us consider a voice communication system based on the automatic speaking machines known as vocoders. The transmitter part of such a system analyzes a speech signal and obtains data to control a speaking machine at the remote receiver. The control signals so obtained are the signals that are sent from the transmitter to the receiver. These control signals operate the distant speaking machine. Excessive noise in the transmission path may cause errors of articulation in the speech the message destination hears.

In this example we come on another concept introduced by Shannon. The vocoder and its control signals must be complex enough to produce speech that meets a fidelity criterion set by the message destination. If we fail to meet the fidelity criterion, the purposes of the communication system will not be fulfilled. If we produce better speech than is necessary, the system will be inefficient.

Thus Shannon's diagram of a communication system can apply to a system that is very complex indeed. Moreover, Shannon's theory can tell the communication engineer something meaningful and useful about any communication system. It gives him a measure of the commodity he is trying to transmit. That measure, a unit of uncertainty or choice, is called a bit. A bit (a contraction of "binary digit") is the uncertainty between "yes" or "no" or "heads" or "tails" when both are equally likely; it is the choice we exercise in choosing "left" or "right" most unpredictably (that is, with equal probability for each). The symbols 0 and 1 (that is, the digits of a binary number) can specify yes or no, heads or tails, left or right.

Shannon showed how in principle to measure the information rate of a message source—a speaker, a person writing, the output of a television camera—in bits per message or bits per second. This quantity is called the entropy or entropy rate of the source.

Shannon also showed how to measure the capacity of a communication channel. Again the measure is bits per second. The entropy rates of different message sources vary widely. Studies conducted by Shannon show that the entropy of English text is probably about one bit per character. The entropy rate of speech is not known. Experiments with vocoders indicate that it is less than (and probably much less than) 1,000 bits per second; in contrast we routinely use a channel (the telephone) capable of transmitting 60,000 bits per second of high-quality speech. A channel capable of transmitting some 60 million bits per second is generally used in transmitting television pictures, but the entropy rate of the picture source must surely be far less than that.

One thing is clear: It is necessarily more costly to transmit a television picture than to transmit speech, and more costly to transmit speech than to transmit text. Transmitting a detailed picture, whatever its worth, is bound to be more than 1,000 times more costly than efficiently transmitting 1,000 words of text.

Shannon contributed a great deal in establishing the bit as a measure of the complexity of message sources and the capabilities of channels. In addition he proved an extraordinary theorem. He showed that if the entropy rate of a message source does not exceed the capacity of a communication channel, then in principle messages from the source can be transmitted over the channel with a vanishingly small probability of error. This can be achieved only by storing an exceedingly long stretch of message before transmitting it [see "Communication Channels," by Henri Busignies, page 63].

Shannon's communication theory has had two chief values. One is rather like the value of the law of conservation of energy. Shannon has made it possible for communication engineers to distinguish between what is possible and what is not possible. Communication theory has disposed of unworkable inventions that are akin to perpetual motion machines. It has directed the attention of engineers to real and soluble problems. It has given them a quantitative mea-

sure of the effectiveness of their systems. Shannon's work has also inspired the invention of many error-correcting codes, by means of which one can attain error-free transmission over noisy communication channels.

Information theory and coding theory are widely pursued areas of research. It is true that many real and significant problems seem too difficult to solve, and that many of the problems that are solved seem made up because they can be solved rather than because they are very significant. Nonetheless, communication theory as Shannon conceived it has enduring importance.

Shannon is an engaging and lucid

writer. In his exposition of what he had done he used amusing as well as enlightening examples. One example was a message source in which the probability of the next letter depended on the preceding letters. Such a source produced "words" such as *grocid*, *pondenome*, *demonstures* and *deamy*. Shannon's choice of technical terms, on the other hand, was evocative as well as apt; it included *information*, *entropy*, *redundancy* and *equivocation*. Surely a theory that dealt with such wide-ranging concepts must have wide-ranging application.

So thought Weaver, as he expressed himself in "Recent Contributions to the Mathematical Theory of Communica-

CHANNEL		CHANNEL BANDWIDTH (HERTZ)	CHANNEL CAPACITY (BITS PER SECOND)
TELEPHONE WIRE (SPEECH)		3,000	60,000
AM RADIO		10,000	80,000
FM RADIO		200,000	250,000
HIGH-FIDELITY PHONOGRAPH OR TAPE		15,000	250,000
COMMERCIAL TELEVISION		6 MILLION	90 MILLION
MICROWAVE RELAY SYSTEM (1,200 TELEPHONE CHANNELS)		20 MILLION	72 MILLION
L-5 COAXIAL-CABLE SYSTEM (10,800 TELEPHONE CHANNELS)		57 MILLION	648 MILLION
PROPOSED MILLIMETER-WAVEGUIDE SYSTEM (250,000 TELEPHONE CHANNELS)		70 BILLION	15 BILLION
HYPOTHETICAL LASER SYSTEM		10 TRILLION	100 BILLION

CAPACITY OF VARIOUS COMMUNICATION CHANNELS can be measured according to Shannon's theory in bits per second, as indicated in the column at the extreme right in this chart. The numbers given for each entry are more or less rough estimates for a particular system (either currently in operation, proposed or merely envisioned); in many cases it is difficult to ascribe even an approximate value for capacity in bits per second to an analogue channel because of the variability of parameters such as signal-to-noise ratio.

tion," his part of the 1949 book. Weaver plausibly divided the problem of communication into three levels: (A) the technical problem: How accurately can the symbols of communication be transmitted? (B) the semantic problem: How precisely do the transmitted symbols convey the desired meaning? (C) the effectiveness problem: How effectively does the received meaning affect conduct in the desired way?

Weaver recognized that Shannon's work pertained to level A, but he argued persuasively that it overlapped and had significance for levels B and C as well. Weaver was intrigued by the idea of using the powerful body of probability theory involving Markoff processes in connection with both languages and semantic studies. Moreover, in pointing out the pertinence of information theory to cryptography, he argued that information theory "contributes to the problem of translation from one language to another."

This brings us to the fascinating story of machine translation. Since most of the details of the story are irrelevant to communication, I shall simply sketch the broad outlines. In brief, when simple machine "dictionary look-up" produced ambiguous, unreadable texts, the proponents of computer translation turned to grammar for a cure. They found that existing grammars were unhelpful. In fact, they found that no attainable grammar cured the persistent ills of machine translation: inaccuracy, ambiguity and unreadability. As Victor H. Yngve, once an associate of Chomsky's, wrote in 1964: "Work in mechanical translation has come up against a semantic barrier. ... We have come face to face with the realization that we will only have adequate mechanical translation when the machine can 'understand' what it is translating and this will be a very difficult task indeed.... 'Understand' is just what I mean.... Some of us are pressing forward undaunted."

Both the Shannon-Weaver book and the search for a syntactical cure for the ills of machine translation led to a reexamination of syntax. In *Syntactic Structures* Chomsky sought an avenue toward a grammar of a language. Letting L stand for a language, he wrote: "The grammar of L will thus be a device that generates all of the grammatical sequences of L and none of the ungrammatical ones. One way to test the adequacy of a grammar proposed for L is to determine whether or not the sentences that it generates are actually grammatical, i.e., acceptable to a native speaker."

Chomsky rejected the Markoff process, which Weaver had mentioned, as being inappropriate and inadequate. Part of his argument was statistical. Although a statistical process can generate sentences, the likelihood that a sentence will occur has nothing to do with whether or not it is grammatical. Indeed, in 1939 Ernest Vincent Wright published a novel, *Gadsby,* in which the letter *e* simply does not occur. Although the text violates the statistics of English, it violates neither grammar nor sense [*see illustration on page 8*].

Another part of Chomsky's argument was that neither the Markoff process nor any existing grammar gave simple, sensible explanations for many obvious features of English, including the passive voice. To this end Chomsky proposed a new grammatical concept: the transformational grammar.

Chomsky's work was important in two ways. It led a number of linguists, Yngve among them, to try to produce transformational grammars of English. This work produced grammars that became larger and larger and less and less intuitive; moreover, none of the grammars produced could generate all grammatical sequences and no ungrammatical sequences.

Another outcome of Chomsky's work was to inspire certain psychologists,

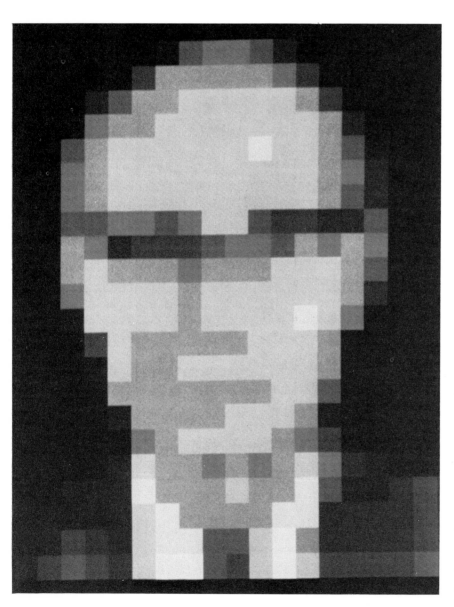

CUBIST PORTRAIT of John R. Pierce, the author of this article, was made by Leon D. Harmon of the Bell Telephone Laboratories as part of a computer experiment designed to determine the least amount of visual information a picture can contain and still be recognizable. The picture is divided into about 200 squares, with each square rendered evenly in one of 16 intensities of gray. For best results the portrait should be viewed from a distance of 15 feet or more; jiggling the picture, squinting or removing one's eyeglasses also helps. Such studies of the information content of a visual image may be useful in devising future systems for storing, transmitting and displaying pictures with the aid of computers.

notably George A. Miller, then at Harvard, to do experimental work on human response to language. At first this line of inquiry seemed very fruitful. For one thing, response to the active voice appeared to be quicker than response to the passive voice, a finding consistent with the view that the passive voice involves an additional transformation. As such work has proceeded it has become complicated and unclear in implication, except for one thing: the importance of meaning in communication [see "Verbal Communication," by Roman Jakobson, page 39].

Remember that Chomsky proposed as a criterion for a sentence's being grammatical that it be "acceptable to a native speaker." When in fact naïve native speakers are asked whether or not a sentence is grammatical, they frequently reject it as being ungrammatical unless it makes sense to them. Conversely, ingenious people will spontaneously and gleefully invent tortured circumstances in which a seemingly meaningless or ungrammatical sentence will actually be acceptable to a native speaker. We are inclined to reject "I is a boy," but what is our reaction to be if we are visiting a school in which all the children are assigned pronouns rather than being called by their names?

Indeed, whether or not a sentence is grammatical or meaningful seems to depend ultimately on the ingenuity of the person who puzzles over it. Even then we are left with Weaver's exception: "Similarly, anyone would agree that the probability is low for such a sequence of words as 'Constantinople fishing nasty pink.' Incidentally, it is low, but not zero; for it is perfectly possible to think of a passage in which one sentence closes with 'Constantinople fishing,' and the next begins with 'Nasty pink.' And we might observe in passing that the unlikely four-word sequence under discussion has occurred in a single good English sentence, namely the one above."

Weaver therefore stresses meaning and effectiveness in communication. We find this search for meaning and effect outside the laboratory both in the myths and magic of antiquity and in our own daily experience. We find meaning in text or speech even when the text is corrupt or the speech scarcely audible. William James had observed this truth in 1899: "When we listen to a person speaking or read a page of print, much of what we think we see or hear is supplied from our memory. We overlook misprints, imagining the right letters, though we see the wrong ones; and how

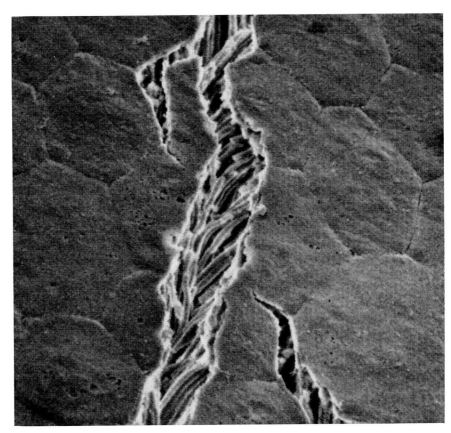

VISUAL-INFORMATION RECEPTORS are represented in this scanning electron micrograph by the outer rod segments seen through a tear in the membrane at the back surface of a rabbit's retina. The micrograph was made by Thomas F. Budinger and Thea Scott of the Lawrence Berkeley Laboratory. The magnification is approximately 4,000 diameters.

AUDITORY-INFORMATION RECEPTORS are shown enlarged some 6,000 diameters in this scanning electron micrograph of the ciliary tufts of hair cells in the sacculus, or inner ear, of a frog. The micrograph was made by James Pawley of the University of California at Berkeley working with a sample prepared by Edwin R. Lewis in his laboratory at Berkeley.

little we actually hear, when we listen to speech, we realize when we go to a foreign theatre; for there what troubles us is not so much that we cannot understand what the actors say as that we cannot hear their words. The fact is that we hear quite as little under similar conditions at home, only our mind, being fuller of English verbal associations, supplies the requisite material for comprehension upon a much slighter auditory hint."

This passage from James gives us a strong clue to understanding where the meaning of language really resides. It is useless to seek the meaning or utility of a book between its covers, or the intent or effect of a speech in the sounds that are uttered. A textbook on physics or mathematics exists in the context of the physics and mathematics of its time. It is not a complete exposition of the physics or mathematics it is intended to teach. Such a text is addressed to a person who already knows a language, something about the world and something about physics and mathematics. It is intended to enable him to learn, understand and use knowledge, skills and insights that the author himself has acquired. Taken out of its environment of language, such a textbook would be completely unintelligible. Taken out of its environment of physics or mathematics, such a textbook might be interpreted symbolically, construed as magic or dismissed as boring nonsense.

Our everyday communication has meaning in a much more restricted context. An order on a battlefield communicates only to a soldier who knows the situation, and the situation cannot be re-created by an examination of the words uttered. Phrases passed back and forth in a discussion may earn John Smith a raise or cost him his job, but the phrases have meaning only with respect to what those who are discussing Smith already know about him. Communication can take place only between people with a common aim, a common problem, a common curiosity, a common interest; in other words, something in common that is meaningful and important or fascinating to both. The process of communication is not one of imparting entire areas of knowledge or of drastically changing views. That is the process of education or training, which makes use of communication but goes far beyond communication as we commonly construe it. Communication in everyday use is a process of adjusting understandings and attitudes, of making them congruent or of ascertaining how and where they agree or disagree. A common language is of extreme advantage in our efforts to communicate, but it is not as important as a common interest and some degree of common understanding.

Yet if we had everything, or almost everything, in common, no communication, or very little communication, would suffice. That is the case with certain animals, such as bees [see "Animal Communication," by Edward O. Wilson, page 29]. The need for communication arises because something unguessable must be imparted concerning our understanding or actions. A little must be added to what we already know or as a basis for modifying what we would otherwise do. It is this element of the unguessable that Shannon measures as entropy. And it is the unguessable, the surprising, that is an essential part of communication, as opposed to the mere repetition of gestures, incantations or prayers.

Meaning can exist only through what we have in common in our lives, minds and language. It is concerning what we share that communication takes place. We cannot be certain that reassurance will be offered, and we are upset if it is not. We are excited by a new discovery or by a tidbit of gossip about someone we love or hate. We spring to a task we understand and feel impelled to undertake. And, as I have observed, we con-

---

XXIX

GADSBY WAS WALKING back from a visit down in Branton Hills' manufacturing district on a Saturday night. A busy day's traffic had had its noisy run; and with not many folks in sight, His Honor got along without having to stop to grasp a hand, or talk; for a Mayor out of City Hall is a shining mark for any politician. And so, coming to Broadway, a booming bass drum and sounds of singing, told of a small Salvation Army unit carrying on amidst Broadway's night shopping crowds. Gadsby, walking toward that group, saw a young girl, back towards him, just finishing a long, soulful oration, saying:—

". . .and I can say this to you, for I know what I am talking about; for I was brought up *in a pool of liquor!!*"

As that army group was starting to march on, with this girl turning towards Gadsby, His Honor had to gasp, astonishingly:—

"Why! Mary Antor!!"

"Oh! If it isn't Mayor Gadsby! I don't run across you much, now-a-days. How is Lady Gadsby holding up during this awful war?"

[201]

IMPROBABLE TEXT, represented by this page copied from the 1939 novel *Gadsby*, by Ernest Vincent Wright, violates the statistics of English, although it violates neither grammar nor sense. Wright's entire novel of more than 50,000 words was written without a single word containing the letter *e*. This extraordinary counterexample serves to symbolize the difficulties associated with a purely statistical approach to the analysis of language. Such problems came into prominence in the course of early attempts at computer translation, leading certain linguistic theorists, such as Noam Chomsky of the Massachusetts Institute of Technology, to undertake a reexamination of syntax in linguistic communication.

tinually search for meaning, whether or not meaning is there.

I believe it is a mixture of surprise and the search for meaning in a familiar context—the English language—that lends charm to Shannon's statistical words *grocid, pondenome, deamy.* They are so like English that we wonder what they mean, or perhaps we feel that we sense some elusive meaning or connotation. I think that it is our straining toward some such extraordinary context or meaning that gives charm to computer-produced "poems" such as those of Marie Borroff:

> *The river*
> *Winks*
> *And I am ravished.*
>
> *Dangerously, intensely, the music*
> *Sins and brightens*
> *And I am woven.*

These poems are not so much out of the world as enticingly on the fringes of it.

We are challenged by what seems almost within our comprehension, but we reject or are bored with whatever completely eludes our grasp. Using computer-generated patterns, Bela Julesz of the Bell Telephone Laboratories has shown that a given degree of order or redundancy (in the sense of information theory) can be detectable or undetectable to the eye, trained or untrained. Here is one point of departure between information theory and problems of human communication.

The information theorist asks: What is a general measure of order, or rather of disorder, in a message source, and how can I take advantage of the order that is there in transmitting messages from that source efficiently? To do this, however, one must adapt the communication equipment to the order that lies in the source. Our eyes, ears and brain, adapted as they may have been through evolution, are with us throughout our lives. We can make use of order only if we can perceive it. Some order we can learn to perceive; some must escape our senses, to be detected only through statistical analysis.

Many artists and musicians who have been inspired by information theory have sought to produce works with an optimum combination of order and randomness. Such a criterion antedates information theory. Beethoven is said to have declared that in music everything must be at once surprising and expected. That is appealing. If too little is surprising, we are bored; if too little is expect-

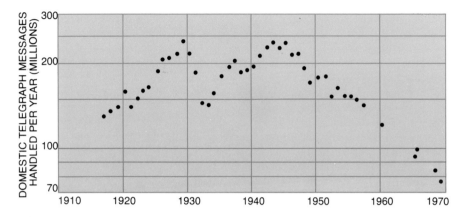

RISE AND FALL of a form of communication, the telegraph, is traced in this graph of the total number of domestic telegraph messages handled in the U.S. from 1917 to 1970.

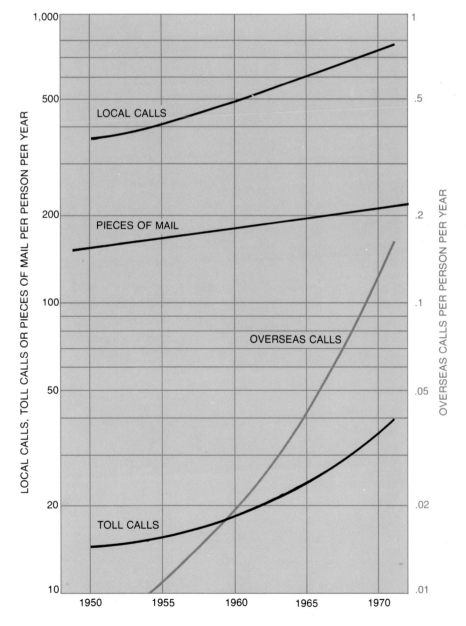

ACCELERATING USE of two other forms of communication, the postal service and the telephone, in recent years has contributed to the decline of telegraphy. The rate of increase for pieces of mail per person is currently about 3.5 percent per year, for local telephone calls per person about 5 percent per year, for toll telephone calls per person about 10 percent per year and for overseas telephone calls per person about 25 percent per year.

ed, we are lost. Communication is possible only through a degree of novelty in a context that is familiar.

Music communicates at once by reassurance and by surprise, but we can be neither reassured nor surprised by what passes unnoticed. Sir Donald Tovey, the British composer and writer, characterized certain contrapuntal devices as "for the eye only" and so implied that they must go unheard and unappreciated by the listener.

Order undetected is order in vain. One contemporary Canadian composer, Gerald Strang, has said that much random music and much totally organized music sound alike: uniformly gray. This would indeed be the consequence of an order undetectable by the ear and brain.

As to what is perceivable order and what is not, there will be long arguments. Some will say that the occurrence of the diatonic musical scale in unrelated cultures argues that it is physically or psychologically suited to man, whereas the only basis for 12-tone music is the fact that the piano has 12 black and white keys per octave. Others will argue that what we expect and what surprises us in older music is entirely cultural; that with sufficient training and effort on the part of the listener today's gray music will come to shimmer with color and startle with surprise, intellectual if not acoustical. It is plausible that what has moved many men may move others; it is less plausible that men will necessarily come to be moved by what has moved no one.

So far in this article I have associated communication entirely with man and communication among men. Another kind of communication is growing up around us: communication among machines. Here we are back to the process of devising, understanding and improving tools. We do not care about the working conditions or interests of computers. In the end we do not care how our credit-card transactions are processed as long as the process is accurate, cheap and prompt. What we do care about is providing a simple, easy-to-use, compact, reliable terminal by means of which a man can send messages to a machine and receive messages from it.

It seems ridiculous to speak a credit-card number into a telephone and have the computer operator key the number into the machine and relay the machine's yes or no answer by voice. It *is* ridiculous, and people are working on machines to read credit cards and communicate with a distant computer directly.

All of us look toward communication with distant computers from the home or the office, but as yet there are no adequate terminals. Teletypewriters are large, clanking and costly. Cathode ray terminals are large, limited and costly. The problem is that we have no cheap and adequate means for display. Keyboards are compact, reliable and easy to use. I for one would rather command a computer through a keyboard than talk to it, even if that science-fiction dream were possible.

The widespread use of computers is held up by lack of cheap, compact, reliable terminals, and by other things as well. The field of data communication and interacting computer systems is powerful and fascinating. It calls into play not only communication theory but also the construction of artificial languages, complete with grammars and the devising of computer programs of great complexity. Such communication is a growing part of our world, but it is remote from the average user of communication, who sees and cares to see only the terminals by means of which he uses such computer systems. As the computer and terminal arts advance, we shall have all kinds of new services in our homes, whether for consulting advertisements, purchasing, making reservations, learning algebra or learning Japanese. All of this and more will come, but when it will come is hard to judge [see "Communication Terminals," by Ernest R. Kretzmer, page 91].

Whatever one may say about communication among machines, human communication takes place within a community of interest made up of human beings. Within that community people think and act, and they communicate in moving others toward or away from what they regard as appropriate thoughts and actions. In terms of information theory only certain messages among all possible messages occur in communication within a community of interest, because only certain messages are appropriate, make sense and will be understood.

In a simple society, an isolated band or a village with a subsistence economy, a community of limited size and complexity provides a community of interest common to all. Speech supplies ade-

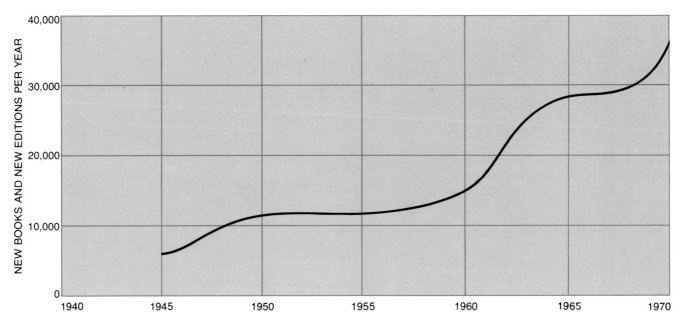

IRREGULAR UPWARD TREND characterizes this plot of the number of new books and new editions of old books issued in the U.S. each year from 1945 to 1970. An initial rise after the end of World War II was followed by a plateau (perhaps associated with a period of postwar practicality and conformism), which in turn gave way to a wavering but very steep rise beginning in about 1960.

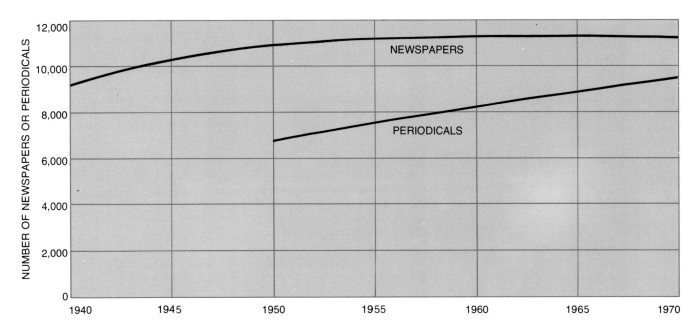

INTERESTING CONTRAST is evident in this graph, which shows that the number of periodicals published in the U.S. over the pe-riod 1950–1970 has increased steadily, whereas the number of newspapers published over the same period has become fairly stable.

quate communication. The family or the clan may be a subsidiary community of interest. Other places, other people and other times must somehow be taken into account in myth and custom. Nonetheless, to a degree all of life (that is, all that is noted) is accessible and intelligible to all members of the community.

Our world has far outgrown the reach of the voice or the comprehension of any one mind. It is divided into countless communities of interest. Increasingly these communities are intellectual rather than geographical. A physicist or a mathematician or a biologist may have more in common with a colleague in a foreign land than he does with his next-door neighbor.

Our multiple communities of interest and the institutions that serve them overlap. A mathematician may be interested in the stock market and in riding unicycles. An engineer may be interested in spectator sports, skiing and music. A science-fiction writer may be interested in local politics. That each man is a member of many communities of interest makes them no less real.

Clearly such communities of interest could not exist without adequate communication. I shall not argue that advances in communication and travel have brought these communities of interest into being, or that conversely wide-ranging interests have stimulated the technologies of travel and communication. What is clear is that communication plays a complex role in a complex way of life. In so serving us modes of communication interact with the people

they serve in many ways [see "Communication and Social Environment," by George Gerbner, page 111].

Some forms of communication serve many communities of interest, ranging from the individual and the family to large business and cultural organizations. The postal service, the telegraph and the telephone are among these forms. The telegraph provides an interesting example of the rise and fall of a form of communication. When one plots the domestic telegraph messages handled from 1917 to 1968, one finds a faltering peak from 1930 to 1935 [see top *illustration on page 9*]. Anyone who has sent or received telegrams can read a variety of economic and social observations into these data. On the one hand one sees competition from the telephone, through direct distance dialing and decreasing long-distance rates. On the other hand one sees that a dispersal of population into suburbia and rising labor costs have combined to make the physical delivery of telegrams uneconomic. Those with long memories may recall the knock of the telegraph boy at the door. They may even recall office switches that would summon telegraph boys to take messages. Such services have vanished, and Western Union is seeking a new mode of life.

Mails and telephony, in contrast, are still on the increase, with the telephone winning out [see *bottom illustration on page 9*]. There are more local calls per person than pieces of mail per person, and the rate of increase is faster. Furthermore, toll calls increase twice as fast as local calls and overseas calls increase

more than twice as fast as toll calls. In such statistics we see a society in which human relations and business transactions both have a shorter time scale. Life has become less leisurely, less planned, more immediate. The increases in toll calls and overseas calls also tell us that communities of interest are becoming more far-flung.

These increases in part reflect advances in technology that have made such calls cheaper and better. Quality is important to the use and success of communications. Overseas calls increased rapidly after 1954, when the first undersea cable made overseas calls more intelligible and useful than they had been in the days of shortwave radio. Cost is equally important. Surely a reduction in the cost of toll calls, and particularly of calls during certain hours, has stimulated such calling.

Although a decrease in cost can stimulate the use of communications, too high a cost can result in no use whatever. Invitations are no longer carried by footmen. And, technological marvel though it is, the Bell System's Picturephone service seems unlikely to sweep the country. The cost is greater than people care to pay, particularly for long-distance calls. So it seems to be with many ambitiously proposed communication systems. The cost is more than the traffic will bear. In time videotelephone and home communication centers will be available to all, but only when radical advances in technology bring the cost down. That time will not be tomorrow.

Telegrams, the postal service and the telephone serve almost all communities of interest. Some modes of communication serve large communities of interest only. Books are among these. Nothing is more diverse than books. With rare exceptions (the Bible is among them) each book reaches a small fraction of the total population. Yet a successful book may reach a large fraction of those deeply interested in a particular area or subject, be it yoga, tennis, the stock market or general relativity. In the last instance a successful book can blanket the real community of interest with a few thousand copies.

A plot of the number of new books and new editions of old books issued each year from 1945 to 1970 reveals that there was an initial rise after the war and then a plateau. We can associate the plateau, if we wish, with postwar practicality and conformism [*see illustration on page 10*]. About 1960 a wavering but very steep rise set in. Does this rise reflect an increasing diversity and a growing number of communities of interest? Or does it reflect a reduction of cost and an increasing number of outlets during the paperback revolution? I am sure that it reflects both, and that both are a part of the interaction of communication and society.

A book can serve a rather narrow community of interest, for example the worldwide community of specialists in some field of science. In general periodical publications must have a larger readership in order to survive. Nonetheless, the number of periodicals published over the period 1950–1970 has increased steadily [*see illustration on preceding page*]. This increase reflects a growth in communities of interest of substantial

size, including the community of interest that is served by this magazine.

I believe that such statistics actually underestimate the true number of periodical publications, and that they omit many that serve very real communities of interest. Particularly in technology and business, there are a large number of highly specialized periodical publications: monthly, quarterly or yearly. They are directed to subjects as special as digests of commercially available computer hardware and analyses of the financial condition and prospects of certain companies. The subscription price for some is extremely high; this factor seems to show that they serve particular communities of interest better than more general technical or financial journals. Other highly specialized and probably uncounted periodicals include the mimeographed science-fiction fan magazines called "fanzines" and endless club and society bulletins and the like. All serve real communities of interest.

It is interesting to note that whereas the number of periodicals is rising, the number of newspapers is static. I think that here too one can read meaning into statistics. As we progress from the mails and the telephone through books, through periodicals and on to newspapers we are considering successively media that necessarily serve larger and larger communities of interest. With the newspaper we have arrived at what survives of the geographical and the national communities of interest. Newspapers must appeal to such interests as we all have in common because we live in a particular community, state or nation.

What is true of newspapers is also true

of radio and television [*see illustrations below*]. Here we see that whereas virtually every home has a radio and a television set, the number of stations is still rising somewhat. With the advent of the communication satellite, television has become a truly international medium. President Nixon's trips to China and the U.S.S.R. and the astronauts' trip to the moon have been hit shows. With the growth in diversity, however, the geographical, the national and indeed the international communities of interest have come to occupy an equivocal place in our lives. Mass communications have come to have an uncertain role in the functioning of society. It can be argued that mass communications are not effective eyes and ears on the world, and that they do not ensure popular participation in government.

Here I come back to Wiener's *Cybernetics,* to which I have scarcely referred since I mentioned it at the beginning of this article. Unlike Shannon's "The Mathematical Theory of Communication," *Cybernetics* does not expound a novel, well-defined and well-implemented body of theory. Rather it is a discussion, partly mathematical and partly popular, of the relation between certain concepts and man and his world.

One prime concept expounded by Wiener is homeostasis: the functioning of an organism or a system so as to correct for adverse disturbances. Homeostasis involves two processes: the detection of deviation from the desired state, and negative feedback, by which the discrepancy between the desired state and the present observed state is cor-

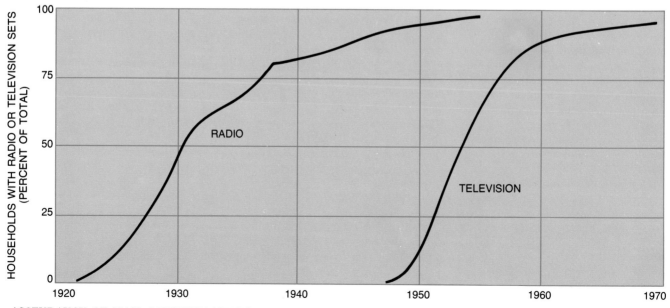

ASCENDANCY OF MASS COMMUNICATIONS is reflected in the graphs on these two pages, which show that whereas virtually

every home in the U.S. now has both a radio and a television set (*left*), the number of radio and television stations is still rising

rected. The process of homeostasis may fail in many ways.

For the overall process to function, we must satisfactorily sense that some correction needs to be made. Beyond that, however, negative feedback may itself result in instability. This happens when there is too much negative feedback, or when it acts too quickly in a system in which some responses are necessarily slow. The normal human being can observe the fallibilities of feedback by trying to carry a shallow pan full of water without spilling it. He had best keep his eyes off the pan as he walks along, however. Efforts guided by the eye ordinarily heighten rather than reduce the sloshing of the water.

Wiener observes that "small, closely knit communities have a very considerable measure of homeostasis; and this, whether they are highly literate communities in a civilized country, or villages of primitive savages. Strange and even repugnant as the customs of many barbarians may seem to us, they generally have a very definite homeostatic value, which it is part of the function of anthropologists to interpret. It is only in the large community, where the Lords of Things as They Are protect themselves from hunger by wealth, from public opinion by privacy and anonymity, from private criticism by the laws of libel and the possession of the means of communication, that ruthlessness can reach its most sublime levels. Of all of these antihomeostatic factors in society, the control of the means of communication is the most effective and most important."

No doubt greed, self-interest and cal-lousness do account for failures of communication in our overall community of interest. We may also observe, however, that the world in which we live and which affects our daily lives has become overwhelmingly complex. We cannot possibly understand it in the sense that we might understand a small, closely knit community. If we do not disregard the larger world, we must perceive it as it is represented by the media of mass communication. Is this, however, a real world, or is it a myth that stands in the place of something we cannot possibly understand?

It seems common that those with special knowledge, be it of science or publishing, distrust mass-media presentations of their own fields while accepting the pictures the media present of other fields. Even in the large a civil war in Nigeria attracted notice and aroused passion, whereas one in the Sudan went unnoticed and left us cold. Can the mass media present a useful picture of an overall community of interest? To what degree does such a community of interest exist? And whose interests are taken into account?

Whatever may be the reality of the overall community of interest people observe, they do react to it strongly and sometimes violently. Even if this reaction were a reaction to the true state of affairs, it would not necessarily result in a return to the desired state, whatever that might be. I think all societies perceive this difficulty of perception and reaction. In totalitarian societies great efforts are made to narrow and control the channels of communication. In open societies the channels of communication are open, but constraints such as due process and checks and balances are put on the speed and magnitude of reaction. Yet, as society becomes ever larger and more complex, the problem of communication and control in the overall community of interest becomes progressively more difficult [see "Communication and Freedom of Expression," by Thomas I. Emerson, page 121].

At times governments show a public awareness of this. One response is to try to make society simpler and more uniform through centralization and drastic restrictive legislation concerning whatever is deemed to be antisocial or unfair or simply unpopular. Another response is to try to make communication and control operate meaningfully and effectively by pushing power toward communities of interest, whether these are intellectual, technological or geographical in the sense that regions, states and cities are.

Long before we took deliberate steps in this latter direction, men's communities of interest had somehow multiplied, differentiated themselves and had in many cases broken their geographical bonds. The amount of communication we use, the distances over which we communicate and the increasing diversity of books and periodicals show this clearly. Still, geography governs some aspects of our lives. However universal our understanding of science or our enjoyment of music may be, we prefer stoves in the Arctic and air conditioners in the Tropics. The world that communication and transportation have built is exceedingly complex and very difficult to govern wisely.

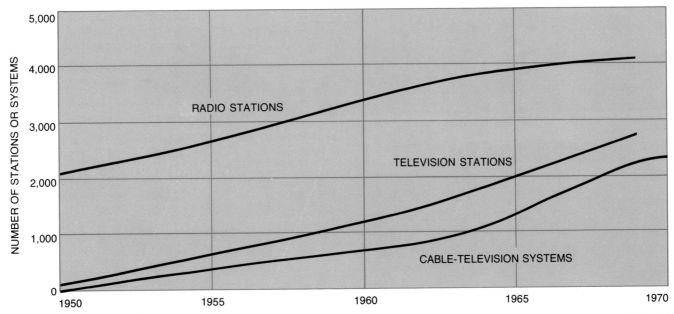

somewhat (*right*). The graphs are derived mainly from two sources: *The American Almanac*, which is published by Grosset & Dunlap in 1972, and *Historical Statistics of the United States: Colonial Times to 1957*, published by the U.S. Department of Commerce.

2

CELLULAR COMMUNICATION

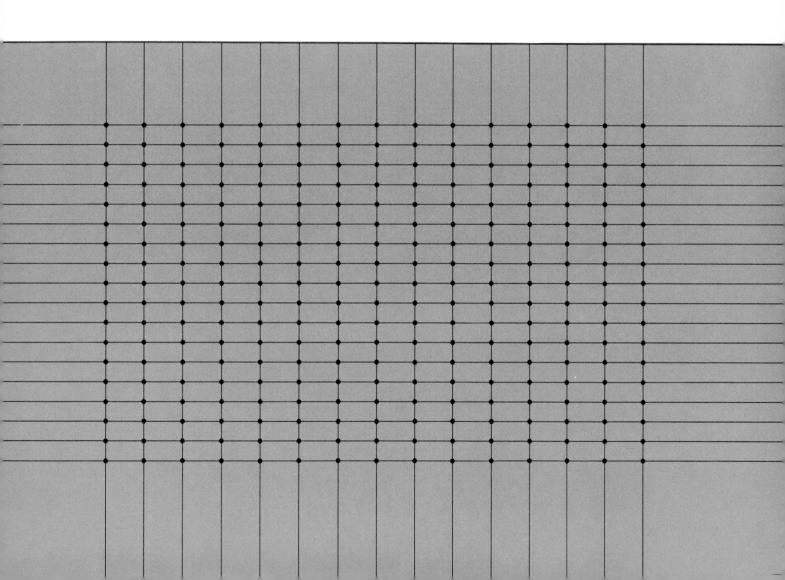

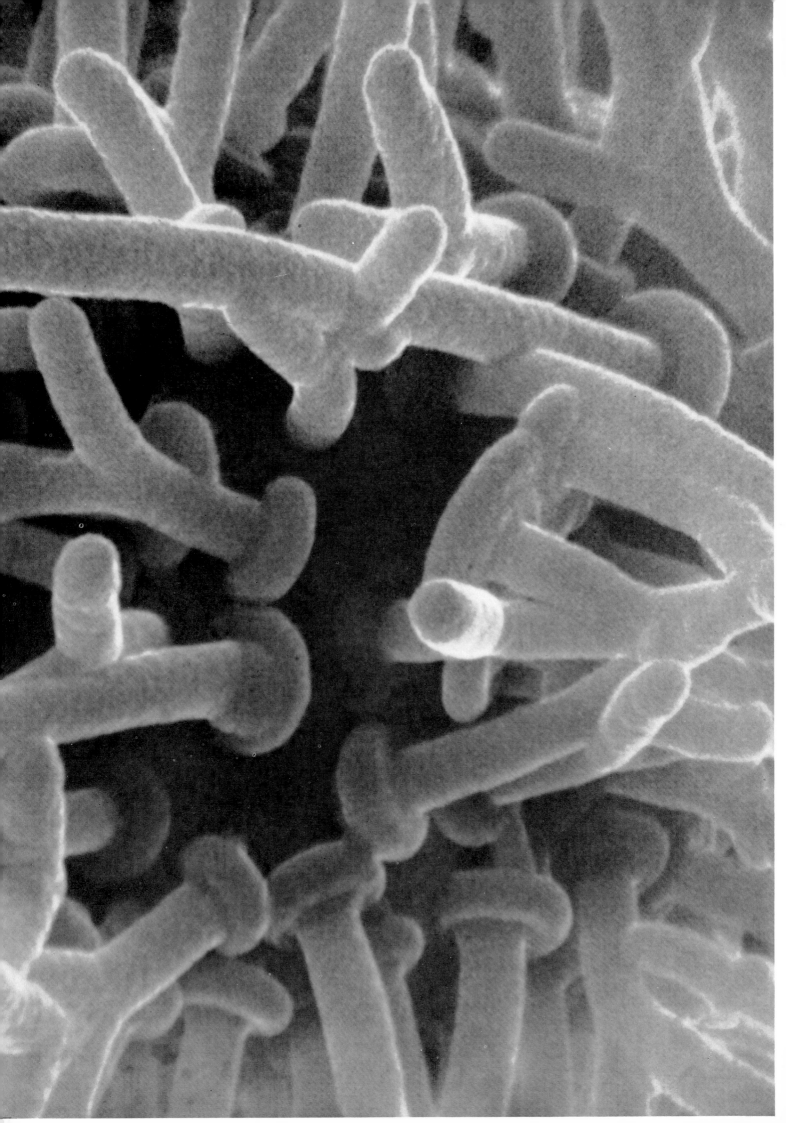

Cellular Communication

GUNTHER S. STENT

Cells communicate by means of hormones and nerve fibers. Such communication and all other forms of communication are founded on the information incorporated in the molecules of nucleic acid.

The capacity to communicate is a fundamental feature of living cells. As John R. Pierce notes in the introduction to this book, the types of information that are the subject of cellular communication can be grouped into three general classes: genetic, metabolic and nervous. The genetic information of an organism is embodied in the precise sequence of the four kinds of nucleotide base—adenine, guanine, thymine and cytosine—in the DNA molecules of the nuclei of its cellular constituency. The meaning of that information is the specification of the precise sequence of the 20 amino acids in a myriad of different kinds of protein molecule. It is the ensemble of cellular proteins that functions to make the cell what it is: an engine built of highly specific structural members and enzymes that carries out a complex network of catalytically facilitated metabolic reactions. In the course of cell reproduction the parental DNA molecules are replicated and each of the two daughter cells is endowed with a complete store of the genetic information of the mother cell.

In addition to this "vertical" inheritance, in which each cell receives its genetic information from only one parent cell, there is a "horizontal" mode of inheritance, in which cells communicate and thus exchange their genetic information to give rise to offspring of mixed parentage. There are at least four different mechanisms by which such communication of genetic information is re-alized. The most primitive is genetic transformation, in which a donor cell simply releases some of its DNA molecules into its surroundings. One of the released donor DNA molecules is then taken up by a recipient cell, which incorporates the molecule into its own genetic structures. The second mechanism is genetic transduction. On the infection of a host cell with a virus one or another of the host-cell DNA molecules is incorporated into the shell of one of the progeny virus particles to which the infection gives rise. After its release from the host cell the bastard virus particle infects a recipient cell and thereby transfers to the new host the donor-cell DNA molecule it brought along for the ride. The third mechanism is genetic conjugation. Here two cells meet and establish a conjugal tube, or thin bridge, between them. In the conjugal act the donor member of the cell pair mobilizes a part of its complement of DNA and passes it through the tube to the recipient member.

The natural occurrence of these three mechanisms has so far been demonstrated only for bacteria, the lowest form of cellular life. Higher forms of life, from fungi and protozoa up to man, employ the fourth and most elaborate mechanism of genetic communication, namely sex. Here two gametes, cell types specialized for just such intercourse, meet, fuse and pool their entire complement of DNA. The process gives rise to offspring to which both parents have com-municated an equal amount of genetic information. This result is to be contrasted with what happens in the first three processes, where the offspring come into possession of only a small fraction of the total donor-cell DNA and are endowed mainly with the genetic information of the recipient cell.

The biological function of genetic communication is to increase the evolutionary plasticity of the species. The ultimate source of the genetic diversity on which natural selection, the motor that drives evolution, feeds are rare changes, or mutations, in the nucleotide base sequence and hence the genetic information contained in the DNA. Thus in the purely vertical mode of inheritance genetic diversity among the members of a cell population all descended from a single ancestral mother cell could be built up very slowly by the accumulation of mutations in the individual lines of descent. In the horizontal mode of inheritance and its intercellular communication, however, there develops quite quickly a rich individual genetic diversity as mutations that have arisen in different lines of descent are continually combined and recombined among the offspring of the interbreeding population. Thus in anticipation of any environmental changes that may affect its fitness the population presents for natural selection a spectrum of diverse types among which one or another may possess a greater fitness for the future state of the species.

Metabolic information is embodied in the quality and concentration of large and small molecules that participate in the chemical processes by which cells reproduce, develop and maintain their living state. In contrast to the communication of genetic information, whose utility pertains to time periods that are long compared with the life-span of the members of populations, the communication of metabolic information is of importance to organized societies of cells over much shorter intervals. Here the mechanism of communication gen-erally consists in the release by a secre-tory cell of one of its constituent mole-cules. The released molecule diffuses through the space occupied by the cell society, and on encountering a target cell it intervenes in some highly specific manner in the metabolism of that cell. Such messenger molecules of metabol-ic information are generally called hor-mones.

The biological function of metabolic communication is mainly twofold. In the first instance hormones control the order-ly development of multicellular animals

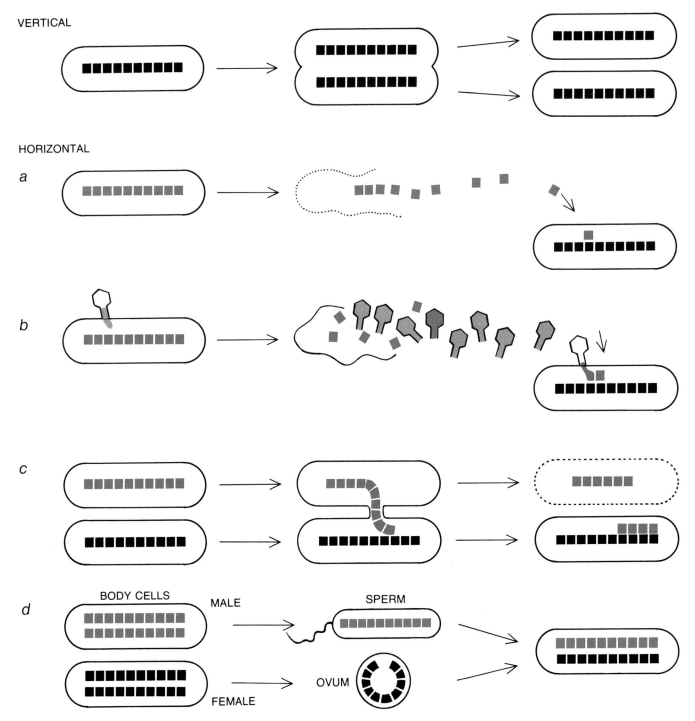

TYPES OF GENETIC COMMUNICATION can be classified as ver-tical or horizontal. In cellular reproduction (top) the communi-cation is vertical; the replication of the parental genes before cell division provides both offspring with complete and identical sets of genetic information. The three simpler kinds of horizontal com-munication are found in bacteria. In transformation (a) the donor cell releases the DNA molecules embodying its genetic information and some of the molecules are taken up by the recipient cell. In transduction (b), which may occur when a virus infects a cell and new viruses are formed, one of the new viruses may incorporate a DNA molecule into its shell; if the new virus now infects another cell, the donor-cell molecule and the information it embodies are transferred to the recipient cell. In conjugation (c) donor and re-cipient cells come into physical contact; a bridge is formed be-tween them and some donor DNA molecules are transferred to the recipient. The fourth and most elaborate kind of horizontal genetic communication (d) is sex. Parental organisms give rise to male (color) and female (black) gametes: specialized cells that contain only half of the information an offspring requires. When these fuse, each parent gives the offspring an equal amount of information.

and plants. These organisms represent societies made up of millions or billions of cells that come into being by a series of successive cycles of cell growth and division from a single fused pair of gametes, for example from the sperm-fertilized egg. This process of cell multiplication is accompanied by the process of cell differentiation, in which each cell acquires the particular molecular ensemble that enables it to play its destined specialized role in the life of the organism. In many cases cells receive from hormones their instructions concerning how and when to differentiate in the developmental sequence that leads to the adult organism. The female sex hormone estrogen, which belongs to the steroid class of molecules, is a well-known example of such a developmental messenger. Estrogen is released by secretory cells in the ovary of the female animal, particularly at the onset of puberty. Estrogen reaches target cells in almost all tissues and induces in these cells the metabolic reactions that eventually lead to the development of the secondary sexual characteristics of the body.

In the second instance hormones serve in the homeostatic processes by means of which all organisms minimize for their internal environment the consequences of changes in the external environment. The protein hormone insulin, well known through its connection with diabetes, is an example of such a homeostatic chemical messenger. The rate of release of insulin by secretory cells of the pancreas is accelerated in response to high glucose concentrations in the blood. On reaching target cells in liver and muscles insulin signals to these organs to remove glucose from the blood and either to store it in the form of glycogen or to burn it. Once, thanks to this increase in removal rates, the glucose blood concentration has returned to its normal level, the release of insulin by the pancreas is slowed down and so is the removal of glucose from the blood by liver and muscles. Thus insulin makes possible the maintenance of a relatively constant blood-sugar concentration in the face of great fluctuations of the animal's rate of sugar intake.

Nervous information is embodied in the activity of a special cell type possessed by all multicellular animals, the nerve cell or neuron. Although the physiological time spans over which the communication of metabolic information is relevant are much shorter than the evolutionary periods for which the communication of genetic information is intended, these physiological time spans still extend over hours, days or weeks. In

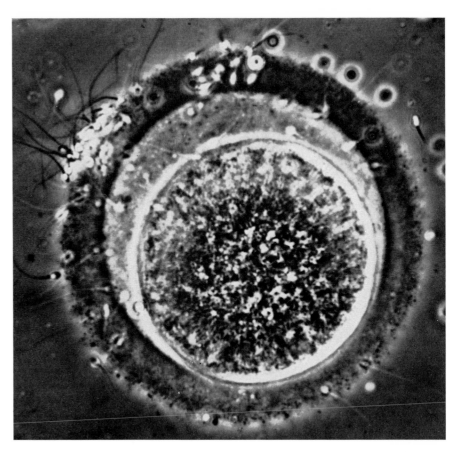

HUMAN OVUM AND SPERM CELLS at the moment of fertilization exemplify the union of gametes and the pooling of an equal amount of genetic information from each parent. Of the numerous sperm cells surrounding the ovum only one will actually deliver the male parental genes. This micrograph, which enlarges the cells some 400 diameters, was made by Landrum B. Shettles of the Columbia University College of Physicians and Surgeons.

order to stay alive, however, most animals must respond to certain events in their environment within time spans of seconds or even milliseconds. And since the diffusion of a molecule such as glucose through the space occupied by the cell society that makes up even so small an animal as a fly requires a few hours, animals must have communication channels that are faster than those provided by hormones. These channels are provided by neurons, and the biological function of the communication of nervous information they perform is to generate the rapid stimulus-response reactions that comprise the animal's behavior.

Neurons are endowed with two singular features that make them particularly suitable for this purpose. First, unlike most other cell types, they possess long and thin extensions: axons. With their axons neurons reach and come into contact with other neurons at distant sites and thereby form an interconnected network extending over the entire animal body. Second, unlike most other cell types, neurons give rise to electrical signals in response to physical or chemical stimuli. They conduct these signals along their axons and transmit them to

other neurons with which they are in contact. The interconnected network of neurons and its traffic of electrical signals forms the nervous system. It is, of course, the nervous system that is both the source and the destination of all the information with which the diverse communication systems under discussion in this issue are concerned.

Like Roman Gaul, the nervous system is divisible into three parts: (1) an input, or sensory, part that informs the animal about its condition with respect to the state of its external and internal environment; (2) an output, or effector, part that produces motion by commanding muscle contraction, and (3) an internuncial part (from the Latin *nuncius*, meaning messenger) that connects the sensory and effector parts. The most elaborate portion of the internuncial part, concentrated in the head of those animals that have heads, is the brain.

The processing of data by the internuncial part consists in the main in making an abstraction of the vast amount of data continuously gathered by the sensory part. This abstraction is the result of a selective destruction of portions of

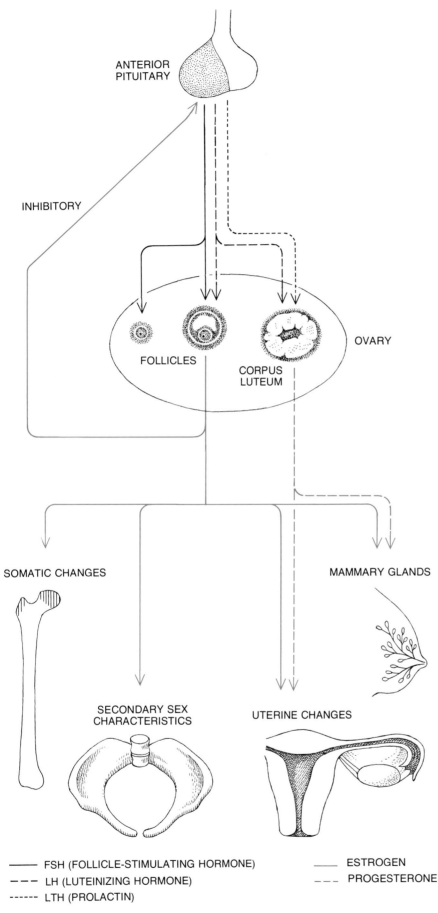

ANTERIOR PITUITARY

INHIBITORY

FOLLICLES

CORPUS LUTEUM

OVARY

SOMATIC CHANGES

MAMMARY GLANDS

SECONDARY SEX CHARACTERISTICS

UTERINE CHANGES

—— FSH (FOLLICLE-STIMULATING HORMONE)

– – – LH (LUTEINIZING HORMONE)

------ LTH (PROLACTIN)

—— ESTROGEN

– – – PROGESTERONE

METABOLIC COMMUNICATION is largely conducted by the messenger molecules known as hormones. One basic role of these chemical messengers is mediation of cell differentiation. Illustrated here is the action of hormones from the anterior pituitary that induce maturation in the human female. The ovarian hormones that are secreted following stimulus by pituitary hormones affect cells in bone, uterine and mammary tissues.

the input data in order to transform these data into manageable categories that are meaningful to the animal. It should be noted that the particular command pattern issued to the muscles by the internuncial part depends not only on here-and-now sensory inputs but also on the history of past inputs. Stated more plainly, neurons can learn from experience. Until not so long ago attempts to fathom how the nervous system actually manages to abstract sensory data and learn from experience were confined mainly to philosophical speculations, psychological formalisms or biochemical naïvetés. In recent years neurophysiologists, however, have made some important experimental findings that have provided for a beginning of a scientific approach to these deep problems. Here I can do no more than describe briefly one example of these recent advances and sketch some of the insights to which it has led.

Before discussing these advances we must give brief consideration to how electrical signals arise and travel in the nervous system. Neurons, like nearly all other cells, maintain a difference in electric potential of about a tenth of a volt across their cell membranes. This potential difference arises from the unequal distribution of the three most abundant inorganic ions of living tissue, sodium (Na^+), potassium (K^+) and chlorine (Cl^-), between the inside of the cell and the outside, and from the low and unequal specific permeability of the cell membrane to the diffusion of these ions. In response to physical or chemical stimulation the cell membrane of a neuron may increase or decrease one or another of these specific ion permeabilities, which usually results in a shift in the electric potential across the membrane. One of the most important of these changes in ion permeability is responsible for the action potential, or nerve impulse. Here there is a rather large transient change in the membrane potential lasting for only one or two thousandths of a second once a prior shift in the potential has exceeded a certain much lower threshold value. Thanks mainly to its capacity for generating such impulses, the neuron (a very poor conductor of electric current compared with an insulated copper wire) can carry electrical signals throughout the body of an animal whose dimensions are of the order of inches or feet. The transient change in membrane potential set off by the impulse is propagated with undiminished intensity along the thin axons. Thus the basic element of signaling in the nervous system is the nerve impulse, and the information transmitted by an axon is encoded in the frequency with which impulses propagate along it.

Neurophysiologists have developed methods by which it is possible to listen to the impulse traffic in a single neuron of the nervous system. For this purpose a recording electrode with a very fine tip (less than a ten-thousandth of an inch in diameter) is inserted into the nervous tissue and brought very close to the surface of a neuron. A neutral electrode is placed at a remote site on the animal's body. Each impulse that arises in the neuron then gives rise to a transient difference in potential between the recording electrode and the neutral electrode. With suitable electronic hardware this transient potential difference can be displayed as a blip on an oscilloscope screen or made audible as a click in a loudspeaker.

The point at which two neurons come into functional contact is called a synapse. Here the impulse signals arriving at the axon terminal of the presynaptic neuron are transferred to the postsynaptic neuron that is to receive them. The transfer is mediated not by direct electrical conduction but by the diffusion of a chemical molecule, the transmitter, across the narrow gap that separates the presynaptic axon terminal from the membrane of the postsynaptic cell. That is to say, the arrival of each impulse at the presynaptic axon terminal causes the release there of a small quantity of transmitter, which reaches the postsynaptic membrane and induces a transient change in its ion permeability. Depending on the chemical identity of the transmitter and the nature of its interaction with the postsynaptic membrane, the permeability change may have one of two diametrically opposite results. On the one hand it may increase the chance that there will arise an impulse in the postsynaptic cell. In that case the synapse is said to be excitatory. On the other hand it may reduce that chance, in which case the synapse is said to be inhibitory. Most neurons of the internuncial part receive synaptic contacts from not just one but many different presynaptic neurons, some axon terminals providing excitatory inputs and others inhibitory ones. Hence the frequency with which impulses arise in any postsynaptic neuron reflects an ongoing process of summation, more exactly a temporal integration, of the ensemble of its synaptic inputs.

We are now ready to proceed to our example of an important advance in the understanding of the internuncial ner-

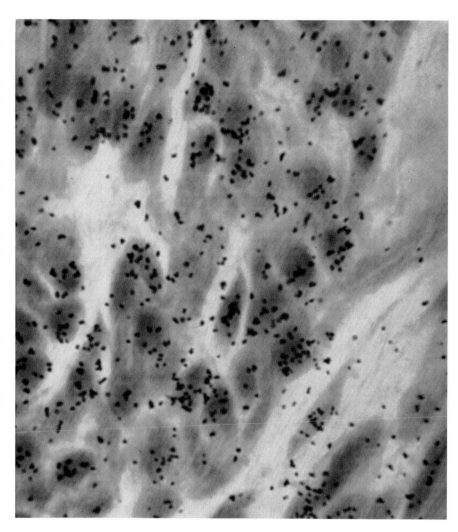

HORMONE AND TARGET CELLS appear in a radioautograph of muscle tissue from a rat uterus. Estradiol, a component of the hormone estrogen that stimulates the growth of uterine muscle, was labeled with tritium; the tissue section was prepared one hour after the hormone was injected. Black dots show concentrations of the hormone. Most are grouped in or near the nuclei of muscle cells. Micrograph was made by W. E. Stumpf, M. Sar and R. N. Prasad of the Laboratories for Reproductive Biology of the University of North Carolina.

vous system, the analysis of the visual pathway in the brain of higher mammals. It is along this pathway that the visual image formed on the retina by light rays entering the eye is transformed into a visual percept, on the basis of which appropriate commands to the muscles are issued. The visual pathway begins at the mosaic of approximately 100 million primary light-receptor cells of the retina. They transform the light image into a spatial pattern of electrical signals, much as a television camera does. Still within the retina, however, the axons of the primary light-receptor cells make synapses with neurons already belonging to the internuncial part of the nervous system. After one or two further synaptic transfers within the retina the signals emanating from the primary light-receptor cells eventually converge on about a million retinal ganglion cells. These ganglion cells send their axons into the optic nerve, which con-

nects the eye with the brain. Thus it is as impulse traffic in ganglion-cell axons that the visual input leaves the eye.

In 1953 Stephen W. Kuffler, who was then working at Johns Hopkins University, discovered that what the impulse traffic in ganglion-cell axons carries to the brain is not raw sensory data but an abstracted version of the primary visual input. This discovery emerged from Kuffler's efforts to ascertain the ganglion-cell receptive field, or that territory of the retinal receptor-cell mosaic whose interaction with incident light influences the impulse activity of individual ganglion cells. For this purpose Kuffler inserted a recording electrode into the immediate vicinity of a ganglion cell in a cat's retina. At the very outset of the study Kuffler made a somewhat unexpected finding, namely that even in the dark, retinal ganglion cells produce impulses at a fairly steady rate (20 to 30 times per second) and that illuminating

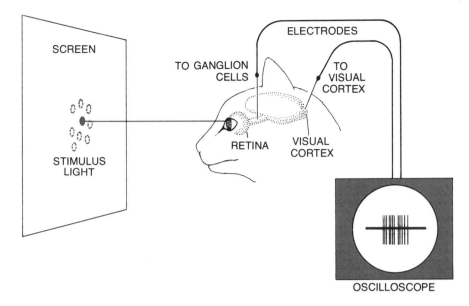

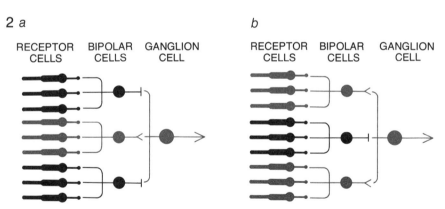

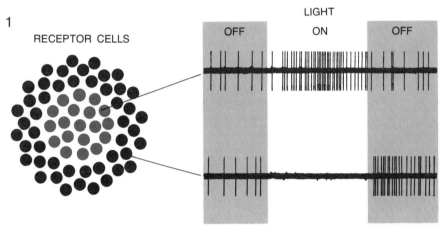

NERVE COMMUNICATION depends for its effectiveness on a process of abstraction that has been demonstrated in studies of visual perception in cats. Use of the experimental situation illustrated at top has revealed the selective destruction of sensory inputs at three successively higher levels of organization within the visual system. At the first of these levels impulses from ganglion cells in the retina, displayed on an oscilloscope, indicate that the cells receive signals from circular arrays of receptor cells. The center and the peripheral cells of the array react differently when stimulated by a spot of light. If the array is an "on center" one (1, *color*), the number of impulses produced by the ganglion cell will increase when light falls on the center but diminish when light falls on the periphery; the reaction is reversed if the array is an "off center" one. An oversimplified diagram of the neuronal circuits involved (2) suggests that in on-center arrays the central receptor cells (*a, color*) feed an excitatory synapse on the ganglion cell while the peripheral cells feed inhibitory synapses. Off-center arrays (*b*) would have the reverse circuitry. Thus the ganglion cell does not report the data on levels of illumination that are collected by the individual receptor cells but sends to the next level of abstraction a summary of the contrast between two concentric regions of the receptive field. The successive stages in this process of selective destruction of sensory inputs are illustrated on the opposite page and on the next two pages.

the entire retina with diffuse light does not have any dramatic effect on that impulse rate. This finding suggested paradoxically that light does not affect the output activity of the retina. Kuffler then, however, projected a tiny spot of light into the cat's eye and moved the image of the spot over various areas of the retina. In this way he found that the impulse activity of an individual ganglion cell does change when the light spot falls on a small circular territory surrounding the retinal position of the ganglion cell. That territory is the receptive field of the cell.

On mapping the receptive fields of many individual ganglion cells Kuffler discovered that every field can be subdivided into two concentric regions: an "on" region, in which incident light increases the impulse rate of the ganglion cell, and an "off" region, in which incident light decreases the impulse rate. Furthermore, he found that the structure of the receptive fields divides retinal ganglion cells into two classes: on-center cells, whose receptive field consists of a circular central "on" region and a surrounding circular "off" region, and off-center cells, whose receptive field consists of a circular central "off" region and a surrounding circular "on" region. In both the on-center and the off-center cells the net impulse activity arising from partial illumination of the receptive field is the result of an algebraic summation: two spots shining on different points of the "on" region give rise to a more vigorous response than either spot alone, whereas one spot shining on the "on" and the other on the "off" region give rise to a weaker response than either spot alone. Uniform illumination of the entire receptive field, the condition that exists under diffuse illumination of the retina, gives rise to virtually no response because of the mutual cancellation of the antagonistic responses from "on" and "off" regions.

It could be concluded, therefore, that the function of retinal ganglion cells is not so much to report to the brain the intensity of light registered by the primary receptor cells of a particular territory of the retina as it is to report the degree of light and dark contrast that exists between the two concentric regions of its receptive field. As can be readily appreciated, such contrast information is essential for the recognition of shapes and forms in the animal's visual field, which is what the eyes are mainly for. Thus we encounter the first example in this discussion of how the nervous system abstracts information by selective destruction of information. The absolute light-intensity data gathered by the primary light-receptor cells are selectively destroyed in the algebraic summation process of "on" and "off" responses and are thereby transformed into the perceptually more meaningful relative-contrast data.

When one thinks about the neuronal circuits that might be responsible for this retinal abstraction process, the first possibility that comes to mind is that they embody the antagonistic function of excitatory and inhibitory synaptic inputs to the same postsynaptic neuron. One might suppose that to produce an on-center receptive field the axon terminals of primary receptor cells from the central "on" territory simply make excitatory synapses with their retinal ganglion cell and primary cells from the peripheral "off" territory make inhibitory synapses [*see illustration on opposite page*]. Detailed analyses of the anatomy and physiology of retinal neurons conducted in recent years have shown that on the one hand the real situation is much more complicated than this simple picture, but that on the other hand the actual neuronal circuits do involve matching of excitatory and inhibitory synapses in the pathways leading from the primary light receptor of antagonistic receptive-field regions to the ganglion cell.

In the late 1950's David H. Hubel and Torsten N. Wiesel, two associates of Kuffler's (who was by then, and still is, at the Harvard Medical School), began to extend these studies on the structure and character of visual receptive fields to the next-highest stage of information processing [see "The Visual Cortex of the Brain," by David H. Hubel; SCIENTIFIC AMERICAN Offprint 168]. For this purpose they examined the further fate of the impulse signals conducted away from the eye by the million or so retinal ganglion-cell axons in the optic nerve to the brain. The optic nerves from the two eyes meet near the center of the head at the optic chiasm. In animals such as cats and men there is a partial crossover of the optic nerves at the optic chiasm; some retinal ganglion-cell axons cross over to the opposite brain hemisphere and some do not. This partial crossover provides the right hemisphere of the brain with the binocular input that the retinas of both eyes receive from the left half of the animal's visual field, and vice versa. Behind the optic chiasm the output of the retinal ganglion cells passes through a way station in the midbrain that for the purposes of this discussion can be considered a simple neuron-to-neuron replay and finally reaches the cerebral cortex at the back of the head. The cortical destination of the visual input is designated as the visual cortex. Here the incoming axons make synaptic contact with the nerve cells of the cortex. The first cortical cells with which the axon projecting from the eye comes in contact in turn send their axons to other cells in the visual cortex for further processing of the visual input. From that point one must still find the trail that eventually leads to the motor centers of the brain, where, if the visual stimulus is to elicit a behavioral act, commands must be issued to the muscles.

Hubel and Wiesel's procedure was to insert a recording electrode into the visual cortex of a cat and to observe the impulse activity of individual cortical neurons in response to various light stimuli projected on a screen in front of the cat's eyes. In this way they found that these higher-order neurons of the visual pathway also respond only to stimuli falling on a limited retinal territory of light-receptor cells. The character of the receptive fields of cortical neurons turned out, however, to be dramatically different from that of the retinal ganglion cells. Instead of having circular receptive fields with concentric "on" and "off" regions, the cortical neurons were found to respond to straight edges of light-dark contrast, such as bright bars on a dark background. Furthermore, for the straight edge to produce its optimum response it must be in a particular orientation in the receptive field. A bright bar projected vertically on the screen that produces a vigorous response in a particular cortical cell will no longer elicit the response as soon as its projection is tilted slightly away from the vertical.

In their first studies Hubel and Wiesel found two different classes of cells in the

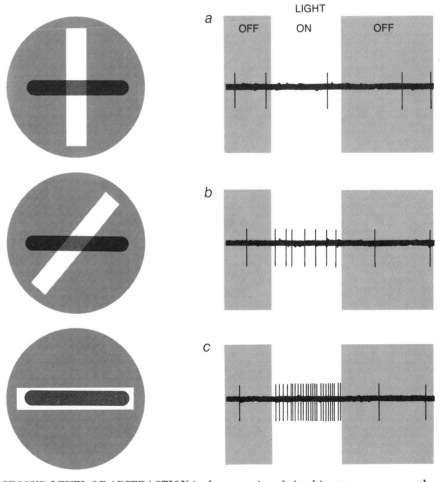

SECOND LEVEL OF ABSTRACTION in the processing of visual inputs occurs among the "simple" cells of the visual cortex, which receive summarized data from many ganglion cells. Cortical-cell impulses increase only when the many retinal receptor cells providing input data are stimulated by light-dark contrast in the form of a straight edge, such as a bar of light shown on a dark background. Moreover, the simple cortical cells fail to react if the edge is not precisely oriented, as the difference in oscilloscope impulse frequencies (a–c) indicates. In effect, by means of selective destruction of input data, the simple cortical cells transform the ganglion-cell information about light-dark contrast at various points in the visual field into information about light-dark contrasts along straight-line sets of points.

visual cortex: simple cells and complex cells. The response of simple cells demands that the straight-edge stimulus must have not only a given orientation but also a precise position in the receptive field. The stimulus requirements of complex cells are less demanding, however, in that their response is sustained on a parallel displacement (but not a tilt) of the straight-edge stimuli within the receptive field. Thus the process of abstraction of the visual input begun in the retina is continued at higher levels in the visual cortex. The simple cells, which are evidently the next abstraction stage, transform the data supplied by the retinal ganglion cells concerning the light-dark contrast at individual points of the visual field into information concerning the contrast present at particular straight-line sets of points. This transformation is achieved by the selective destruction of the information concerning just how much contrast exists at just which point of the straight-line set. The complex cells carry out the next stage of abstraction. They transform the contrast data concerning particular straight-line sets of visual-field points into information concerning the contrast present at parallel sets of straight-line point sets. In other words, here there is a selective destruction of the information concerning just how much contrast exists at each member of a set of parallel straight lines.

The neuronal circuits responsible for these next stages of abstraction of the visual input can now be fathomed. Let us consider first the simple cell of the visual cortex that responds best to a bright bar on a dark background projected in a particular orientation and position on the retinal receptor-cell mosaic. Here we may visualize the simple cell being so connected to the output of

the retina that it receives synaptic inputs from axons reporting the impulse activity of a set of on-center retinal ganglion cells with receptive fields arranged in a straight line. Therefore a bright bar falling on all the central "on" regions of this row of receptive fields but on none of the peripheral "off" regions will activate the entire set of retinal ganglion cells and provide maximal excitation for the simple cortical cell. If the retinal projection of the bar is slightly displaced or tilted, however, some light will also strike the peripheral "off" regions and the excitation provided for the simple cell is diminished.

We next consider the response of a complex cortical cell to a bright bar of a particular orientation in any one of several parallel positions in the receptive field. This response can be easily explained on the basis that the complex cell receives its synaptic inputs from the axons of a set of simple cortical cells. All the simple cells of this set would have receptive fields that respond optimally to a bright bar projected in the same field orientation, but they differ in the field position of their optimal response. A suitably oriented bright bar projected anywhere in the complex receptive field will always activate one of the component simple cells and so also the complex cell.

In their later work Hubel and Wiesel were able to identify cells in the visual cortex whose optimal stimuli reflect even higher levels of abstraction than parallel straight lines, such as straight-line ends and corners. It is not so clear at present how far this process of abstraction by convergence of communication channels ought to be imagined as going. In particular, should one think that there exists for every pattern of whose specific recognition an animal is capable at least

one particular cell in the cerebral cortex that responds with impulse activity when that pattern appears in the visual field? In view of the vast number of such patterns we recognize in a lifetime, that might seem somewhat improbable. So far, however, no other plausible explanation of perception capable of advancing neurophysiological research appears to have been put forward.

Admittedly, ever since the discipline of neurophysiology was founded more than a century ago, there have been adherents of a "holistic" theory of the brain. This theory envisions specific functions of the brain, including perception, depending not on the activity of particular localized cells or centers but flowing instead from general and widely distributed activity patterns. With the discovery of functionally specialized brain loci such as the visual cortex the holistic theory has had to retreat from its original extreme position, yet it may still hold in some more limited way. Quite aside from being hard to fathom, however, the theory seems to be better suited to inspiring experiments that show the defects of the localization concept than to explaining how the brain might actually work.

In any case the findings on the nature of nervous communication described here have some important general implications, in that they lend physiological support to the latter-day philosophical view that has come to be known as "structuralism." In recent years the structuralist view emerged more or less simultaneously, independently and in different guises in diverse fields of study, for example in analytical psychology, cognitive psychology, linguistics and anthropology. The names most often associated with each of these developments are those of Carl Jung, Wolfgang Köhler, Noam Chomsky and Claude Lévi-Strauss. The emergence of structuralism represents the overthrow of "positivism" (and its psychological counterpart "behaviorism") that held sway since the late 19th century and marks a return to Immanuel Kant's late-18th-century critique of pure reason. Structuralism admits, as positivism does not, the existence of innate ideas, or of knowledge without learning. Furthermore, structuralism recognizes that information about the world enters the mind not as raw data but as highly abstract structures that are the result of a preconscious set of step-by-step transformations of the sensory input. Each transformation step involves the selective destruction of information,

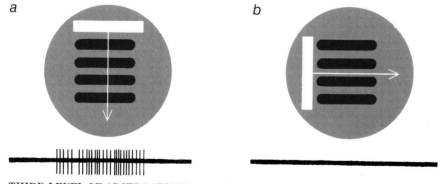

a   b

THIRD LEVEL OF ABSTRACTION occurs when data from the simple cortical cells reach the complex cortical cells. These higher nerve cells increase their impulses only when the retinal stimulus consists of a bar of light in motion across the visual field. Moreover, only the vertical movement of a horizontal bar through the field (a) induces the complex cells of the cortex to respond; a vertical bar moved horizontally (b) goes unnoticed. A diagram of the circuitry responsible for this type of abstraction appears on the opposite page.

according to a program that preexists in the brain. Any set of primary sense data becomes meaningful only after a series of such operations performed on it has transformed the data set into a pattern that matches a preexisting mental structure. These conclusions of structuralist philosophy were reached entirely from the study of human behavior without recourse to physiological observations. As the experimental work discussed in this article shows, however, the manner in which sensory input into the retina is processed along the visual pathway corresponds exactly to the structuralist tenets.

It should be mentioned in this connection that studies on the visual cortex of monkeys have led to results entirely analogous to those obtained with cats, namely that there are simple and complex cells responding to parallel straight-line patterns in the visual field. It is therefore reasonable to expect that the organization of the human visual cortex follows the same general plan. That is to say, our own visual perception of the outer world is filtered through a stage in which data are processed in terms of straight parallel lines, thanks to the way in which the input channels coming from the primary light-receptors of the retina are hooked up to the brain. This fact cannot fail to have profound psychological consequences; evidently a geometry based on straight parallel lines, and hence by extension on plane surfaces, is most immediately compatible with our mental equipment. It need not have been this way, since (at least from the neurophysiological point of view) the retinal ganglion cells could just as well have been connected to the higher cells in the visual cortex in such a way that their concentric on-center and off-center receptive fields form arcs rather than straight lines. If evolution had given rise to that other circuitry, curved rather than plane surfaces would have been our primary spatial concept. Thus neurobiology has now shown why it is human—and all too human—to hold Euclidean geometry and its nonintersecting coplanar parallel lines to be a self-evident truth. Non-Euclidean geometries of convex or concave surfaces, although our brain is evidently capable of conceiving them, are more alien to our built-in spatial-perception processes. Apparently a beginning has now been made in providing, in terms of cellular communication, an explanation for one of the deepest of all philosophical problems: the relation between reality and the mind.

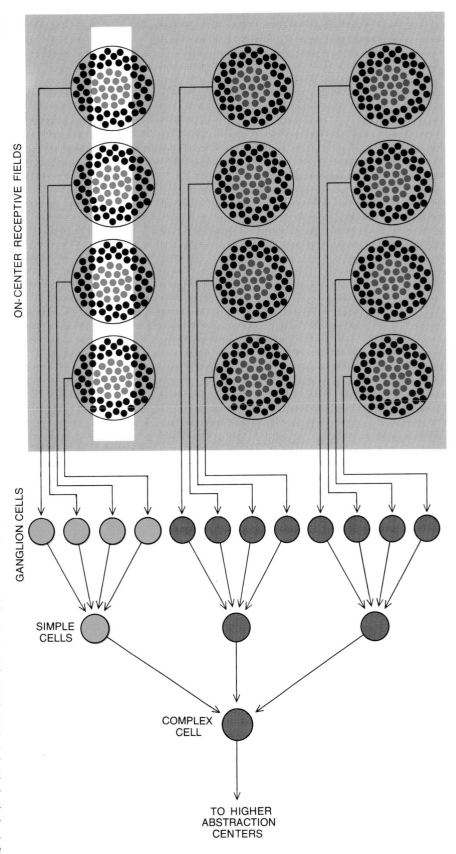

CIRCUITRY OF ABSTRACTION inferred to exist within a cat's visual cortex is illustrated schematically. It begins with a rectangular array of receptive fields. The array is comprised of three parallel vertical rows and each row contains four receptive fields. The axons from the retinal ganglion cells that correspond to each row converge on one of three simple cortical cells; the axons from the simple cells then converge on one complex cortical cell. A bar of light (*left*) falling on a row of receptive fields excites the four ganglion cells corresponding to that row and also the simple cortical cell connected to them (*color*).

3

ANIMAL COMMUNICATION

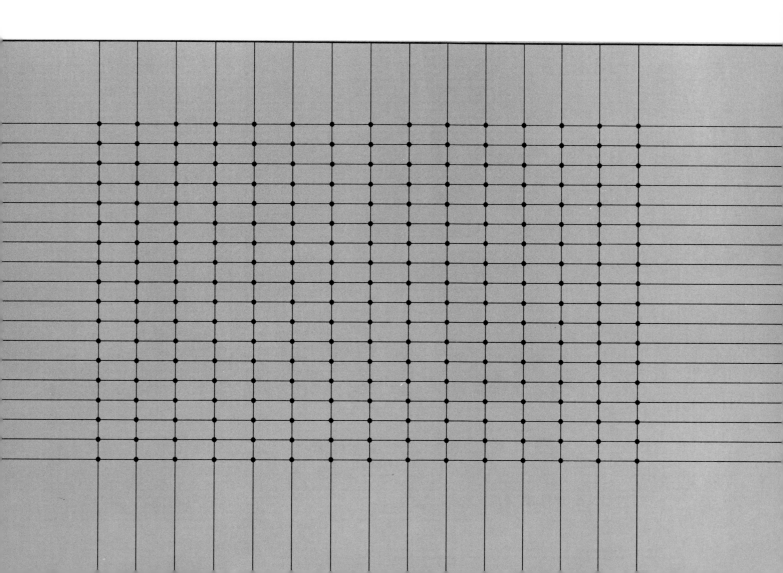

Animal Communication
EDWARD O. WILSON

Animals ranging from insects to mammals communicate by means of chemicals, movements, and sounds. Man also uses these modes of communication, but he adds his own unique kind of language.

The most instructive way to view the communication systems of animals is to compare these systems first with human language. With our own unique verbal system as a standard of reference we can define the limits of animal communication in terms of the properties it rarely—or never—displays. Consider the way I address you now. Each word I use has been assigned a specific meaning by a particular culture and transmitted to us down through generations by learning. What is truly unique is the very large number of such words and the potential for creating new ones to denote any number of additional objects and concepts. This potential is quite literally infinite. To take an example from mathematics, we can coin a nonsense word for any number we choose (as in the case of the googol, which designates a 1 followed by 100 zeros). Human beings utter their words sequentially in phrases and sentences that generate, according to complex rules also determined at least partly by the culture, a vastly larger array of messages than is provided by the mere summed meanings of the words themselves. With these messages it is possible to talk about the language itself, an achievement we are utilizing here. It is also possible to project an endless number of unreal images: fiction or lies, speculation or fraud, idealism or demagogy, the definition depending on whether or not the communicator informs the listener of his intention to speak falsely.

Now contrast this with one of the most sophisticated of all animal communication systems, the celebrated waggle dance of the honeybee (*Apis mellifera*), first decoded in 1945 by the German biologist Karl von Frisch. When a foraging worker bee returns from the field after discovering a food source (or, in the course of swarming, a desirable new nest site) at some distance from the hive, she indicates the location of this target to her fellow workers by performing the waggle dance. The pattern of her movement is a figure eight repeated over and over again in the midst of crowds of sister workers. The most distinctive and informative element of the dance is the straight run (the middle of the figure eight), which is given a particular emphasis by a rapid lateral vibration of the body (the waggle) that is greatest at the tip of the abdomen and least marked at the head.

The complete back-and-forth shake of the body is performed 13 to 15 times per second. At the same time the bee emits an audible buzzing sound by vibrating its wings. The straight run represents, quite simply, a miniaturized version of the flight from the hive to the target. It points directly at the target if the bee is dancing outside the hive on a horizontal surface. (The position of the sun with respect to the straight run provides the required orientation.) If the bee is on a vertical surface inside the darkened hive, the straight run points at the appropriate angle away from the vertical,

so that gravity temporarily replaces the sun as the orientation cue.

The straight run also provides information on the distance of the target from the hive, by means of the following additional parameter: the farther away the goal lies, the longer the straight run lasts. In the Carniolan race of the honeybee a straight run lasting a second indicates a target about 500 meters away, and a run lasting two seconds indicates a target two kilometers away. During the dance the follower bees extend their antennae and touch the dancer repeatedly. Within minutes some begin to leave the nest and fly to the target. Their searching is respectably accurate: the great majority come down to search close to the ground within 20 percent of the correct distance.

Superficially the waggle dance of the honeybee may seem to possess some of the more advanced properties of human language. Symbolism occurs in the form of the ritualized straight run, and the communicator can generate new messages at will by means of the symbolism. Furthermore, the target is "spoken of" abstractly: it is an object removed in time and space. Nevertheless, the waggle dance, like all other forms of nonhuman communication studied so far, is severely limited in comparison with the verbal language of human beings. The straight run is after all just a reenactment of the flight the bees will take, complete with wing-buzzing to represent the actual motor activity required. The separate messages are not devised arbitrarily. The rules they follow are genetically fixed and always designate, with a one-to-one correspondence, a certain direction and distance.

In other words, the messages cannot be manipulated to provide new classes of information. Moreover, within this

COURTSHIP RITUAL of grebes is climaxed by the "penguin dance" shown on the opposite page. In this ritual the male and the female present each other with a beakful of the waterweed that is used as a nest-building material. A pair-bonding display, the dance may have originated as "displacement" behavior, in this instance a pantomime of nest-building triggered by the conflict within each partner between hostility and sexual attraction. The penguin dance was first analyzed in 1914 by Julian Huxley, who observed the ritual among great crested grebes in Europe. Shown here are western grebes in southern Saskatchewan.

rigid context the messages are far from being infinitely divisible. Because of errors both in the dance and in the subsequent searches by the followers, only about three bits of information are transmitted with respect to distance and four bits with respect to direction. This is the equivalent of a human communication system in which distance would be gauged on a scale with eight divisions and direction would be defined in terms of a compass with 16 points. Northeast could be distinguished from north by northeast, or west from west by southwest, but no more refined indication of direction would be possible.

The waggle dance, in particular the duration of the straight run denoting distance, illustrates a simple principle that operates through much of animal communication: the greater the magnitude to be communicated, the more intense and prolonged the signal given. This graduated (or analogue) form of communication is perhaps most strikingly developed in aggressive displays among animals. In the rhesus monkey, for example, a low-intensity aggressive display is a simple stare. The hard look a human receives when he approaches a caged rhesus is not so much a sign of curiosity as it is a cautious display of hostility.

Rhesus monkeys in the wild frequent-ly threaten one another not only with stares but also with additional displays on an ascending scale of intensity. To the human observer these displays are increasingly obvious in their meaning. The new components are added one by one or in combination: the mouth opens, the head bobs up and down, characteristic sounds are uttered and the hands slap the ground. By the time the monkey combines all these components, and perhaps begins to make little forward lunges as well, it is likely to carry through with an actual attack. Its opponent responds either by retreating or by escalating its own displays. These hostile exchanges play a key role in maintaining dominance relationships in the rhesus society.

Birds often indicate hostility by ruffling their feathers or spreading their wings, which creates the temporary illusion that they are larger than they really are. Many fishes achieve the same deception by spreading their fins or extending their gill covers. Lizards raise their crest, lower their dewlaps or flatten the sides of their body to give an impression of greater depth. In short, the more hostile the animal, the more likely it is to attack and the bigger it seems to become. Such exhibitions are often accompanied by graded changes both in color and in vocalization, and even by the release of characteristic odors.

The communication systems of insects, of other invertebrates and of the lower vertebrates (such as fishes and amphibians) are characteristically stereotyped. This means that for each signal there is only one response or very few responses, that each response can be evoked by only a very limited number of signals and that the signaling behavior and the responses are nearly constant throughout entire populations of the same species. An extreme example of this rule is seen in the phenomenon of chemical sex attraction in moths. The female silkworm moth draws males to her by emitting minute quantities of a complex alcohol from glands at the tip of her abdomen. The secretion is called bombykol (from the name of the moth, *Bombyx mori*), and its chemical structure is *trans*-10-*cis*-12-hexadecadienol.

Bombykol is a remarkably powerful biological agent. According to estimates made by Dietrich Schneider and his coworkers at the Max Planck Institute for Comparative Physiology at Seewiesen in Germany, the male silkworm moths start searching for the females when they are immersed in as few as 14,000 molecules of bombykol per cubic centimeter of air. The male catches the molecules on some 10,000 distinctive sensory hairs on each of its two feathery antennae. Each hair is innervated by one or two receptor cells that lead inward to the main antennal nerve and ultimately through connecting nerve cells to centers in the brain. The extraordinary fact that emerged from the study by the Seewiesen group is that only a single molecule of bombykol is required to activate a receptor cell. Furthermore, the cell will respond to virtually no stimulus other than molecules of bombykol. When about 200 cells in each antenna are activated, the male moth starts its motor response. Tightly bound by this extreme signal specificity, the male performs as little more than a sexual guided missile, programmed to home on an increasing gradient of bombykol centered on the tip of the female's abdomen—the principal goal of the male's adult life.

Such highly stereotyped communication systems are particularly important in evolutionary theory because of the possible role the systems play in the origin of new species. Conceivably one small change in the sex-attractant molecule induced by a genetic mutation, together with a corresponding change in the antennal receptor cell, could result in the creation of a population of individuals that would be reproductively isolated from the parental stock. Persuasive

WAGGLE DANCE of the honeybee, first decoded by Karl von Frisch in 1945, is performed by a foraging worker bee on its return to the hive after the discovery of a food source. The pattern of the dance is a repeated figure eight. During the straight run in the middle of the figure the forager waggles its abdomen rapidly and vibrates its wings. As is shown in the illustrations on the opposite page, the direction of the straight run indicates the line of flight to the food source. The duration of the straight run shows workers how far to fly.

evidence for the feasibility of such a mutational change has recently been adduced by Wendell L. Roelofs and Andre Comeau of Cornell University. They found two closely related species of moths (members of the genus *Bryotopha* in the family Gelechiidae) whose females' sex attractants differ only by the configuration of a single carbon atom adjacent to a double bond. In other words, the attractants are simply different geometric isomers. Field tests showed not only that a *Bryotopha* male responds solely to the isomer of its own species but also that its response is inhibited if some of the other species' isomer is also present.

A qualitatively different kind of specificity is encountered among birds and mammals. Unlike the insects, many of these higher vertebrates are able to distinguish one another as individuals on the basis of idiosyncrasies in the way they deliver signals. Indigo buntings and certain other songbirds learn to discriminate the territorial calls of their neighbors from those of strangers that occupy territories farther away. When a recording of the song of a neighbor is played near them, they show no unusual reactions, but a recording of a stranger's song elicits an agitated aggressive response.

Families of seabirds depend on a similar capacity for recognition to keep together as a unit in the large, clamorous colonies where they nest. Beat Tschanz of the University of Bern has demonstrated that the young of the common murre (*Uria aalge*), a large auk, learn to react selectively to the call of their parents in the first few days of their life and that the parents also quickly learn to distinguish their own young. There is some evidence that the young murres can even learn certain aspects of the adult calls while they are still in the egg. An equally striking phenomenon is the intercommunication between African shrikes (of the genus *Laniarius*) recently analyzed by W. H. Thorpe of the University of Cambridge. Mated pairs of these birds keep in contact by calling antiphonally back and forth, the first bird vocalizing one or more notes and its mate instantly responding with a variation of the first call. So fast is the exchange, sometimes taking no more than a fraction of a second, that unless an observer stands between the two birds he does not realize that more than one bird is singing. In at least one of the species, the boubou shrike (*Laniarius aethiopicus*), the members of the pair learn to sing duets with each other. They work out combinations of phrases that are sufficiently individual

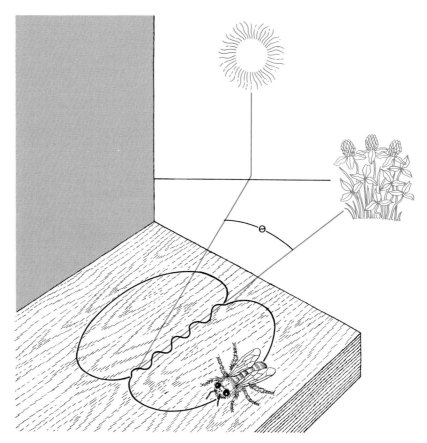

DANCING OUTSIDE THE HIVE on a horizontal surface, the forager makes the straight run of its waggle dance point directly at the source of food. In this illustration the food is located some 20 degrees to the right of the sun. The forager's fellow workers maintain the same orientation with respect to the sun as they leave for the reported source of food.

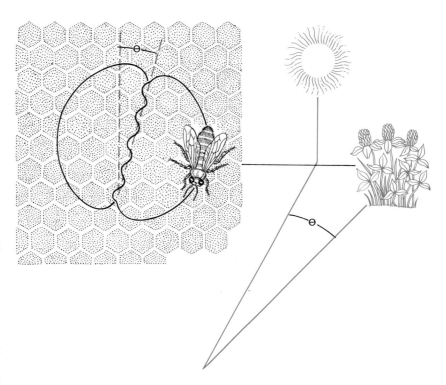

DANCING INSIDE THE HIVE on the vertical face of the honeycomb, the forager uses gravity for orientation. The straight line of the waggle dance that shows the line of flight to the source of food is oriented some 20 degrees away from the vertical. On leaving the hive, the bee's fellow workers relate the indicated orientation angle to the position of the sun.

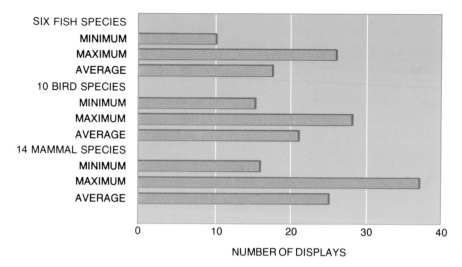

SIX FISH SPECIES
MINIMUM
MAXIMUM
AVERAGE
10 BIRD SPECIES
MINIMUM
MAXIMUM
AVERAGE
14 MAMMAL SPECIES
MINIMUM
MAXIMUM
AVERAGE

0   10   20   30   40

NUMBER OF DISPLAYS

COMMUNICATIVE DISPLAYS used by 30 species of vertebrate animals whose "languages" have been studied vary widely within each of the classes of animals represented: fishes, birds and mammals. The average differences between the classes, however, are comparatively small. The largest and smallest number of displays within each class and the average for each class are shown in this graph. Six of the fish species that have been studied use an average of some 17 displays, compared with an average of 21 displays used by 10 species of birds and an average of 25 displays among 14 species of mammals. Martin H. Moynihan of the Smithsonian Institution compiled the display data. The 30 vertebrates and the number of displays that each uses are illustrated on the opposite page and on page 34.

to enable them to recognize each other even though both are invisible in the dense vegetation the species normally inhabits.

Mammals are at least equally adept at discriminating among individuals of their own kind. A wide range of cues are employed by different species to distinguish mates, offspring and in the case of social mammals the subordinate or dominant rank of the peers ranged around them. In some species special secretions are employed to impart a personal odor signature to part of the environment or to other members in the social group. As all dog owners know, their pet urinates at regular locations within its territory at a rate that seems to exceed physiological needs. What is less well appreciated is the communicative function this compulsive behavior serves: a scent included in the urine identifies the animal and announces its presence to potential intruders of the same species.

Males of the sugar glider (*Petaurus breviceps*), a New Guinea marsupial with a striking but superficial resemblance to the flying squirrel, go even further. They mark their mate with a secretion from a gland on the front of their head. Other secretions originating in glands on the male's feet, on its chest and near its arms, together with its saliva, are used to mark its territory. In both instances the odors are distinctive enough for the male to distinguish them from those of other sugar gliders.

As a rule we find that the more highly social the mammal is, the more complex the communication codes are and the more the codes are utilized in establishing and maintaining individual relationships. It is no doubt significant that one of the rare examples of persistent individual recognition among the lower animals is the colony odor of the social insects: ants and termites and certain social bees and wasps. Even here, however, it is the colony as a whole that is recognized. The separate members of the colony respond automatically to certain caste distinctions, but they do not ordinarily learn to discriminate among their nestmates as individuals.

By human standards the number of signals employed by each species of animal is severely limited. One of the most curious facts revealed by recent field studies is that even the most highly social vertebrates rarely have more than 30 or 35 separate displays in their entire repertory. Data compiled by Martin H. Moynihan of the Smithsonian Institution indicate that among most vertebrates the number of displays varies by a factor of only three or four from species to species. The number ranges from a minimum of 10 in certain fishes to a maximum of 37 in the rhesus monkey, one of the primates closest to man in the complexity of their social organization. The full significance of this rule of relative inflexibility is not yet clear. It may be that the maximum number of messages any animal needs in order to be fully adaptive in any ordinary environment, even a social one, is no more than

30 or 40. Or it may be, as Moynihan has suggested, that each number represents the largest amount of signal diversity the particular animal's brain can handle efficiently in quickly changing social interactions.

In the extent of their signal diversity the vertebrates are closely approached by social insects, particularly honeybees and ants. Analyses by Charles G. Butler at the Rothamsted Experimental Station in England, by me at Harvard University and by others have brought the number of individual known signal categories within single species of these insects to between 10 and 20. The honeybee has been the most thoroughly studied of all the social insects. Apart from the waggle dance its known communicative acts are mediated primarily by pheromones: chemical compounds transmitted to other members of the same species as signals. The glandular sources of these and other socially important substances are now largely established. Other honeybee signals include the distinctive colony odor mentioned above, tactile cues involved in food exchange and several dances that are different in form and function from the waggle dance.

Of the known honeybee pheromones the "queen substances" are outstanding in the complexity and pervasiveness of their role in social organization. They include *trans*-9-keto-2-decenoic acid, which is released from the queen's mandibular glands and evokes at least three separate effects according to the context of its presentation. The pheromone is spread through the colony when workers lick the queen's body and regurgitate the material back and forth to one another. For the substance to be effective in the colony as a whole the queen must dispense enough for each worker bee to receive approximately a tenth of a microgram per day.

The first effect of the ketodecenoic acid is to keep workers from rearing larvae in a way that would result in their becoming new queens, thus preventing the creation of potential rivals to the mother queen. The second effect is that when the worker bees eat the substance, their own ovaries fail to develop; they cannot lay eggs and as a result they too are eliminated as potential rivals. Indirect evidence indicates that ingestion of the substance affects the corpora allata, the endocrine glands that partly control the development of the ovaries, but the exact chain of events remains to be worked out. The third effect of the pheromone is that it acts as a sex attractant. When a virgin queen flies from

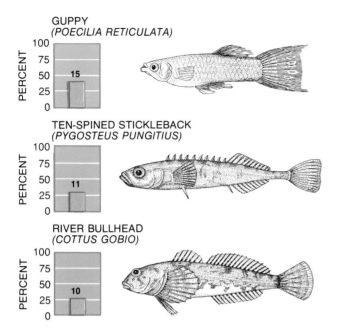

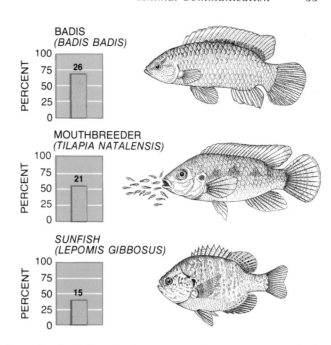

DISPLAYS BY FISHES range from a minimum of 10, used by the river bullhead (*bottom left*), to a maximum of 26, used by the badis (*top right*). The badis repertory is thus more extensive than those of eight of the 10 birds and nine of the 14 mammals studied. The bar beside each fish expresses the number of its displays in percent; 37 displays, the maximum in the study, equal 100 percent.

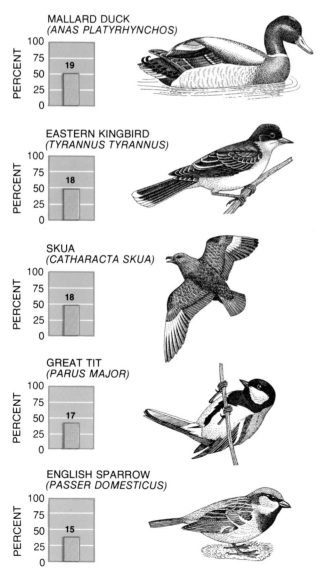

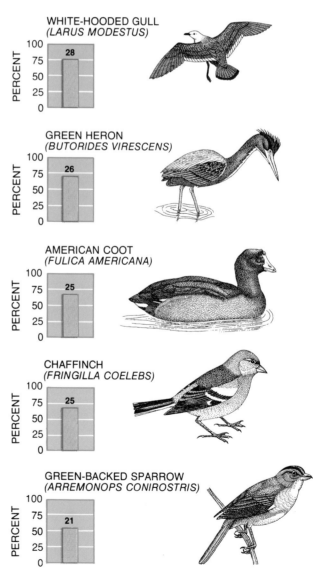

DISPLAYS BY BIRDS range from a minimum of 15, used by the English sparrow (*bottom left*), to a maximum of 28, used by the white-headed gull (*top right*). The maximum repertory among birds thus proves to be little greater than the fishes' maximum.

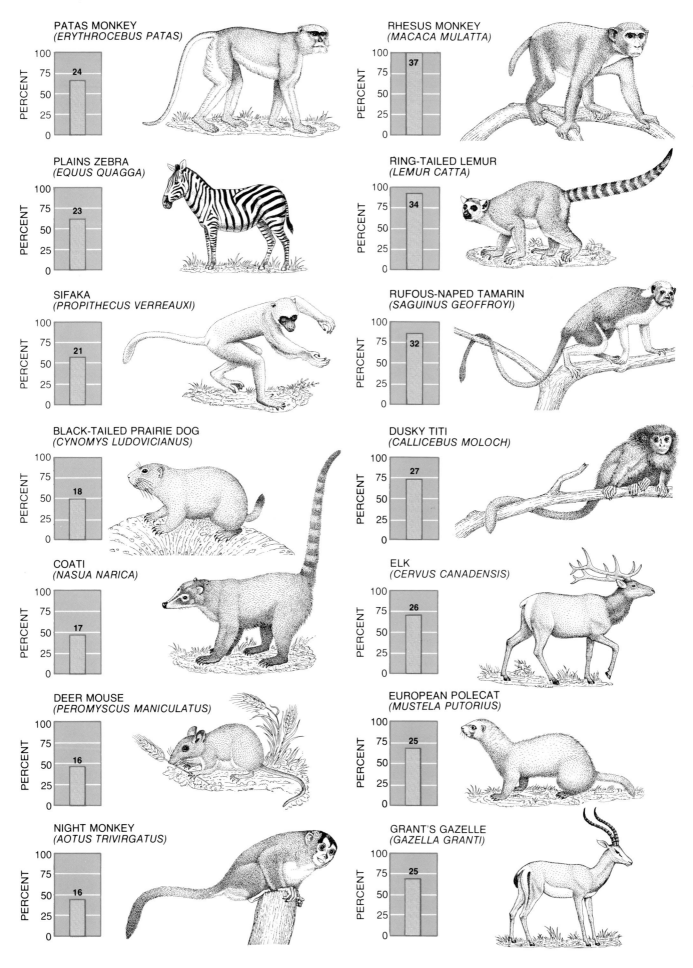

PATAS MONKEY
(*ERYTHROCEBUS PATAS*)

PLAINS ZEBRA
(*EQUUS QUAGGA*)

SIFAKA
(*PROPITHECUS VERREAUXI*)

BLACK-TAILED PRAIRIE DOG
(*CYNOMYS LUDOVICIANUS*)

COATI
(*NASUA NARICA*)

DEER MOUSE
(*PEROMYSCUS MANICULATUS*)

NIGHT MONKEY
(*AOTUS TRIVIRGATUS*)

RHESUS MONKEY
(*MACACA MULATTA*)

RING-TAILED LEMUR
(*LEMUR CATTA*)

RUFOUS-NAPED TAMARIN
(*SAGUINUS GEOFFROYI*)

DUSKY TITI
(*CALLICEBUS MOLOCH*)

ELK
(*CERVUS CANADENSIS*)

EUROPEAN POLECAT
(*MUSTELA PUTORIUS*)

GRANT'S GAZELLE
(*GAZELLA GRANTI*)

DISPLAYS BY MAMMALS range from a minimum of 16, used both by the deer mouse and by the night monkey (*left, bottom and next to bottom*), to a maximum of 37, used by the rhesus monkey (*top right*). Two other primates rank next in number of displays.

the hive on her nuptial flight, she releases a vapor trail of the ketodecenoic acid in the air. The smell of the substance not only attracts drones to the queen but also induces them to copulate with her.

Where do such communication codes come from in the first place? By comparing the signaling behavior of closely related species zoologists are often able to piece together the sequence of evolutionary steps that leads to even the most bizarre communication systems. The evolutionary process by which a behavior pattern becomes increasingly effective as a signal is called "ritualization." Commonly, and perhaps invariably, the process begins when some movement, some anatomical feature or some physiological trait that is functional in quite another context acquires a secondary value as a signal. For example, one can begin by recognizing an open mouth as a threat or by interpreting the turning away of the body in the midst of conflict as an intention to flee. During ritualization such movements are altered in some way that makes their communicative function still more effective. In extreme cases the new behavior pattern may be so modified from its ancestral state that its evolutionary history is all but impossible to imagine. Like the epaulets, shako plumes and piping that garnish military dress uniforms, the practical functions that originally existed have long since been obliterated in order to maximize efficiency in display.

The ritualization of vertebrate behavior commonly begins in circumstances of conflict, particularly when an animal is undecided whether or not to complete an act. Hesitation in behavior communicates the animal's state of mind—or, to be more precise, its probable future course of action—to onlooking members of the same species. The advertisement may begin its evolution as a simple intention movement. Birds intending to fly, for example, typically crouch, raise their tail and spread their wings slightly just before taking off. Many species have ritualized these movements into effective signals. In some species white rump feathers produce a conspicuous flash when the tail is raised. In other species the wing tips are flicked repeatedly downward, uncovering conspicuous areas on the primary feathers of the wings. The signals serve to coordinate the movement of flock members, and also may warn of approaching predators.

Signals also evolve from the ambivalence created by the conflict between two or more behavioral tendencies.

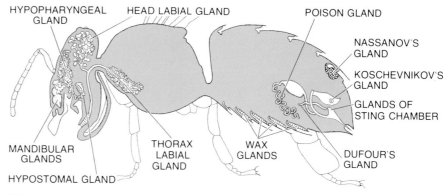

PHEROMONES OF THE HONEYBEE are produced by the glands shown in this cutaway figure of a worker. The glands perform different functions in different castes. In workers, for example, the secretion of the mandibular glands serves as an alarm signal. In a queen, however, the mandibular secretion that is spread through the colony as a result of grooming inhibits workers from raising new queens and also prevents workers from becoming egg-layers. It is also released as a vaporous sex attractant when the new queen leaves the hive on her nuptial flight. The "royal jelly" secreted by the hypopharyngeal gland serves as a food and also acts as a caste determinant. The labial glands of head and thorax secrete a substance utilized for grooming, cleaning and dissolving. Action of the hypostomal-gland secretion is unknown, as is the action of Dufour's gland. The wax glands yield nest-building material, the poison gland is for defense and the sting-chamber glands provide an alarm signal. The secretion of Nassanov's gland assists in assembling workers in conjunction with the waggle dance; that of Koschevnikov's gland renders queens attractive to workers.

When a male faces an opponent, unable to decide whether to attack or to flee, or approaches a potential mate with strong tendencies both to threaten and to court, he may at first make neither choice. Instead he performs a third, seemingly irrelevant act. The aggression is redirected at a meaningless object nearby, such as a pebble, a blade of grass or a bystander that serves as a scapegoat. Or the animal may abruptly commence a "displacement" activity: a behavior pattern with no relevance whatever to the circumstance in which the animal finds itself. The animal may preen, start ineffectual nest-building movements or pantomime feeding or drinking.

Such redirected and displacement activities have often been ritualized into strikingly clear signals. Two classic examples involve the formation of a pair bond between courting grebes. They were among the first such signals to be recognized; Julian Huxley, the originator of the concept of ritualization, analyzed the behavior among European great crested grebes in 1914. The first ritual is "mutual headshaking." It is apparently derived from more elementary movements, aimed at reducing hostility, wherein each bird simply directs its bill away from its partner. The second ritual, called by Huxley the "penguin dance," includes headshaking, diving and the mutual presentation by each partner to its mate of the waterweeds that serve as nesting material. The collection and presentation of the waterweeds may have evolved from displacement nesting behavior initially produced by the conflict between hostility and sexuality.

A perhaps even more instructive example of how ritualization proceeds is provided by the courtship behavior of the "dance flies." These insects include a large number of carnivorous species of dipterans that entomologists classify together as the family Empididae. Many of the species engage in a kind of courtship that consists in a simple approach by the male; this approach is followed by copulation. Among other species the male first captures an insect of the kind that normally falls prey to empids and presents it to the female before copulation. This act appears to reduce the chances of the male himself becoming a victim of the predatory impulses of the female. In other species the male fastens threads or globules of silk to the freshly captured offering, rendering it more distinctive in appearance, a clear step in the direction of ritualization.

Increasing degrees of ritualization can be observed among still other species of dance flies. In one of these species the male totally encloses the dead prey in a sheet of silk. In another the size of the offered prey is smaller but its silken covering remains as large as before: it is now a partly empty "balloon." The male of another species does not bother to capture any prey object but simply offers the female an empty balloon. The last display is so far removed from the original behavior pattern that its evolutionary origin in this empid species might have remained a permanent mystery if biolo-

AGGRESSIVE DISPLAYS by a rhesus monkey (*top*) and a green heron (*bottom*) illustrate a major principle of animal communication: the greater the magnitude to be communicated, the more prolonged and intense the signal is. In the rhesus what begins as a display of low intensity, a hard stare (*left*), is gradually escalated as the monkey rises to a standing position (*middle*) and then, with an open mouth, bobs its head up and down (*right*) and slaps the ground with its hands. If the opponent has not retreated by now, the monkey may actually attack. A similarly graduated aggressive display is characteristic of the green heron. At first (*middle*) the heron raises the feathers that form its crest and twitches the feathers of its tail. If the opponent does not retreat, the heron opens its beak, erects its crest fully, ruffles all its plumage to give the illusion of increased size and violently twitches its tail (*right*). Thus in both animals the likelier the attack, the more intense the aggressive display. Andrew J. Meyerriecks of the University of South Florida conducted the study of heron display and Stuart A. Altmann of the University of Chicago conducted the rhesus display study.

gists had not discovered what appears to be the full story of its development preserved step by step in the behavior of related species.

One of the most important and most difficult questions raised by behavioral biology can be phrased in the evolutionary terms just introduced as follows: Can we hope to trace the origin of human language back through intermediate steps in our fellow higher primates—our closest living relatives, the apes and monkeys—in the same way that entomologists have deduced the origin of the empty-balloon display among the dance flies? The answer would seem to be a very limited and qualified yes. The most probable links to investigate exist within human paralinguistics: the extensive array of facial expressions, body postures, hand signals and vocal tones and emphases that we use to supplement verbal speech. It might be possible to match some of these auxiliary signals with the more basic displays in apes and monkeys. J. A. R. A. M. van Hooff of the State University of Utrecht, for example,

has argued persuasively that laughter originated from the primitive "relaxed open-mouth display" used by the higher primates to indicate their intention to participate in mock aggression or play (as distinct from the hostile open-mouth posture described earlier as a low-intensity threat display in the rhesus monkey). Smiling, on the other hand, van Hooff derives from the primitive "silent bared-teeth display," which denotes submission or at least nonhostility.

What about verbal speech? Chimpanzees taught from infancy by human trainers are reported to be able to master the use of human words. The words are represented in some instances by sign language and in others by metal-backed plastic symbols that are pushed about on a magnetized board. The chimpanzees are also capable of learning rudimentary rules of syntax and even of inventing short questions and statements of their own. Sarah, a chimpanzee trained with plastic symbols by David Premack at the University of California at Santa Barbara, acquired a vocabulary of 128 "words," including a different "name"

for each of eight individuals, both human and chimpanzee, and other signs representative of 12 verbs, six colors, 21 foods and a rich variety of miscellaneous objects, concepts, adjectives and adverbs. Although Sarah's achievement is truly remarkable, an enormous gulf still separates this most intelligent of the anthropoid apes from man. Sarah's words are given to her, and she must use them in a rigid and artificial context. No chimpanzee has demonstrated anything close to the capacity and drive to experiment with language that is possessed by a normal human child.

The difference may be quantitative rather than qualitative, but at the very least our own species must still be ranked as unique in its capacity to concatenate a large vocabulary into sentences that touch on virtually every experience and thought. Future studies of animal communication should continue to prove useful in helping us to understand the steps that led man across such a vast linguistic chasm in what was surely the central event in the evolution of the human mind.

4

VERBAL COMMUNICATION

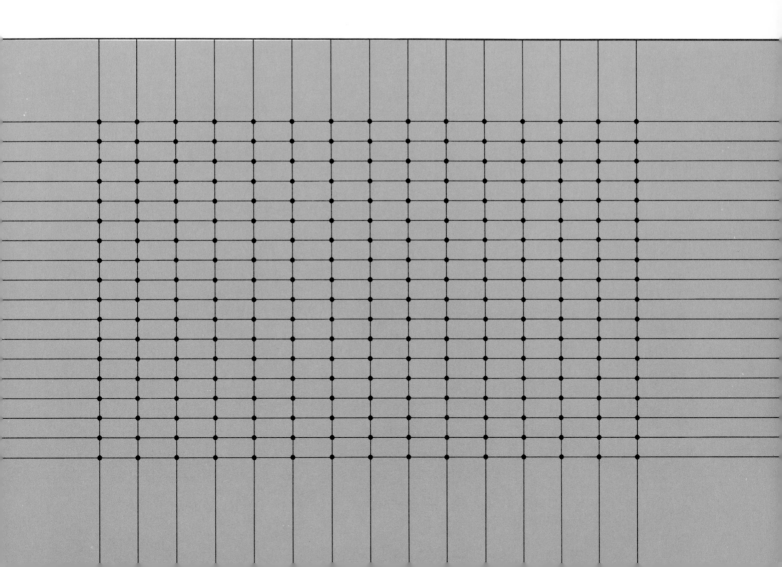

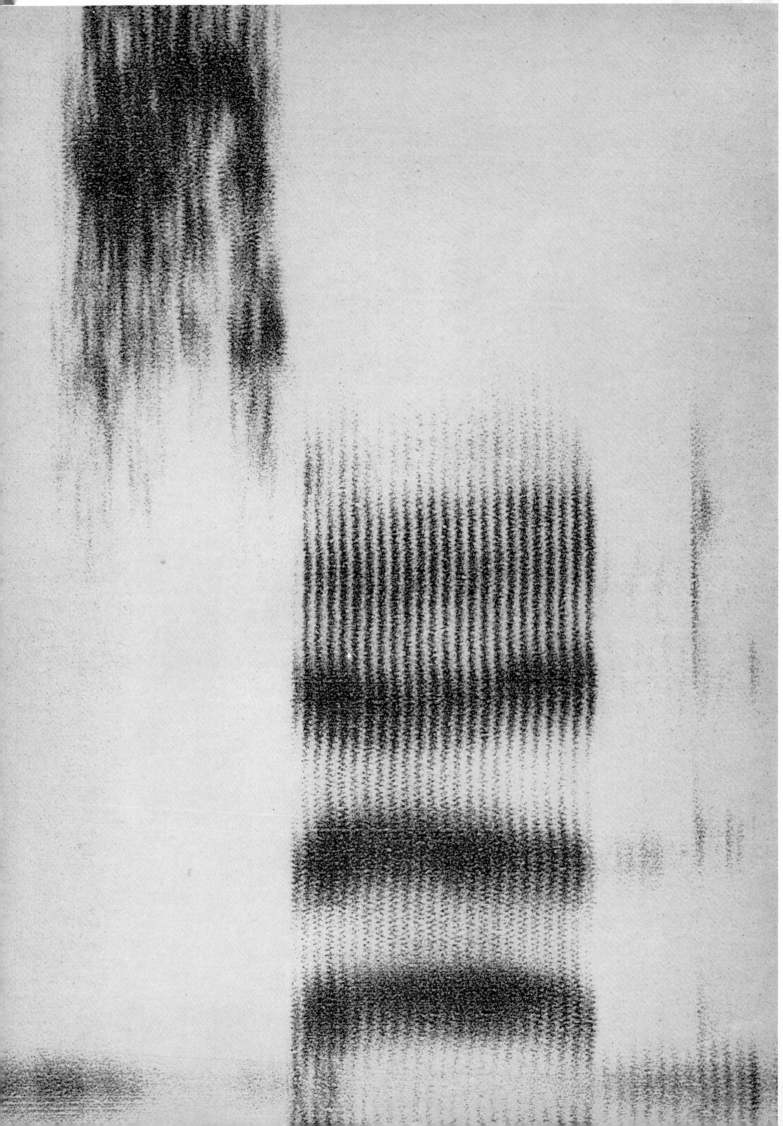

Verbal Communication

ROMAN JAKOBSON

The ability of human language to convey an infinite number of messages and to form and develop new concepts is based on the unique and universal properties of the verbal code.

For all human beings, and only for human beings, language is the vehicle of mental life and communication. It is natural that the study of this explicit and effective instrument, together with the rudiments of mathematics, is among the oldest sciences. The earliest linguistic work we possess, a Sumerian grammar of nearly 4,000 years ago, was succeeded by continuous efforts in various countries to interpret the makeup of the locally privileged language and the verbal network in general, as well as by speculations on the mysterious gift and confusion of tongues. If we concentrate our attention on the Indic and Greco-Latin tradition, beginning with the pre-Christian centuries, we can hardly find a single period without persistent inquiries into some facet of language. In many cases discoveries were made only to be temporarily swept away. Thus, for instance, the historic attainments of the Schoolmen's linguistic (particularly semantic) theory were dismissed after, as Charles Sanders Peirce used to say, "a barbarous rage against medieval thought broke out."

The variety of languages in space and time was the focal point of investigatory interest throughout the 19th century. Linguistics was held to be exclusively comparative, and the genetic relationship of kindred languages going back to a supposedly uniform parent language was considered the chief or only goal of linguistic comparison. The regularity of changes undergone by each of these languages at any given time was the acknowledged theoretical prerequisite for a conversion of the observed diversity of languages into their conjectured original unity.

This tenet was worked out meticulously by the Neogrammarian trend that dominated European (primarily German) linguistics during the last third of the 19th century. The "linguistic philosophy" of the Neogrammarians was viewed by their champion Karl Brugmann (1849–1919) as an antidote to "the arbitrariness and error to which a crude empiricism is everywhere exposed." This philosophy implied the acceptance of two uniformities, each concerned with successive stages: (1) the antecedent uniformity and subsequent plurality and (2) a uniform, "exceptionless" mutation from an earlier stage to a later one within any given speech community. Thus the question of likeness and divergence was applied primarily or even solely to the temporal sequence of linguistic phenomena, whereas the coexistence and simultaneous interplay of invariance and variation within any given state of language remained unnoticed.

The same epoch that brought the rise of this influential school saw the emergence of several geographically scattered investigators and theoreticians of language who had outgrown the standard beliefs of their time and environment. These bold precursors of the present-day linguistic quest were born in the middle decades of the century; their remarkably original and mutually independent but basically convergent theses appeared in the 1870's and at the beginning of the 1880's. Methodological and philosophical preconditions for an immediate implementation of their novel ideas were still lacking, yet the vital problems they raised show a remarkable parallelism in time and essence with the ideas that underlie the development of modern mathematics and physics.

It was in the 1870's that both in mathematics and in the research work of the *avant-garde* linguists the conjugate notions of invariance and variation assumed ever greater importance and brought forward the corollary task of eliciting relational invariants from a flux of variables. The historic proposal "to study the constituents of a multiplicity with regard to those properties which are not affected by the transformations of the given group" in Felix Klein's (1849–1925) Erlanger Programm of 1872 was aimed at developing a generalized geometry. A similar principle inspired the linguistic outposts of the same age, in particular the few initial publications of Henry Sweet (1845–1912), Jan Baudouin de Courtenay (1845–1929), Jost Winteler (1846–1929), Mikolaj Kruszewski (1851–1887) and Ferdinand de Saussure (1857–1913). All of them considered the Neogrammarian doctrine either unsuitable or insufficient for a more general and immanent science of language, as Kruszewski wrote to Baudouin in a sagacious letter of 1882. To quote the conclusion of my own survey of Sweet's arduous struggle, each of these spirited trailblazers who ventured to look far ahead "bears a stamp of tragedy on his whole life," owing to the resistance of a conservative milieu and perhaps even more to the ideological tenor of the Victorian

THE WORD "SAID" appears in the sound spectrogram on the opposite page. The sound spectrogram analyzes speech sounds into a series of frequency bands, with the lowest frequencies at the bottom and the highest at the top. The time axis of the presentation runs from left to right. The trace at upper left is the "s" sound; the trace at lower right, the "aid." The spectrogram was made by Dennis Klatt of the Massachusetts Institute of Technology.

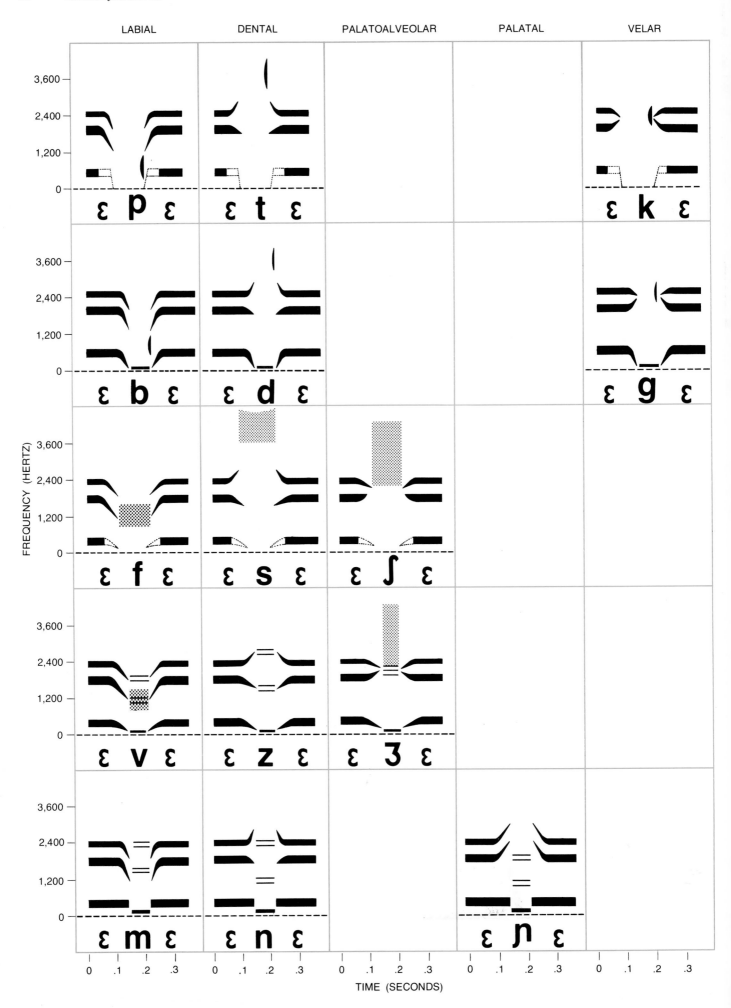

era, which impeded the concrete application and further development of daring designs and unwonted approaches.

At the beginning of the 1930's N. S. Trubetzkoy (1890–1938), a wise, inquisitive linguist of the era between the world wars, came by pure chance on Winteler's dissertation. In a letter of January, 1931, Trubetzkoy extolled the remarkable foresight of Winteler, whose unprecedented vistas and methods had met with a disappointing lack of comprehension and had doomed him to the lot of a mere schoolteacher. Winteler's book *Die Kerenzer Mundart des Kantons Glarus in ihren Grundzügen dargestellt*, completed in 1875 and published a year later in Leipzig, contains an analysis of his native Swiss-German dialect "outlined in its fundamentals" and shows a rare depth and insight into the essentials of linguistic structure, particularly in cardinal questions of sound-patterning.

The memoirs of the septuagenarian Winteler written for the Zurich fortnightly *Wissen und Leben* in 1916 quote a judgment he heard four years after the appearance of his dissertation: "If only one would have started differently, then one could have become a university professor, while now one has to stay a life-long schoolmaster." The retired instructor of the cantonal school in Aarau confesses how often he grieved over his cruel fate. Even Winteler's modest career was clouded by incomprehension and endangered by accusations of his being "redder than the socialists."

The adolescent Albert Einstein, who had left the regimented gymnasium in Munich he so deeply detested, sought admission to the Federal Institute of Technology in Zurich but failed the entrance examination and in 1895 took refuge in the liberal cantonal school at Aarau, some 25 miles from Zurich. A recent essay by Gerald Holton in *American Scholar* (Vol. 41, No. 1, Winter, 1971–72), indicates that the Aarau days were "a crucial turning point" in Einstein's development, and Einstein re-

peatedly acknowledged their beneficial import. Adopted as a boarder and treated as a member of the family in Jost Winteler's household, Einstein met, as his biographers say, his "lucky star." Even when he moved to Zurich for graduate studies, he missed no opportunity to call on his dear old friend in Aarau. Forty years later, during Einstein's stay at the Institute for Advanced Study in Princeton, he still remembered and praised "the clairvoyant Papa Winteler."

It was in the relaxed atmosphere of the Aarau school that the young Einstein recovered his repressed bent for science. When we read about the "thought experiment" that was performed there by the prodigious teen-ager and that gradually led him to his theory of relativity, the question of what influence was exerted on him by his daily conversations with the lucid scholar suggests itself. Winteler remained true to the principle of "configurational relativity" (*Relativität der Verhältnisse*) that had been disclosed in his dissertation with special reference to the sound pattern of language. In particular his theory required a consistent distinction between the relational invariants and variables within language, respectively termed "essential" and "accidental" properties. According to Winteler's insight, speech sounds cannot be evaluated in isolation but only in their relation to all other sound units of the given language and to the linguistic functions assigned to them in such a manifold. Correspondingly, the symmetry properties of the whole pattern were explicitly recognized and examined by the audacious "autodidact," as the author of the *Kerenzer Mundart* introduced himself.

Einstein, the future proponent of "empathy [*Einfühlung*] into external experience," obviously felt a spiritual affinity with such an ardent devotee of science as Winteler, who had dared in 1875 to preface his book with the farsighted declaration: "My work in its essence is

addressed solely to those who are able to grasp the verbal form as a revelation of the human mind that stands to the mind in much more inner and sweeping relations than even the best products of a most consummate literature. Thus the addressees of my work must conceive the inquiry into the latent powers which determine the continual motion of the verbal form as a task which, in its interest and relevance, competes with any other field of knowledge."

Reports about the free and spirited exchange of opinions that reigned in Winteler's family circle enhance the certainty of the deep imprint left by his exciting ideas on Einstein's responsive mind. Hence the parable of a seed doomed "to die without having borne any fruit," the gloomy vision that haunted Winteler's imagination from his youth, seems to have met with a luminous refutation.

The story of Winteler and Einstein provides us with a new and significant example of the suggestive interconnections between linguistics and mathematics, of their historical parallelism and particularly of an equally radical difference between two stages in the development undergone by each of these sciences. As historians of mathematical ideas have repeatedly stated, the concept of invariance has found a wide scientific application only in our century, after "the reverse side of invariance," the idea of relativity and its corollaries, had been gradually disclosed and mastered. The emergence of Einstein's theory and the advances in the analysis of purely topological relations indeed find striking correspondences in the simultaneous unfolding of similar linguistic conceptions and methods. The present manifestly constructive period in the history of linguistic science has ensued as a sequel to anticipations raised by Winteler and other pioneers.

In the Neogrammarian tradition the notions and labels "comparative" and "general" linguistics nearly merged, and the comparative method was confined to a merely historical or, strictly speaking, genealogical study of cognate dialects and languages. Today virtually any linguistic problem whatever has received a thoroughly comparative treatment. Any question of language and languages is conceived of as being a comparative operation in search of the equivalent relations that underlie the structure of a given language, and that furthermore allow us to interpret the structural affinities and divergences between languages, however distant they may be in origin

DISTINCTIVE FEATURES of French consonants that remain invariant under variable combinations with other concurrent or sequential features are shown in the sound-spectrographic patterns charted on the opposite page. The chart was made by the French phonetician Pierre Delattre. The acoustic formants (concentrations of acoustic energy) are represented by the three horizontal bands. The downward direction of the upper formant distinguishes all labial consonants (*first column of the chart*) from the upward direction of the same formant in the dental consonants (*second column*). The remaining three columns show the palatoalveolar, palatal and velar consonants. These consonants, in spite of their articulatory and acoustic diversity, have in common an upward direction or reinforcement in the middle formant. This feature opposes them to all the consonants in the first and second columns, which move off or weaken the middle formant in relation to the upper one. Symbols to left and right of symbols for consonants are the surrounding open-front vowels.

and location. The decisive procedure for scientific inquiry into the different levels of linguistic structure is a consistent elicitation and identification of relational invariants amid the multitude of variations. The variables are investigated with reference to the set of diverse transformations that they undergo and that can and must be specified.

Whatever level of language we deal with, two integral properties of linguistic structure force us to use strictly relational, topological definitions. First, every single constituent of any linguistic system is built on an opposition of two logical contradictories: the presence of an attribute ("markedness") in contraposition to its absence ("unmarkedness"). The entire network of language displays a hierarchical arrangement that within each level of the system follows the same dichotomous principle of marked terms superposed on the corresponding unmarked terms. And second, the continual, all-embracing, purposeful interplay of invariants and variations proves to be

an essential, innermost property of language at each of its levels.

These two dyads—markedness/unmarkedness and variation/invariance—are indissolubly tied to the be-all and end-all of language, to the fact, as Edward Sapir (1884–1939) put it, that "language is the communicative process par excellence in every known society." Everything language can and does communicate stands first and foremost in a necessary, intimate connection with meaning and always carries semantic information. The promotion of meaning to a pivotal point of structural analysis has been an ever stronger claim of international linguistic endeavors during the past five decades. Thus, for instance, 20 years ago the French linguist Émile Benveniste, one of the leading figures of the structural trend, declared in a programmatic study that in the last account careful reflection on the makeup of any language points to the "central question of meaning," and that a deepening insight into this problem will open the way to

the future discovery of "transformational laws in linguistic structures."

True, various reductionist experiments were conducted in America. At first repeated efforts were made "to analyze linguistic structure without reference to meaning." Some later tests confined the removal of meaning to the study of grammatical structures under such slogans as "Linguistic description minus grammar equals semantics." All these tentative operations were undoubtedly of considerable interest, particularly because they succeeded in providing us with a graphic demonstration of the omnipresent semantic criterion, no matter what level and constituent of language is examined. One can no longer continue to play hide-and-seek with meaning and to evaluate linguistic structures independently of semantic problems. Whatever end of the linguistic spectrum we deal with, from the phonic components of verbal signs to the discourse as a whole, we are compelled to bear in mind that everything in language is endowed with a certain significative and transmissible value.

Thus in approaching speech sounds we must take into account the fact that they are cardinally different from all other audible phenomena. An astounding discovery of the recent past is that when two sounds are presented simultaneously to both ears, any verbal signals such as words, nonsense syllables and even separate speech sounds are better discerned and identified by the right ear and all other acoustical stimuli such as music and environmental noises are better recognized by the left ear. The phonic components of language owe their particular position in the cortical area, and correspondingly in the aural area, solely to their verbal functions, and henceforth a constant regard for these functions must guide any fruitful study of speech sounds.

In its sound pattern any language contains a certain limited number of "distinctive features," discrete and ultimate relational invariants that can, under a set of transformations, endure even drastic alterations in every respect save their defining attributes. "The categorial nature of perceptual identification," pointed out by the psychologist Jerome S. Bruner in his memorable study "Neural Mechanisms in Perception" (1956), maintains the constancy and validity of these features in verbal communication, where they exercise the fundamental faculty of semantic discrimination.

The pattern of distinctive features is a powerful and economical code: each

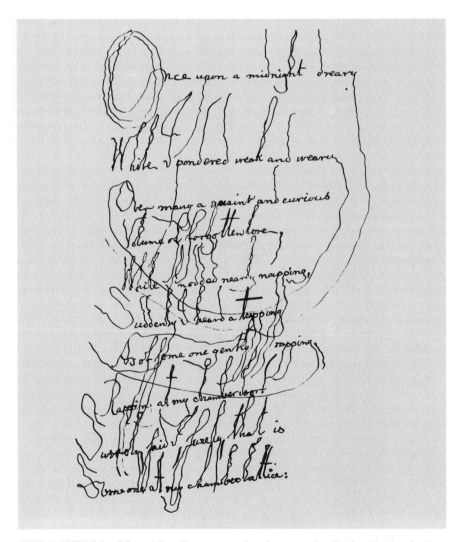

"THE RAVEN," by Edgar Allan Poe, was rendered autographically by Charles Sanders Peirce. He intended to show how ties between sound and meaning, transformed by poetic function of language, can be transmuted into autonomous interplay of letter and meaning.

feature is a binary opposition of a present mark and a missing mark. The selection and interconnection of distinctive features within any given language reveal a remarkable congruity. A comparison of the existing phonological structures with the laws underlying the development of children's language enables us to outline the typology of feature systems and the rules of their internal hierarchical arrangement. The communicative relevance of distinctive features, which is based on their semantic value, brings to naught any chance occurrence and contingency in their patterning. The list of distinctive features that exist in the languages of the world is supremely restricted, and the coexistence of features within one language is restrained by implicational laws.

The most plausible explanation of these either totally or nearly universal principles in regard to the admissibility and interconnection of features apparently lies in the internal logic of communication systems that are endowed with a self-regulating and self-steering capacity. The quest for a universal table of distinctive features must certainly apply the same method of extracting invariants that has been used with respect to single languages: in the context of different languages the same feature with unaltered categorial attributes may vary in its physical implementation.

Transformations that provide the invariants with diverse concomitant variations can be roughly divided into two kinds of alteration: contextual and stylistic. Contextual variants point to the concurrent or consecutive neighborhood of the given feature, whereas stylistic variants add a marked—emotive or poetic—annex to the neutral, purely cognitive information of the distinctive feature. Both of these invariants and variations belong to the common verbal code that endows interlocutors with the competence to understand one another.

For the study of verbal communication it is necessary to face the fact that any speech community and any existing verbal code lack uniformity; everyone belongs simultaneously to several speech communities of different extent; he diversifies his code and blends distinct codes. At each level of the verbal code we observe a scale of transitions that range from maximum explicitness to the briefest elliptic structure, and this scale is subject to a set of rigorous transformational rules. The cardinal property of language noted by the initiator of semiotics, Charles Sanders Peirce (1839–1914), namely the translatability of any verbal sign into another, more explicit one, renders an effective service to communication in that it counteracts ambiguities caused by lexical and grammatical homonymy or by the overlapping of elliptic forms.

People usually display a narrower competence as senders of verbal messages and a wider competence as receivers. The differences in patterning and extent between the codes of the addresser and the addressee attract ever closer attention from students and teachers of language. The core of this divergence was grasped by St. Augustine: "In me it is the word which takes precedence over the sound [*In me prius est verbum, posterior vox*], but for thee who looks to understand me, it is first the sound that comes to thine ear in order to insinuate the word into thy mind." The two-way transformations that make it possible to determine the state of the outputs from that of the inputs and vice versa are an essential prerequisite for all genuine intercommunication.

Both spatial and temporal factors play a significant role in the structure of our verbal code. Various forms of interdialectal code-switchings are among the daily devices in our verbal intercourse. Bilingualism or multilingualism, which allows total or partial shifts from one language to another, cannot be rigidly separated from interdialectal fluctuations. The interaction and interpenetration of single languages in a polyglot's use follow the same rules that apply in the case of translations from one language into another.

As for the time factor, I refer to my earlier objections to the tenacious belief in the static character of the verbal code: Any change first appears in linguistic synchrony as a coexistence and purposive alternation of more archaic and new-fashioned dictions. Thus linguistic synchrony proves to be dynamic; any verbal code at all its levels is convertible, and in any conversion one of the competing alternants is endowed with a supplementary informational value and hence displays a marked status, in contradistinction to the neutral, unmarked character of the other. A historical phonology and grammar, for example the millennial history of the English sound, word and sentence pattern, develop into a study of extractable constants and temporal transformations that both demand an adequate explanation.

The unparalleled expediency of language is rooted in a consistent superposition of several interconnected levels, each of which is differently structured.

The system of a few distinctive features serves to build a more differentiated morphological code of entities endowed with inherent meaning, namely words and, in those languages where words are decomposable, their minimal meaningful constituents (roots and affixes), termed morphemes. The analysis of the morphological units once again reveals a system of relational invariants—binary oppositions of marked and unmarked grammatical categories—but there is a difference of basic importance between a phonological and a grammatical opposition: in the former case the coupled contradictories reside in the perceptible side of language (*signans*, or "signifier"), whereas in the latter they lie in its intelligible side (*signatum*, or "signified").

To illustrate this difference let us first cite an opposition of a phonological mark and its absence: nasalized/nonnasalized implemented by such pairs of consonants as *m/b* and *n/d* or the French nasal vowel in *bon* as opposed to *beau*. On the other hand, in a grammatical opposition such as preterit/present the first, marked tense signals the precedence of the narrated event over the speech act, whereas the general meaning of the unmarked present tense carries no information about the relation between the narrated event and the speech act. This relation varies and its specification depends on the context. Compare the diverse contextual meanings of the same present-tense form in the four sentences "Spring begins today"; "A year from today he begins a new trip"; "With the death of Caesar a new era begins for Rome"; "Life begins at 50."

Here again as when treating the sound pattern we come across the momentous property of natural languages, namely their context-sensitivity. Precisely this property sets them apart from their formalized, artificial superstructures, which tend to a context-freedom. The significant difference between context-free and context-sensitive sign systems had been perspicuously noted by Noam Chomsky, but as Daniel A. Walters complains in *Information and Control* (1970), the specific properties of context-sensitive grammar still receive much less attention than context-free grammars. It is the context-sensitivity of a natural language at *all* levels that provides it with a unique abundance of free variations. The dialectical tension between invariants and variables, which in their own way also appear to be pertinent, ensures the creativity of language.

Morphology answers the phonological pattern of *distinctive* features with an equally coherent and steplike organization of equally binary *conceptual* features; they remain invariant while undergoing a set of transformations that convert the general meanings of grammatical categories into varied contextual (including situational) meanings. In this way we proceed from one grammatical area to a superior one, namely from morphology as a study of totally coded units to the analysis of syntactic structures that combine coded matrixes with a free or, as is always the case in verbal communication, *relatively* free selection of words that fill them up.

Words display two patently distinct kinds of semantic value. Their compulsory *grammatical* meaning, a categorial relational concept or group of concepts that words constantly carry, is supplemented in all autonomous words by a *lexical* meaning. Like grammatical meanings, any general lexical meaning is in turn an invariant that under diverse contextual and situational transformations generates what Leonard Bloomfield (1887–1949) precisely defined as "marginal, transferred" meanings. They are sensed as derivative of the unmarked general meaning, and these tropes either stand in agreement with the verbal code or they are an *ad hoc* digression from it.

The rules of syntax are ordered, and these rules and their order itself determine a "grammatical process" that never fails to impart a "grammatical concept," in accordance with the subtle terms introduced by Sapir. Any syntactic structure is a member of a transformational chain and any two partially synonymous constructions display an interrelation of markedness and unmarkedness. For example, in English the passive is marked in relation to the unmarked active mood. Hence an expression such as "Lions are hunted by natives," similar to but not identical in meaning with the sentence "Natives hunt lions," marks a shift in semantic perspective from the agent to the goal by focusing on "lions" and allowing the omission of the agent, namely "lions are hunted."

In its general meaning any noun is a generic term relating to all members of a class or to all stages of a dynamic whole. The contextual as well as situational application of these characteristics to particulars is a transformation of widest range. This interplay of universals and particulars, which is often underrated by linguists, has for ages been discussed among logicians and philosophers of language, such as the 12th-century Schoolman John of Salisbury, to whose formula—*Nominantur singularia*

sed universalia significantur ("Particulars are named but universals are signified") —Peirce repeatedly refers.

When we observe the highly instructive process of a child's gradual advance in the acquisition of language, we see how decisively important the emergence of the subject-predicate sentence is. It liberates speech from the here and now and enables the child to treat events distant in time and space or even fictitious. This capacity, which mechanists sometimes label "displaced speech," is in fact the first affirmation of language's autonomy. In sign systems other than natural or artificial languages there are no parallels to the formulation of general and particularly equational propositions, no capacity for building logical judgments.

The progress of a child's language depends on his ability to develop a metalanguage, that is, to compare verbal signs and to talk about language. Metalanguage as a part of language is again a structural trait that has no analogues in other sign systems. The founder of the Moscow linguistic school, F. F. Fortunatov (1848–1914), stressed that "the phenomena of language themselves appertain to the phenomena of thought." Interpersonal communication, which is one of the indispensable preconditions for the infant's access to speech, is gradually supplemented by an internalization of language. Inner speech, one's dialogue with oneself, is a powerful superstructure on our verbal intercourse. As the study of language disturbances shows, impairments of inner speech take a conspicuous place among verbal disorders. A lesser dependence on the environmental censorship contributes to the active role of inner speech in the rise and shaping of new ideas.

The equivalence relation that under various names—transformation, transference, translation and transposition—has since the interwar era been gradually approached by linguists at different ends of the world proves to be the mainspring of language. In the light of this relation several controversial questions of verbal communication may receive a more exact and explicit treatment.

Written language is an evident transform of oral speech. All sane human beings talk, but almost half of the world's people are totally illiterate, and the actual use of reading and writing is an asset of a scarce minority. Yet even then literacy is a secondary acquisition. Whatever script is employed, as a rule it refers to the spoken word. Along with invariants common to the oral and written language, each of the two systems in its

constitution and use shows a number of pertinent peculiarities. In particular, those properties that depend on the spatiality of written texts separate them from the purely temporal structure of oral utterances. The comparative study both of verbal patterns and of their roles in social communication is an urgent task that can no longer be neglected. Many hasty generalizations will be dismissed. Thus, for instance, the role of schooling and continual transmission, far from being confined to the world of letters, is attested as well in oral traditions and rhetorical art. The wider diffusion of the written word in the recent past is now being matched by such technical devices of oral messages "to whom it may concern" as radio, television and instruments for recording speech.

In a study "Linguistics and Poetics" I attempted to outline the six basic functions of verbal communication: referential, emotive, conative, poetic, phatic and metalingual. The interaction of these functions and in particular the consequent grammatical transformations cannot receive an adequate linguistic treatment unless survivals of mechanistic views are discarded. For example, the extension of the referential (alias ideational) function at the expense of the conative function leads our language from secondary, obviously marked translations of imperative primary forms such as "Go!" into circumlocutions such as "I wish you would go," "I order you to go," "You must go" or "You should go" with a truth-value forcibly imposed on the conative expression. Efforts to interpret imperatives as transforms of declarative propositions falsely overturn the natural hierarchy of linguistic structures.

Finally, the analysis of grammatical transformations and of their import should include the poetic function of language, because the core of this function is to push transformations into the foreground. It is the purposeful poetic use of lexical and grammatical tropes and figures that brings the creative power of language to its summit. Such a marked innovation as the inverse temporal perspective recently used by three Russian poets independently of one another is hardly fortuitous. "The future for you is trustworthy and definite. You say: Tomorrow we went to the forest" (A. Voznesenskij); "It happened that I found myself tomorrow" (S. Kirsanov); "It was tomorrow" (G. Glinka). In a letter dated March 21, 1955, four weeks before his death, Einstein wrote: "The separation between past, present, and future has only the meaning of an illusion, albeit a tenacious one."

5

THE VISUAL IMAGE

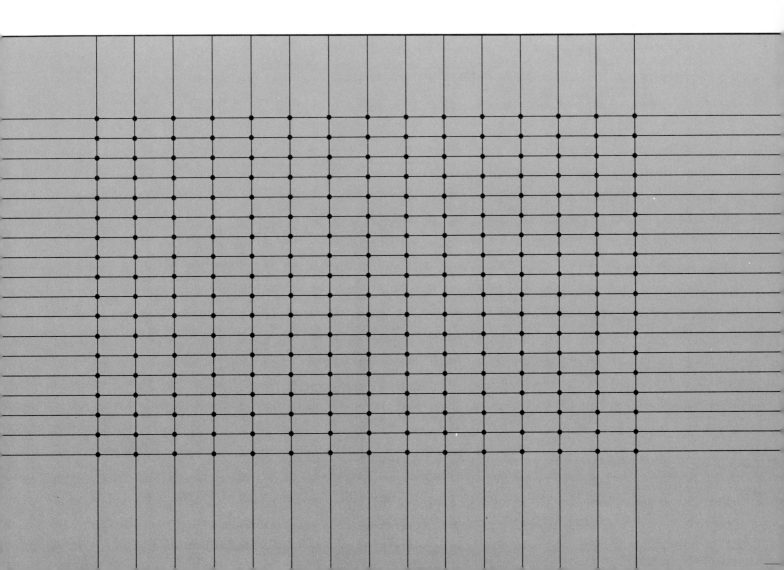

The Visual Image
E. H. GOMBRICH

What a picture means to the viewer is strongly dependent on his past experience and knowledge. In this respect the visual image is not a mere representation of "reality" but a symbolic system.

Ours is a visual age. We are bombarded with pictures from morning till night. Opening our newspaper at breakfast, we see photographs of men and women in the news, and raising our eyes from the paper, we encounter the picture on the cereal package. The mail arrives and one envelope after the other discloses glossy folders with pictures of alluring landscapes and sunbathing girls to entice us to take a holiday cruise, or of elegant menswear to tempt us to have a suit made to measure. Leaving our house, we pass billboards along the road that try to catch our eye and play on our desire to smoke, drink or eat. At work it is more than likely that we have to deal with some kind of pictorial information: photographs, sketches, catalogues, blueprints, maps or at least graphs. Relaxing in the evening, we sit in front of the television set, the new window on the world, and watch moving images of pleasures and horrors flit by. Even the images created in times gone by or in distant lands are more easily accessible to us than they ever were to the public for which they were created. Picture books, picture postcards and color slides accumulate in our homes as souvenirs of travel, as do the private mementos of our family snapshots.

No wonder it has been asserted that we are entering a historical epoch in which the image will take over from the written word. In view of this claim it is all the more important to clarify the potentialities of the image in communication, to ask what it can and what it cannot do better than spoken or written language. In comparison with the importance of the question the amount of attention devoted to it is disappointingly small.

Students of language have been at work for a long time analyzing the various functions of the prime instrument of human communication. Without going into details we can accept for our purpose the divisions of language proposed by Karl Bühler, who distinguished between the functions of expression, arousal and description. (We may also call them symptom, signal and symbol.) We describe a speech act as expressive if it informs us of the speaker's state of mind. Its very tone may be symptomatic of anger or amusement; alternatively it may be designed to arouse a state of mind in the person addressed, as a signal triggering anger or amusement. It is important to distinguish the expression of an emotion from its arousal, the symptom from the signal, particularly since common parlance fails to do this when speaking of the "communication" of feeling. It is true that the two functions can be in unison and that the audible symptoms of a speaker's anger may arouse anger in me, but they may also cause me to be amused. On the other hand, someone may contrive in cold blood to move me to anger. These two functions of communication are shared by human beings with their fellow creatures lower down on the evolutionary scale. Animal communications may be symptomatic of emotive states or they may function as signals to release certain reactions. Human language can do more: it has developed the descriptive function (which is only rudimentary in animal signals). A speaker can inform his partner of a state of affairs past, present or future, observable or distant, actual or conditional. He can say it rains, it rained, it will rain, it may rain, or "If it rains, I shall stay here." Language performs this miraculous function largely through such little particles as "if," "when," "not," "therefore," "all" and "some," which have been called logical words because they account for the ability of language to formulate logical inferences (also known as syllogisms).

Looking at communication from the vantage point of language, we must ask first which of these functions the visual image can perform. We shall see that the visual image is supreme in its capacity for arousal, that its use for expressive purposes is problematic, and that unaided it altogether lacks the possibility of matching the statement function of language.

The assertion that statements cannot be translated into images often meets with incredulity, but the simplest demonstration of its truth is to challenge the doubters to illustrate the proposition they doubt. You cannot make a picture of the concept of statement any more than you can illustrate the impossibility of translation. It is not only the degree of abstraction of language that eludes the visual medium; the sentence from the primer "The cat sits on the mat" is certainly not abstract, but although the primer may show a picture of a cat sitting on a mat, a moment's reflection will show that the picture is not the equivalent of the statement. We cannot express pictorially whether we mean "the" cat (an individual) or "a cat" (a member of a class); moreover, although the sentence may be one possible description of the picture, there are an infinite number of other true descriptive statements you could make such as "There is a cat seen from behind," or for that matter "There

STAINED-GLASS LANCET WINDOWS below the south rose window of the cathedral at Chartres (*opposite page*) exemplify the transformation of a metaphor (the doctrine that the Apostles stand on the shoulders of Old Testament prophets) into a memorable image.

is no elephant on the mat." When the primer continues with "The cat sat on the mat," "The cat will sit on the mat," "The cat sits rarely on the mat," "If the cat sits on the mat..." and so on ad infinitum, we see the word soaring away and leaving the picture behind.

Try to say the sentence to a child and then show him the picture and your respect for the image will soon be restored. The sentence will leave the child unmoved; the image may delight him almost as much as the real cat. Exchange the picture for a toy cat and the child may be ready to hug the toy and take it to bed. The toy cat arouses the same reactions as a real cat—possibly even stronger ones, since it is more docile and easier to cuddle.

This power of dummies or substitutes to trigger behavior has been much explored by students of animal behavior, and there is no doubt that organisms are "programmed" to respond to certain visual signals in a way that facilitates survival. The crudest models of a predator or a mate need only exhibit certain distinctive features to elicit the appropriate pattern of action, and if these features are intensified, the dummy (like the toy) may be more effective than the natural stimulus. Caution is needed in comparing these automatisms to human reactions, but Konrad Z. Lorenz, the pioneer of ethology, has surmised that certain preferred forms of nursery art that are described as "cute" or "sweet" (including many of Walt Disney's creations) generate parental feelings by their structural similarity to babies.

Be that as it may, the power of visual impressions to arouse our emotions has been observed since ancient times. "The mind is more slowly stirred by the ear than by the eye," said Horace in his *Art of Poetry* when he compared the impact of the stage with that of the verbal narrative. Preachers and teachers preceded modern advertisers in the knowledge of the ways in which the visual image can affect us, whether we want it to or not. The succulent fruit, the seductive nude, the repellent caricature, the hair-raising horror can all play on our emotions and

MOSAIC OF A DOG found at the entrance of a house in Pompeii has the inscription *Cave Canem* (Beware of the Dog). Without the inscription the message intended to be communicated by the mosaic is less certain. The mosaic is now in the National Museum in Naples.

engage our attention. Nor is this arousal function of sights confined to definite images. Configurations of lines and colors have the potential to influence our emotions. We need only keep our eyes open to see how these potentialities of the visual media are used all around us, from the red danger signal to the way the décor of a restaurant may be calculated to create a certain "atmosphere." These very examples show that the power of arousal of visual impressions extends far

beyond the scope of this article. What is usually described as communication is concerned with matter rather than with mood.

A mosaic found at the entrance of a house in Pompeii shows a dog on a chain with the inscription *Cave Canem*, Beware of the Dog [*see illustration above*]. It is not hard to see the link between such a picture and its arousal function. We are to react to the picture as we might to a real dog that barks at us. Thus the picture effectively reinforces the caption that warns the potential intruder of the risk he is running. Would the image alone perform this function of communication? It would, if we came to it with a knowledge of social customs and conventions. Why if not as a communication to those who may be unable to read should there be this picture at the entrance hall? But if we could forget what we know and imagine a

TWO PAINTINGS BY VINCENT VAN GOGH suggest that the emotion aroused in someone viewing a work of art may not be the same emotion that inspired the artist. To van Gogh his painting "Bedroom at Arles" (*top illustration on opposite page*) was expressive of tranquillity and undisturbed rest. To achieve this he simplified his technique, adopting stylistic features of Georges Seurat and of Japanese prints. For him this modification stood in clear opposition to the characteristic style found, for instance, in "The Night Café" (*bottom illustration on opposite page*). In that painting van Gogh wanted to show a place where one could go mad. Without prior knowledge of the context and the artist's code naïve subjects rarely can hit on the intended meaning. "Bedroom at Arles" is reproduced courtesy of the Art Institute of Chicago and "The Night Café" courtesy of Yale University Art Gallery.

member of an alien culture coming on such an image, we could think of many other possible interpretations of the image. Could not the man have wanted to advertise a dog he wished to sell? Was he perhaps a veterinarian? Or could the mosaic have functioned as a sign for a public house called "The Black Dog"? The purpose of this exercise is to remind ourselves how much we take for granted when we look at a picture for its message. It always depends on our prior knowledge of possibilities. After all, when we see the Pompeiian mosaic in the museum in Naples we do not conclude that there is a dog chained somewhere. It is different with the arousal function of the image. Even in the museum the image might give us a shadow of a fright, and I recently heard a child of five say when turning the pages of a book on natural history that she did not want to touch the pictures of nasty creatures.

Naturally we cannot adequately respond to the message of the mosaic unless we have read the image correctly. The medium of the mosaic is well suited to formulate the problem in terms of the theory of information. Its modern equivalent would be an advertising display composed of an array of light bulbs in which each bulb can be turned either on or off to form an image. A mosaic might consist of standardized cubes (*tesserae*) that are either dark or light. The amount of visual information such a medium can transmit will depend on the size of the cubes in relation to the scale of the image. In our case the cubes are small enough for the artist to indicate the tufts of hair on the dog's legs and tail, and the individual links of the chain. The artist

might confine himself to a code in which black signifies a solid form seen against a light ground. Such a silhouette could easily be endowed with sufficiently distinctive features to be recognized as a dog. But the Pompeiian master was trained in a tradition that had gone beyond the conceptual method of representation and he included in the image information about the effects of light on form. He conveys the white and the glint of the eye and the muzzle, shows us the teeth and outlines the ears; he also indicates the shadows of the forelegs on the patterned background. The meaning so far is easy to decode, but the white patches on the body and, most of all, the outline of the hind leg set us a puzzle. It was the convention in his time to model the shape of an animal's body by indicating the sheen of the fur, and this must be the origin of these features. Whether their actual shape is due to clumsy execution or to inept restoration could only be decided by viewing the original.

The difficulty of interpreting the meaning of the dog mosaic is instructive because it too can be expressed in terms of communication theory. Like verbal messages, images are vulnerable to the random interference engineers call "noise." They need the device of redundancy to overcome this hazard. It is this built-in safeguard of the verbal code that enables us to read the inscription *Cave Canem* without hesitation even though the first *e* is incomplete. As far as image recognition is concerned it is the enclosing contour that carries most of the information. We could not guess the length of the tail if the black cubes were missing. The individual cubes of the patterned ground and inside the out-

line are relatively more redundant, but those indicating the sheen occupy a middle position; they stand for a feature that is elusive even in reality, although the configuration we now see could never occur.

However automatic our first response to an image may be, therefore, its actual reading can never be a passive affair. Without a prior knowledge of possibilities we could not even guess at the relative position of the dog's two hind legs. Although we have this knowledge, other possibilities are likely to escape us. Perhaps the picture was intended to represent a particular breed that Romans would recognize as being vicious. We cannot tell by the picture.

The chance of a correct reading of the image is governed by three variables: the code, the caption and the context. It might be thought that the caption alone would make the other two redundant, but our cultural conventions are too flexible for that. In an art book the picture of a dog with the caption E. Landseer is understood to refer to the maker of the image, not to the species represented. In the context of a primer, on the other hand, the caption and the picture would be expected to support each other. Even if the pages were torn so that we could only read "og," the fragment of the drawing above would suffice to indicate whether the missing letter was a *d* or an *h*. Jointly the media of word and image increase the probability of a correct reconstruction.

We shall see that this mutual support of language and image facilitates memorizing. The use of two independent channels, as it were, guarantees the ease of reconstruction. This is the basis of the

SIGNS FOR THE 1968 OLYMPIC GAMES in Mexico are self-explanatory because the number of possible meanings is restricted.

The use of pictorial images in international events overcomes the problem of communicating to people who speak diverse languages.

ancient "art of memory" (brilliantly explored in a book by Frances Yates) that advises the practitioner to translate any verbal message into visual form, the more bizarre and unlikely the better. If you want to remember the name of the painter Hogarth, picture to yourself a *hog* practicing his *art* by painting an *h*. You may dislike the association, but you may find it hard to get rid of.

There are cases where the context alone can make the visual message unambiguous even without the use of words. It is a possibility that has much attracted organizers of international events where the Babylonian confusion of tongues rules out the use of language. The set of images designed for the Olympic Games in Mexico in 1968 appears to be self-explanatory; indeed it is, given the limited number of expected messages and the restriction of the choice that is exemplified best by the first two signs of the array [*see illustration on opposite page*]. We can observe how the purpose and context dictate a simplification of the code by concentrating on a few distinctive features. The principle is brilliantly exemplified by the pictorial signs for the various sports and games designed for the same event.

We should never be tempted to forget, however, that even in such usages context must be supported by prior expectations based on tradition. Where these links break, communication also breaks down. Some years ago there was a story in the papers to the effect that riots had broken out in an underdeveloped country because of rumors that human flesh was being sold in a store. The rumor was traced to food cans with a grinning boy on the label. Here it was the switch of context that caused the confusion. As a rule the picture of fruit, vegetable or meat on a food container does indicate its contents; if we do not draw the conclusion that the same applies to a picture of a human being on the container, it is because we rule out the possibility from the start.

In the above examples the image was expected to work in conjunction with other factors to convey a clear-cut message that could be translated into words. The real value of the image, however, is its capacity to convey information that cannot be coded in any other way. In his important book *Prints and Visual Communication* William M. Ivins, Jr., argued that the Greeks and the Romans failed to make progress in science because they lacked the idea of multiplying images by some form of printing. Some of his philosophical points can hardly be sustained

OPERA HOUSE in Sydney, Australia, is so unfamiliar a structure that it is difficult to tell from a single photograph what the inclinations and relations of the various components are.

(the ancient world knew of the multiplication of images through the seal impression and the cast), but it is certainly true that printed herbals, costume books, newssheets and topographical views were a vital source of visual information about plants, fashions, topical events and foreign lands. But study of this material also brings home to us that printed information depends in part on words. The most lifelike portrait of a king will mislead us if it is incorrectly labeled as being somebody else, and publishers of other times sometimes supplied an old woodcut with a new caption on the principle that if you have seen one earthquake, you have seen them all. Even today it is only our confidence in certain informants or

institutions that allays our doubts that a picture in a book, a newspaper or on the screen really shows what it purports to show. There was the notorious case of the German scientist Ernst Haeckel, who was accused of having tried to prove the identity of human and animal development by labeling a photograph of a pig's fetus as that of a human embryo. It is in fact fatally easy to mix up pictures and captions, as almost any publisher knows to his cost.

The information extracted from an image can be quite independent of the intention of its maker. A holiday snapshot of a group on a beach may be scrutinized by an intelligence officer preparing a landing, and the Pompeiian mosaic

DEPTH REVERSAL occurs when some pictures are viewed upside down because the eye assumes that light is coming from the top. The valleys and ridges in the picture on the left (an aerial side-looking-radar view of the Appalachians) turn into ridges and valleys (*right*).

might provide new information to a historian of dog breeding.

It may be convenient here to range the information value of such images according to the amount of information about the prototype that they can encode. Where the information is virtually complete we speak of a facsimile or replica. These may be produced for deception rather than information, fraudulently in the case of a forged banknote, benevolently in the case of a glass eye or an artificial tooth. But the facsimile of a note in a history book is intended for instruction, and so is the cast or copy of an organ in medical teaching.

Even facsimile duplication would not be classed as an image if it shared with its prototype all characteristics including the material of which it is made. A flower sample used in a botany class is not an image, but an artificial flower used for demonstration purposes must be described as an image. Even here the border line is somewhat fluid. A stuffed animal in a showcase is not an image, but the taxidermist is likely to have made his personal contribution through selecting and modifying the carcass. However faithful an image that serves to convey visual information may be, the process of selection will always reveal the maker's interpretation of what he considers relevant. Even the wax effigy of a celebrity must show the sitter in one particular attitude and role; the photographer of people or events will carefully sift his material to find the "telltale" picture.

Interpretation on the part of the image maker must always be matched by the interpretation of the viewer. No image tells its own story. I remember an exhibit in a museum in Lincoln, Neb., showing skeletons and reconstructions

STRIKING IMAGE OF CHRIST is created by a single spiraling line that thickens and thins to form features, shapes, shadings and background. The illustration is a detail from "The Napkin of St. Veronica," engraved in 1649 by the French artist Claude Mellan.

of the ancestor of the horse. By present equine standards these creatures were diminutive, but they resembled our horse in everything but the scale. It was this encounter that brought home to me how inevitably we interpret even a didactic model and how hard it is to discard certain assumptions. Being used to looking at works of sculpture, including small bronze statuettes of horses, I had slipped into the mental habit of discounting scale when interpreting the code. In other words, I "saw" the scale model of a normal horse. It was the verbal description and information that corrected my reading of the code.

Here as always we need a jolt to remind us of what I have called the "beholder's share," the contribution we make to any representations from the stock of images stored in our mind. Once more it is only when this process cannot take place because we lack memories that we become aware of their role. Looking at a picture of a house, we do not normally fret about the many things the picture does not show us unless we are looking for a particular aspect that was hidden from the camera. We have seen many similar houses and can supplement the information from our memory, or we think we can. It is only when we are confronted with a totally unfamiliar kind of structure that we are aware of the puzzle element in any representation. The new opera house in Sydney, Australia, is a structure of a novel kind, and a person who sees only a photograph of it will feel compelled to ask a number of questions the photograph cannot answer [*see top illustration on page 51*]. What is the inclination of the roof? Which parts go inward, which outward? What, indeed, is the scale of the entire structure?

The hidden assumptions with which we generally approach a photograph are most easily demonstrated by the limited information value of shadows on flat images. They only yield the correct impression if we assume that the light is falling from above and generally from the left; reverse the picture and what was concave looks convex and vice versa. That we read the code of the black-and-white photograph without assuming that it is a rendering of a colorless world may be a triviality, but behind this triviality lurk other problems. What colors or tones could be represented by certain grays in the photograph? What difference will it make to, say, the American flag whether it is photographed with an orthochromatic or a panchromatic film?

Interpreting photographs is an important skill that must be learned by all who

TREE OF AFFINITIES was used in medieval times to determine the relation that a husband and a wife each bears to the kin of the other. The illustration, a woodcut made in 1473 by Johannes Andrei, is reproduced with the permission of the Pierpont Morgan Library.

have to deal with this medium of communication: the intelligence officer, the surveyor or archaeologist who studies aerial photographs, the sports photographer who wishes to record and to judge athletic events and the physician who reads X-ray plates. Each of these must know the capacities and the limitations of his instruments. Thus the rapid movement of a slit shutter down the photographic plate may be too slow to show the correct sequence of events it is meant to capture, or the grain of a film may be too coarse to register the desired detail in a photograph. It was shown by the late Gottfried Spiegler that the demand for an easily legible X-ray plate may conflict with its informative function. Strong contrast and definite outlines may

obscure valuable clues. Needless to say, there is the further possibility of retouching a photographic record in the interest of either truth or falsehood. All these intervening variables make their appearance again on the way from the negative to the print, from the print to the photoengraving and then to the printed illustration. The most familiar of these is the density of the halftone screen. As in the case of the mosaic, the information transmitted by the normal illustration process is granular, smooth transitions are transformed into discrete steps and these steps can either be so few that they are obtrusively visible or so small that they can hardly be detected by the unaided eye.

Paradoxically it is the limited power

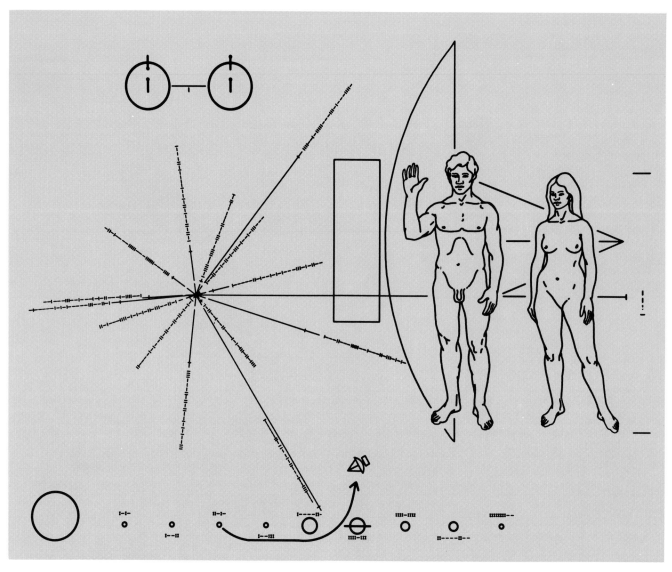

PICTORIAL PLAQUE on the *Pioneer* spacecraft is designed to tell "scientifically educated inhabitants of some other star system" who launched the craft. Without prior knowledge of our use of symbols, however, the inhabitants would not be able to decipher the message.

TRIDENT TRADEMARK adopted for North Sea gas in Britain combines a symbol of the sea, Neptune's trident, with burning gas.

Initially the idea was done realistically (*illustration at left*). Later it was encoded in an abstract form, making it easier to remember.

of vision that has made television possible: the changing intensities of one luminous dot sweeping across the screen build up the image in our eye. Long before this technique was conceived the French artist Claude Mellan displayed his virtuosity by engraving the image of Christ with one spiraling line swelling and contracting to indicate shape and shading [*see illustration on page 52*].

The very eccentricity of this caprice shows how readily we learn to fall in with the code and to accept its conventions. We do not think for a moment that the artist imagined Christ's face to have been lined with a spiral. Contrary to the famous slogan, we easily distinguish the medium from the message.

From the point of view of information this ease of distinction can be more vital than fidelity of reproduction. Many students of art regret the increased use of color reproductions for that reason. A black-and-white photograph is seen to be an incomplete coding. A color photograph always leaves us with some uncertainty about its information value. We cannot separate the code from the content.

The easier it is to separate the code from the content, the more we can rely on the image to communicate a particular kind of information. A selective code that is understood to be a code enables the maker of the image to filter out certain kinds of information and to encode only those features that are of interest to the recipient. Hence a selective representation that indicates its own principles of selection will be more informative than the replica. Anatomical drawings are a case in point. A realistic picture of a dissection not only would arouse aversion but also might easily fail to show the aspects that are to be demonstrated. Even today surgeons sometimes employ "medical artists" to record selective information that color photographs might fail to communicate. Leonardo da Vinci's anatomical studies are early examples of deliberate suppression of certain features for the sake of conceptual clarity. Many of them are not so much portrayals as functional models, illustrations of the artist's views about the structure of the body. Leonardo's drawings of water and whirlpools are likewise intended as visualizations of the forces at work.

Such a rendering may be described as a transition from a representation to diagrammatic mapping, and the value of the latter process for the communication of information needs no emphasis. What is characteristic of the map is the addition of a key to the standardized code. We are told which particular heights are represented by the contour lines and what particular shade of green stands for fields or forests. Whereas these are examples of visible features, standardized for the sake of clarity, there is no difficulty in entering on the map other kinds of feature, such as political frontiers, population density or any other desired information. The only element of genuine representation (also called iconicity) in such a case is the actual shape of the geographical features, although even these are normalized according to given rules of transformation to allow a part of the globe to be shown on a flat map.

It is only a small step from the abstraction of the map to a chart or diagram showing relations that are originally not visual but temporal or logical. One of the oldest of these relational maps is the family tree. The kinship table was often shown in medieval manuscripts of canon law because the legitimacy of marriages and the laws of inheritance were in part based on the degree of kinship [*see illustration on page 53*]. Genealogists also seized on this convenient means of visual demonstrations. Indeed, the family tree demonstrates the advantages of the visual diagram to perfection. A relation that would take so long to explain in words we might lose the thread ("She is the wife of a second cousin of my stepmother") could be seen on a family tree at a glance. Whatever the type of connection, whether it is a chain of command, the organization of a corporation, a classification system for a library or a network of logical dependencies, the diagram will always spread out before our eyes what a verbal description could only present in a string of statements.

Moreover, diagrams can easily be combined with other pictorial devices in charts to show pictures of things in logical rather than spatial relationships. Attempts have also been made to standardize the codes of such charts for the purpose of visual education (particularly by Otto and Marie Neurath of Vienna, who sought to vivify statistics by such a visual code). Readers of *Scientific American* need scarcely be told at length about the mutual support of text and image in illustration.

Whether the developed practice of such visual aids is as yet matched by an adequate theory is another matter. According to press releases, the National Aeronautics and Space Administration has equipped a deep-space probe with a pictorial message "on the off chance that somewhere on the way it is intercepted

OSIRIS in Egyptian hieroglyphics is a rebus with an eye, a throne and a divine scepter.

GREAT SEAL of the United States has the ancient symbol of the eye of Providence.

YIN AND YANG symbol in Chinese cosmology represents the dynamic balance of the female principle (yin) and the male (yang).

by intelligent scientifically educated beings" [*see top illustration on page 54*]. It is unlikely that their effort was meant to be taken quite seriously, but what if we try? These beings would first of all have to be equipped with "receivers" among their sense organs that respond to the same band of electromagnetic waves as our eyes do. Even in that unlikely case they could not possibly get the message. We have seen that reading an image, like the reception of any other message, is dependent on prior knowledge of possibilities; we can only recognize what we know. Even the sight of the awkward naked figures in the illustration cannot be separated in our mind from our knowledge. We know that feet are for standing and eyes are for looking and we project this knowledge onto these configurations, which would look "like nothing on earth" without this prior information. It is this information alone that enables us to separate the code from the message; we see which of the lines are intended as contours and which are intended as conventional modeling. Our "scientifically educated" fellow creatures in space might be forgiven if they saw the figures as wire constructs with loose bits and pieces hovering weightlessly in between. Even if they deciphered this aspect of the code, what would they make of the woman's right arm that tapers off like a flamingo's neck and beak? The creatures are "drawn to scale against the outline of the spacecraft," but if the recipients are supposed to understand foreshortening, they might also expect to see perspective and conceive the craft as being farther back, which would make the scale of the manikins minute. As for the fact that "the man has his right hand raised in greeting" (the female of the species presumably being less outgoing), not even an earthly Chinese or Indian would be able to correctly interpret this gesture from his own repertory.

The representation of humans is accompanied by a chart: a pattern of lines beside the figures standing for the 14 pulsars of the Milky Way, the whole being designed to locate the sun of our universe. A second drawing (how are they to know it is not part of the same chart?) "shows the earth and the other planets in relation to the sun and the path of Pioneer from earth and swinging past Jupiter." The trajectory, it will be noticed, is endowed with a directional arrowhead; it seems to have escaped the designers that this is a conventional symbol unknown to a race that never had the equivalent of bows and arrows.

The arrow is one of a large group of graphic symbols that occupy the zone between the visual image and the written sign. Any comic strip offers examples of these conventions, the history of which is still largely unexplored. They range from the pseudonaturalistic streaking lines indicating speed to the conventional dotted track indicating the direction of the gaze, and from the hallucinatory medley of stars before the eyes after a blow to the head to the "balloon" that contains a picture of what the person has in mind or perhaps only a question mark to suggest puzzlement. This transition from image to symbol reminds us of the fact that writing itself evolved from the pictograph, although it became writing only when it was used to transform the fleeting spoken word into a permanent record.

It is well known that a number of ancient scripts for this purpose drew on both the resources of illustration and the

POLITICAL CARTOONS are a special branch of symbolic imagery. They often lose their impact as the circumstances that engendered them are forgotten. The wit of Vicky's 1942 cartoon "Achilles' Heel" is lost on those who do not know the situation to which it refers.

principle of the rebus: the use of homophones for the rendering of abstract words. Both in ancient Egypt and in China these methods were ingeniously combined to signify sounds and facilitate reading by classifying them according to conceptual categories. Thus the name of the god Osiris was written in hieroglyphics as a rebus with a picture of a throne (*'usr*) and a picture of an eye (*'iri*) to which was adjoined a picture of the divine scepter to indicate the name of a god [*see top illustration on page 55*]. But in all ancient civilizations writing represents only one of several forms of conventional symbolism the meaning of which has to be learned if the sign is to be understood.

Not that this learning need be an intellectual exercise. We can easily be conditioned to respond to signs as we respond to sights. The symbols of religion such as the cross or the lotus, the signs of good luck or danger such as the horseshoe or the skull and crossbones, the national flags or heraldic signs such as the stars and stripes and the eagle, the party badges such as the red flag or the swastika for arousing loyalty or hostility—all these and many more show that the conventional sign can absorb the arousal potential of the visual image.

It may be an open question how far the arousal potential of symbols taps the unconscious significance of certain configurations that Freud explored and Jung was to link with the esoteric traditions of symbolism in mysticism and alchemy. What is open to the observation of the historian is the way the visual symbol has so often appealed to seekers after revelation. To such seekers the symbol is felt to both convey and conceal more than the medium of rational discourse. One of the reasons for this persistent feeling was no doubt the diagrammatic aspect of the symbol, its ability to convey relations more quickly and more effectively than a string of words. The ancient symbol of yin and yang illustrates this potential and also suggests how such a symbol can become the focus of meditation. Moreover, if familiarity breeds contempt, unfamiliarity breeds awe. A strange symbol suggests a hidden mystery, and if it is known to be ancient, it is felt to embody some esoteric lore too sacred to be revealed to the multitudes. The awe surrounding the ancient Egyptian hieroglyphs in later centuries exemplifies this reaction. Most of the meanings of the hieroglyphs had been forgotten, but it was remembered that the name of the god Osiris was written as an eye and a scepter, a fact interpreted to signify that the god symbolized

the sun. The reader need not look further than a U.S. dollar bill to see how this association was tapped by the founding fathers in the design of the Great Seal. Following the advice of the English antiquarian Sir John Prestwich, the design expresses in words and image the hopes and aspirations of the New World for the dawn of a new era. *Novus ordo seclorum* alludes to Virgil's prophecy of a return of the Golden Age, and so does the other Latin tag, *Annuit coeptis*, "He [God] favored the beginning." But it is the image of the unfinished pyramid rising toward heaven and the ancient symbol of the eye suggesting the eye of Providence that gives the entire design the character of an ancient oracle close to fulfillment.

Interesting as the historian must find the continuity of a symbol, such as the eye on the Great Seal, reaching back over more than 4,000 years, the case is somewhat exceptional. More frequently the past influences symbolism through the stories and lore in the language. Cupid's darts, Herculean labors, the sword of Damocles and Achilles' heel

UNEXPECTED IMAGES are frequently used in advertisements to arouse and hold attention. An excellent example is the offset lithograph poster "Astral Peinture Émail," by Raymond Savignac, reproduced here with the permission of the Museum of Modern Art.

come to us from classical antiquity, the olive branch and the widow's mite from the Bible, sour grapes and the lion's share from Aesop's fables, a paper tiger and losing face from the Far East. Such allusions or clichés enable us to "cut a long story short" because we do not have to spell out the meaning. Almost any story or event that becomes the common property of a community enriches language with new possibilities of condensing a situation into a word, whether it is the political term "Quisling" or the scientific term "fallout." Moreover, language carries old and new figures of speech that are rightly described as images: "The sands are running out," "The pump must be primed," "Wages should be pegged," "The dollar should be allowed to float." The literal illustration of these metaphors offers untold possibilities for that special branch of symbolic imagery, the art of the cartoonist. He too can condense a comment into a few pregnant images by the use of the language's stock figures and symbols. Vicky's cartoon showing Italy as Hitler's "Achilles' heel" is a case in point [*see illustration on page 56*].

Like the successful pun that finds an unexpected but compelling meaning in the sound of a word, Vicky's cartoon reminds us that Italy has a "heel," and what else could it be but an Achilles' heel? But even if we can count on some familiarity with the shape of Italy and the story of Achilles, the aptness of the cartoon might need a good deal of spelling out 30 years after its initial appearance. If there is one type of image that remains mute without the aid of context, caption and code, it is the political cartoon. Its wit must inevitably be lost on those who do not know the situation on which it comments.

A glance at the imagery that surrounds us does not bear out the claim that our civilization lacks inventiveness in this field. Whether we approve or disapprove of the role advertising has come to play in our society, we can enjoy the ingenuity and wit used by commercial artists in the use of old symbols and the invention of fresh ones. The trademark adopted for North Sea gas in Britain cleverly combines the trident, that old symbol of Neptune, with the picture of a gas burner. It is interesting to watch how

this idea was first coded as a realistic representation and then reduced to essentials, the increase in distinctiveness making both more memorable and easier to reproduce.

Freud's analysis of the kinship between verbal wit and dreamwork could easily be applied, as Ernst Kris has shown, to the condensation of visual symbols in advertising and cartoons. Where the aim is first and foremost to arrest the attention, condensation and selective emphasis are used both for their power of arousal and for their surprise effects. The incomplete image and the unexpected image set the mind a puzzle that makes us linger, enjoy and remember the solution, where the prose of purely informational images would remain unnoticed or unremembered [*see illustration on preceding page*].

It might be tempting to equate the poetry of images with the artistic use of visual media, but it is well to remember that what we call art was not invariably produced for purely aesthetic effects. Even in the sphere of art the dimensions of communication are observable,

MARTYRDOM OF ST. LAWRENCE is depicted in the central portal of the cathedral of Genoa. Below the traditional image of Christ enthroned is the saint, marked with a halo, on a grid. The ruler on the left prompts executioners to fan flames with bellows.

although in more complex interaction. Here too it is the arousal function of the image that determines the use of the medium. The cult image in its shrine mobilizes the emotions that belong to the prototype, the Divine being. In vain did the Hebrew prophets remind the faithful that the heathen idols were only sticks and stones. The power of such images is stronger than any rational consideration. There are few who can escape the spell of a great cult image in its setting.

The strength of the visual image posed a dilemma for the Christian church. The church feared idolatry but hesitated to renounce the image as a means of communication. The decisive papal pronouncement on this vital issue was that of Pope Gregory the Great, who wrote that "pictures are for the illiterates what letters are for those who can read." Not that religious images could function without the aid of context, caption and code, but given such aid the value of the medium was easily apparent. Take the main porch of the cathedral of Genoa, with its traditional rendering of Christ enthroned between the four symbols of the Evangelists (derived from the prophet Ezekiel's vision of the throne of the Lord as it is described in the Bible). The relief underneath will tell the faithful from afar to which saint the church is dedicated. It represents the martyrdom of St. Lawrence. For all its impressive lucidity the image could not be read by anyone unfamiliar with the code, that is, with the style of medieval sculpture. That style disregards the relative size of figures for the sake of emphasizing importance through scale, and it represents every object from the most telling angle. Hence the naked man is not a giant hovering sideways in front of a grid. We must understand that he is stretched out on an instrument of torture while the ruler commands an executioner to fan the flames with his bellows. The truly illiterate, of course, could not know that the sufferer is not a malefactor but a saint who is marked by the symbol of the halo, or that the gestures made by the onlookers indicate compassion.

But if the image could not tell the worshiper a story he had never heard of, it was admirably suited to remind him of the stories he had been told in sermons or lessons. Once he had become familiar with the legend of St. Lawrence even the picture of a man with a gridiron would remind him of the saint. It only needed a change in the means and aims of art to enable a great master to make us feel the heroism and the suffering of the martyr in images of great emotional appeal. In this way pictures could in-

ALLEGORICAL IMAGES can communicate abstract thought, as Michelangelo demonstrated in his famous sculpture "Night," with its symbolic star, owl and sleep-inducing poppies.

deed keep the memory of sacred and legendary stories alive among the laity, whether or not they were able to read. Pictures still serve the purpose. There must be many whose aquaintance with these legends started from images.

We have touched briefly on the mnemonic power of the image, which is certainly relevant to many forms of religious and secular art. The windows of Chartres show the power of symbolism to transform a metaphor into a memorable image with their vivid portrayal of the doctrine that the apostles stand on the shoulders of the Old Testament prophets. The whole vast genre of allegorical images testifies to this possibility of turning an abstract thought into a picture. Michelangelo's famous statue of Night, with her symbolic attributes of the star, the owl and the sleep-inducing poppies, is not only a pictograph of a concept but also a poetic evocation of nocturnal feelings.

The capacity of the image to purvey a maximum of visual information could be exploited only in periods where the styles of art were sufficiently flexible and rich for such a task. Some great artists met the demands of naturalistic portraiture and faithful views with consummate mastery, but the aesthetic needs for selective emphasis could also clash with these more prosaic tasks. The idealized

portrait or the revealing caricature was felt to be closer to art than the wax facsimile could ever be, and the romantic landscape that evoked a mood was similarly exalted over the topographic painting.

The contrast between the prose and the poetry of image making often led to conflicts between artists and patrons. The conflict increased in acerbity when the autonomy of art became an issue. It was the Romantic conception of genius in particular that stressed the function of art as self-expression (even though the catchword is of later date). It is precisely this issue that remains to be discussed here, since it will be remembered that the expressive symptom of emotions was distinguished in the theory of communication from the dimension of arousal or description. Popular critics who speak of art as communication often imply that the same emotions that give rise to the work of art are transmitted to the beholder, who feels them in his turn. This naïve idea has been criticized by several philosophers and artists, but to my knowledge the most succinct criticism was a drawing that appeared some years ago in *The New Yorker* [see illustration on next page]. Its target is the very setting in which the term self-expression has had the greatest vogue. A little dancer fondly believes she is communicating her idea of a flower, but observe what arises instead in the minds of the various onlookers. A series of experiments made by Reinhard Krauss in Germany some decades ago confirms the skeptical view portrayed in the cartoon. Subjects were asked to convey through drawn abstract configurations some emotion or idea for others to guess at. Not surprisingly it was found that such guessing was quite random. When people were given a list of various possible meanings, their guesses became better, and they improved progressively with a reduction in the number of alternatives with which they were confronted. It is easy to guess whether a given line is intended to convey grief or joy, or stone or water.

Many readers will know the painting by van Gogh of his humble bedroom painted in Arles in 1888 [*see top illustration on page 48*]. It happens to be one of the very few works of art where we know the expressive significance the work held for the artist. In van Gogh's wonderful correspondence there are three letters dealing with this work that firmly establish the meaning it held for him. Writing to Gauguin in October, 1888, he says:

"Still for the decoration (of my house) I have done... my bedroom with its furniture of whitewood which you know. Well, it amused me enormously to do that interior with nothing in it, with a simplicity à la Seurat: with flat paint but coarsely put on, the neat pigment, the walls a pale violet...."

"I wanted to express an absolute calm with these very different tones, you see, where there is no white except in the mirror with its black frame...."

A letter to his brother Theo confirms his intention and explains it further:

"My eyes are still strained, but at last I have a new idea in my head.... This time it is quite simply my bedroom, color alone must carry it off, by imparting through simplification a grander style to things, it should be suggestive of rest and sleep in general. In other words, the sight of the picture should rest the head, or rather the imagination.... The walls are pale violet, the floor tiles red... the doors are green, that is all. There is nothing in the room with the shutters closed. The squareness of the furniture should also express the undisturbed rest.... The shadows and modeling are suppressed, it is colored with flat tints like the Japanese prints. This will contrast, for instance,

with the *diligence* of Tarascon and the Night Café."

Here we have an important clue. Van Gogh had written of "The Night Café" [*see bottom illustration on page 48*] that he wanted to show that it was a place where one could go mad. To him, in other words, his little room was a haven after the strain of work, and it was this contrast that made him stress its tranquillity. The manner of simplification he adopted from Seurat and from the Japanese print stood for him in clear opposition to the expressive graphological brushwork that had become so characteristic of his style. This is what he stresses in still another letter to his brother. "No stippling, no hatching, nothing, flat areas, but in harmony." It is this modification of the code that van Gogh experiences as being expressive of calm and restfulness. Does the painting of the bedroom communicate this feeling? None of the naïve subjects I have asked hit on this meaning; although they knew the caption (van Gogh's bedroom), they lacked the context and the code. Not that this failure of getting the message speaks against the artist or his work. It only speaks against the equation of art with communication.

NONVERBAL COMMUNICATION of ideas and emotions is unlikely to take place unless there are some prior hints about what the possibilities are. This skeptical view is portrayed in a cartoon by CEM, which appeared in *The New Yorker*, copyright 1961.

6

COMMUNICATION CHANNELS

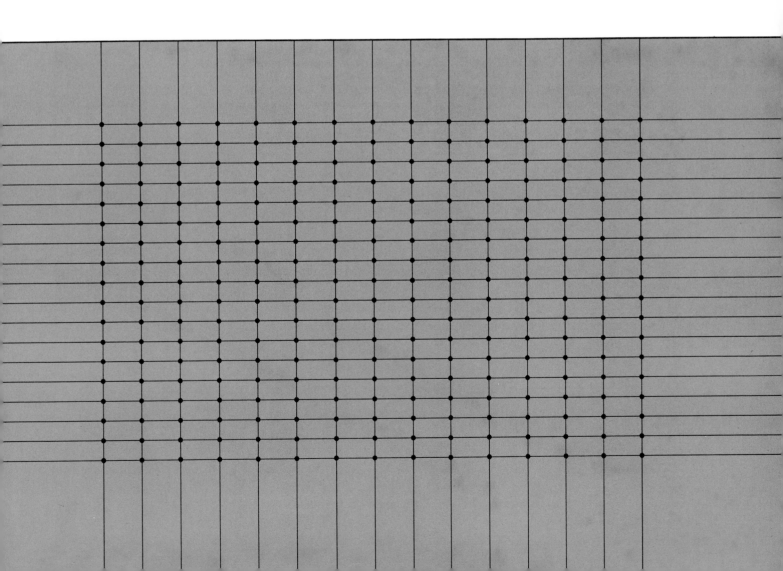

Communication Channels

HENRI BUSIGNIES

Wires, coaxial cables and radio waves provide the principal channels for telecommunications. In the near future optical channels should make it possible to transmit information in any conceivable volume.

Channels of communication take many forms and have many subtle properties. They differ enormously in length and capacity and in the speed and fidelity with which they can transmit signals. Most interpersonal communication is accomplished at distances of a few feet through a channel provided by molecules of air. The channel is usually noisy and limited both in capacity and in transmission speed. The overwhelming bulk of information we receive and act on in our waking moments is carried by electromagnetic radiation in the form of light waves that travel from a few inches (for example the print on this page) to a few hundred yards (for example traffic signals) through a channel that pervades all space. Although the channel is extremely noisy in certain parts of the electromagnetic spectrum and in certain parts of the universe, its capacity is virtually infinite and it transmits signals over any distance at the highest velocity known: 3×10^{10} centimeters, or 186,000 miles, per second.

Perhaps the most remarkable channels of all are those in the nervous system of vertebrate animals, where at any given instant hundreds of millions or billions of impulses, all essentially identical, are traveling from the organs of sight, hearing, touch, smell and taste (and also from the muscles and various internal organs) to the brain at speeds ranging from a few meters to about 100

meters per second. Each bundle of nerve fibers has its own characteristic conduction speed; for example, the signals conveying muscle position travel at the highest velocity, presumably because balance and quick movement are absolutely vital, whereas pain signals are among the slowest. One cannot doubt that the varying transmission speeds represent an optimization of the total biological communication system, achieved over millenniums by progressive evolution.

In developing technical means of communication inventors and engineers have naturally sought to exploit channels that carry messages at the highest possible speed. The most widely used channels are twisted pairs of wires, coaxial cables (metal tubes about 3/8 inch in diameter surrounding a thin central conductor) and the free space between two antennas, one for transmitting a signal and one—or millions—for receiving it. In limited service so far are the high-capacity electromagnetic channels known as waveguides: carefully fabricated tubes of round or rectangular cross section that efficiently carry radio waves whose length is measured in centimeters or millimeters. In the laboratory much work is being done on channels with vastly higher capacities, "pipes" of various kinds for carrying light: thin metal tubes, glass fibers or ceramic fibers filled with liquid [*see illustration on opposite page*].

The use of light to carry information goes back at least as far as the smoke signals used by the American Indians. In the 1790's Claude Chappe built a communication network of semaphore stations on the top of hills throughout France. He also devised an alphabet code based on the positions of the semaphore arms, which were mechanically set by an operator at each relay point. Although the scheme Chappe used for modulating and demodulating signals was extremely slow, the signals themselves traveled as fast as the microwave signals beamed today between antenna towers that occupy some of the same hills Chappe had used for his semaphores. Plus ça change, plus c'est la même chose.

Electrical communication at a substantial distance was first demonstrated in 1844 by Samuel F. B. Morse, who sent a dot-dash message over a single wire strung on poles between Baltimore and Washington, with the earth serving as a return conductor. In 1876 Alexander Graham Bell demonstrated that the human voice could be electrically transmitted over wires. The first transatlantic telegraph cable was completed in 1858, and the first radiotelegraph message was sent across the Atlantic in 1901. Commercial transatlantic radiotelephony was introduced in 1923, but high cost, limited capacity (one voice channel) and limited national distribution discouraged its use.

Transatlantic telephone calls finally became popular with the opening of the high-quality 36-channel cable in 1956. Six years later the first active experimental communication satellite, Telstar, relayed the first live television pictures between the U.S. and Europe. In 1965 Early Bird was placed in commercial transatlantic service with 240 telephone

GLASS-FIBER CHANNELS, or similar "light pipes" now under development, are potentially capable of carrying a prodigious volume of information. Operating at the frequency of visible light or infrared radiation, a single optical channel should be able to carry millions of voice signals or thousands of television signals. The fiber is 175 microns in diameter and in the photograph on the opposite page is carrying light of a wavelength of 6,328 angstroms produced by a helium-neon laser. The optical fiber is shown about actual size.

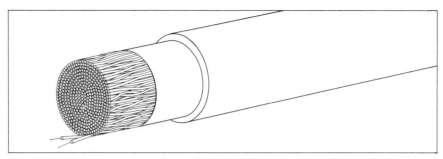

PAIRS OF TWISTED WIRES provide the standard channels for carrying telephone conversations. With time-division multiplexing (*see second illustration from top on page 71*) two wire pairs can carry 24 voice channels up to 50 miles with the aid of repeaters.

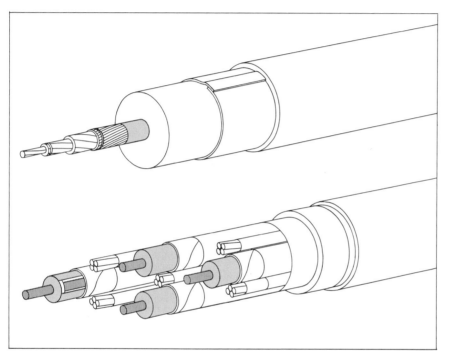

COAXIAL CABLES were introduced in the early 1940's to carry from 12 to 24 voice conversations a few hundred miles. A coaxial cable for suboceanic use (*top*) consists of a central conductor of copper surrounded by polyethylene insulation, all inside a copper cylinder. The latest transoceanic cables can carry 1,840 two-way conversations with the aid of repeaters spaced every few kilometers. Cables for use underground (*bottom*) contain from four to 20 or more coaxial cables, along with a number of wire pairs, inside a single sheath. Each pair of cables can accommodate up to 2,700 two-way telephone conversations.

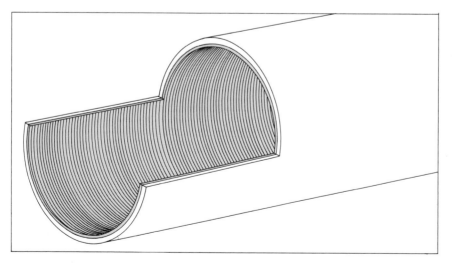

WAVEGUIDES, carefully fabricated tubes some 7.5 centimeters in diameter, are efficient carriers of radio waves ranging in length from about seven millimeters to less than three millimeters. Waveguides have a potential capacity of 250,000 two-way voice channels.

circuits. Today more than eight communication satellites are in synchronous ("stationary") orbits over the Atlantic, Pacific and Indian oceans, beaming telephone, television, telegraph, facsimile and other signals to ground stations in 39 countries. In 1957 the total number of international voice channels was only 1,000. There are now more than 25,000 such channels, and it is predicted that the number will grow tenfold in the next 10 years.

Two related concepts are fundamental in discussing channels of electrical communication: bandwidth and frequency. Both are related to the rate at which a source generates information. Let us imagine that the information source is a mechanically activated "printer" that punches holes a millimeter in diameter in a paper tape, creating a coded message consisting of holes or the absence of holes and representing bits or the absence of bits of information. If the printer can punch up to 10 consecutive holes per second and if the tape is used for transmission at that rate, the bandwidth necessary for transmission is at least 10 cycles per second (10 hertz). If the printer can punch a million holes per second, and again if the tape is used for transmission at the equivalent rate, the source will be said to have a bandwidth of a million hertz. By the same token, in order to carry a signal of that bandwidth one needs a channel able to accommodate frequencies of up to a million hertz in order to transmit the information at the rate at which it is produced.

This rule of a minimum bandwidth of one hertz for one bit of information can be transcended by some elaborate combinations of modulation techniques. In general, however, no more than one piece of information can be "printed" on each wave of a signal. Therefore if one desires to transmit the human voice, most of whose frequencies lie between 300 and 4,000 hertz, one must use an electrical signal with a frequency or bandwidth of at least 4,000 hertz. (In some cases the voice-channel bandwidth is limited to 3,000 hertz, which still provides adequate quality.) The human ear, however (when it is young and healthy), responds to frequencies as high as 15,000 hertz or even 20,000. If one wishes to transmit music with high fidelity, the required bandwidth is 15,000 hertz. The bandwidth required for television is much higher. Each U.S. television station is assigned a bandwidth of six megahertz (million hertz), of which the color-picture signal effectively uses about 4.5

megahertz. The digital data produced by computers can also require bandwidths of up to several megahertz.

The total process of electrical communication involves not only choosing an adequate bandwidth but also selecting a method for multiplexing signals or modulating carrier waves, minimizing the noise introduced by various components in the system and designing repeaters for amplifying signals to raise their level periodically in order to compensate for transmission losses over long pathways. It is obvious that costly communication pathways (between microwave towers, for example) cannot be dedicated to handling a single message but must provide for the simultaneous transmission of many messages: telephone conversations, computer and business data, television signals and so on. This is done either by frequency-division multiplexing or time-division multiplexing.

In frequency-division multiplexing the original frequencies of a number of signals are transposed and arranged side by side to constitute in effect one wideband signal. In time-division multiplexing, a more recent development, the various input signals are sampled repetitively and their instantaneous amplitudes (or the digital equivalents of their amplitudes) are transmitted sequentially. At the receiving terminal the samples are reassembled to reconstruct the original signals [*see top illustration on page 71*]. In this way thousands of signals, often of different kinds, are transmitted simultaneously with negligible interference among them.

When signals of the same bandwidth or different bandwidths are multiplexed by either method, the total bandwidth or frequency required cannot be less than the sum of the individual bandwidths (together with a little margin to provide separation). This is most easily seen in frequency-division multiplexing. For example, 10,000 voice channels of 4,000 hertz (margins included) would require 10,000 times 4,000 hertz, or 40 megahertz. Ten U.S. television channels, each with a bandwidth of six megahertz including margins, would require a bandwidth of 60 megahertz. To handle 10 television channels in addition to 10,000 voice channels would require a bandwidth of at least 100 megahertz, plus substantial margins. An energy carrier, whatever it may be, must have a frequency definitely higher than the total bandwidth of all the signals it is supposed to carry. A carrier signal is used in all forms of radio transmission. In coaxial-cable transmission no carrier is

EXTREMELY LOW FREQUENCY (ELF)	30–300 HERTZ
VOICE FREQUENCY (VF)	300–3,000 HERTZ
VERY LOW FREQUENCY (VLF)	3–30 KILOHERTZ
LOW FREQUENCY (LF)	30–300 KILOHERTZ
MEDIUM FREQUENCY (MF)	300–3,000 KILOHERTZ
HIGH FREQUENCY (HF)	3–30 MEGAHERTZ
VERY HIGH FREQUENCY (VHF)	30–300 MEGAHERTZ
ULTRAHIGH FREQUENCY (UHF)	300–3,000 MEGAHERTZ
SUPERHIGH FREQUENCY (SHF)	3–30 GIGAHERTZ
EXTREMELY HIGH FREQUENCY (EHF)	30–300 GIGAHERTZ

ONE MICRON	1/1,000 OF A MILLIMETER
ONE ANGSTROM	1/10,000 OF A MICRON
ONE HERTZ	ONE CYCLE PER SECOND
ONE KILOHERTZ	1,000 HERTZ
ONE MEGAHERTZ	1,000,000 (10^6) HERTZ
ONE GIGAHERTZ	1,000,000,000 (10^9) HERTZ
ONE TERAHERTZ	1,000,000,000,000 (10^{12}) HERTZ
ONE VU	VOICE UNIT OF 4-KILOHERTZ BANDWIDTH ASSIGNMENT
ONE TVU	TELEVISION UNIT OF 6-MEGAHERTZ BANDWIDTH ASSIGNMENT

SPECIAL TERMINOLOGY has grown up to designate various segments of the radio-frequency spectrum from 30 hertz (cycles per second) to 300 gigahertz (billion cycles per second). U.S. television stations, for example, have been assigned 12 channels in the VHF region and another 70 channels in the UHF region. The informal contractions VU, for "voice units," and TVU, for "television units," are used in the illustrations on the next three pages as a measure of the potential channel capacity of various frequency bands.

used; the signals are simply added after frequency transposition so that they occupy adjacent regions of the total transmitted bandwidth.

The most widely used processes of modulation are amplitude modulation (AM), frequency modulation (FM), pulse amplitude modulation (PAM) and pulse code modulation (PCM). The several modulation schemes can also be combined in various ways. The energy being modulated can be in the form of direct current, alternating current and currents of higher and higher frequency up to many millions of hertz. The energy can be transmitted on electrical conductors (such as telephone wire pairs and coaxial cables) or through space in the form of electromagnetic waves extending over an enormous range of frequencies, from as low as 10,000 hertz to 40 gigahertz (billion hertz) and beyond. Radio waves with frequencies between 20 and 90 gigahertz are well suited for transmission in waveguides. Electromagnetic waves in the infrared and visible region of the spectrum, with frequencies in the vicinity of 500,000 gigahertz (500 terahertz), are conveniently carried in optical waveguides or by optical fibers.

A carrier's energy can be modulated in various ways. The first modulation system to be developed for radio was amplitude modulation, in which the original signal, say a sound wave, direct-

ly alters the carrier wave's power or amplitude, that is, its up-and-down oscillation [*see illustration on page 69*]. As is well known, AM radio signals are subject to many sources of "static," or atmospheric noise. The noise is generated by electrical storms, by the aurora borealis, by the sun or by radio-emitting objects in galactic or extragalactic space and by electrical devices of all kinds. In the early 1930's Edwin H. Armstrong introduced the idea of using frequency modulation as a way of reducing noise and improving the quality of the received radio signal. In FM the frequency rather than the amplitude of the carrier wave is modulated [*see top illustration on page 70*]. In practice, to obtain the desired benefits an FM radio signal must have a bandwidth several times as wide as an AM signal. The engineer says that FM trades bandwidth for noise. In AM if the amplitude of modulation is to be increased, the power must be increased proportionately. In FM the amplitude of the frequency modulation can be increased without increasing the power at all. This is the basic difference between the two systems. In addition, since the amplitude of the FM carrier is constant, limiters can be used to reduce impulse noise.

AM was adopted for the transmission of the video part of the commercial television signal partly because it was considered easier to generate than an FM signal but chiefly because it requires considerably less space' in the radio spectrum. On the other hand, the audio part of the television signal is transmitted by FM. Most coaxial-cable systems successfully employ single-side-band AM signals because they require a minimum of bandwidth. With the development of microwave-relay systems, however, FM was adopted for much the same reasons that it is preferred for transmitting audio signals in radio and television.

Each repeater used in coaxial cables and each relay station used in microwave links adds some noise, mostly from its input circuits. The total must be less than values specified as acceptable by committees of the International Telecommunication Union of the United Nations (ITU).

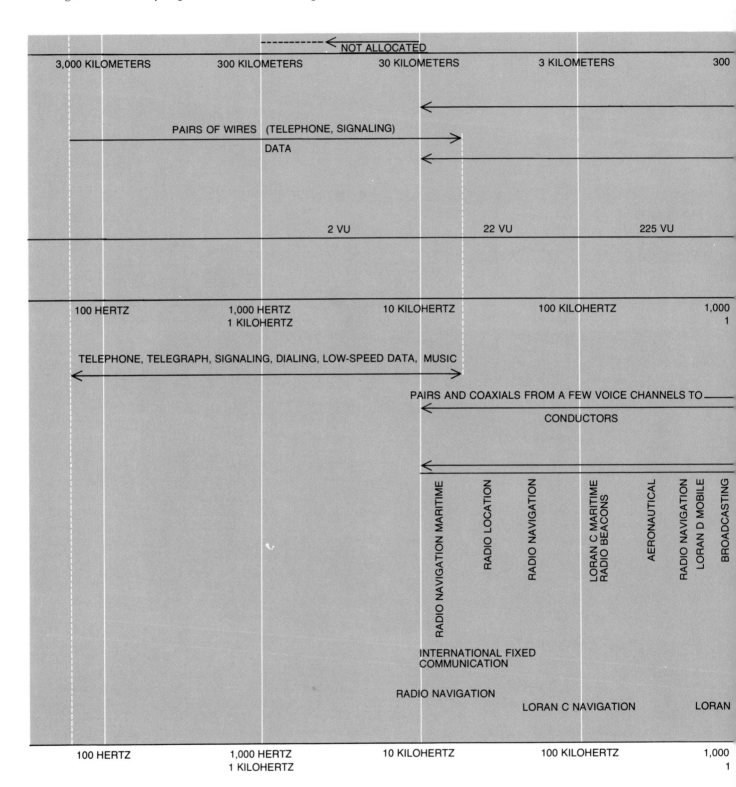

RADIO-FREQUENCY SPECTRUM is precisely allocated among a wide variety of competing communication services by international agreements. The part of the total electromagnetic spectrum potentially useful for telecommunications is depicted on these two pages and continues on the next page. The officially allocated part of the spectrum extends from 10 kilohertz (wavelength 30 kilometers) to 40 gigahertz (wavelength 7.5 millimeters, or 7,500 microns). The wavelengths corresponding to the various other frequencies are shown along the top of the illustration. The region between 10 kilohertz and 40 gigahertz is densely populated by communication services of various kinds, the most important of which are identified in the lower half of the illustration. Although this frequency region of

The existing technologies for designing against noise, distortion and interference from outside sources are complex but well understood. The main problem is to find solutions that are economically acceptable. For example, one of the newest and most noise-resistant transmission methods, the pulse code modulation (PCM) invented more than 30 years ago by Alec H. Reeves of Britain, has been made increasingly attractive by the development of solid-state-circuit technologies also incorporated in computers. In pulse code modulation the signal consists of a rapid sequence of pulses of constant amplitude arranged in binary-code groups (sequences of 0's and 1's) that correspond to numerical values [*see bottom illustration on page 70*]. The numerical values represent the amplitude values needed to re-create the shape of

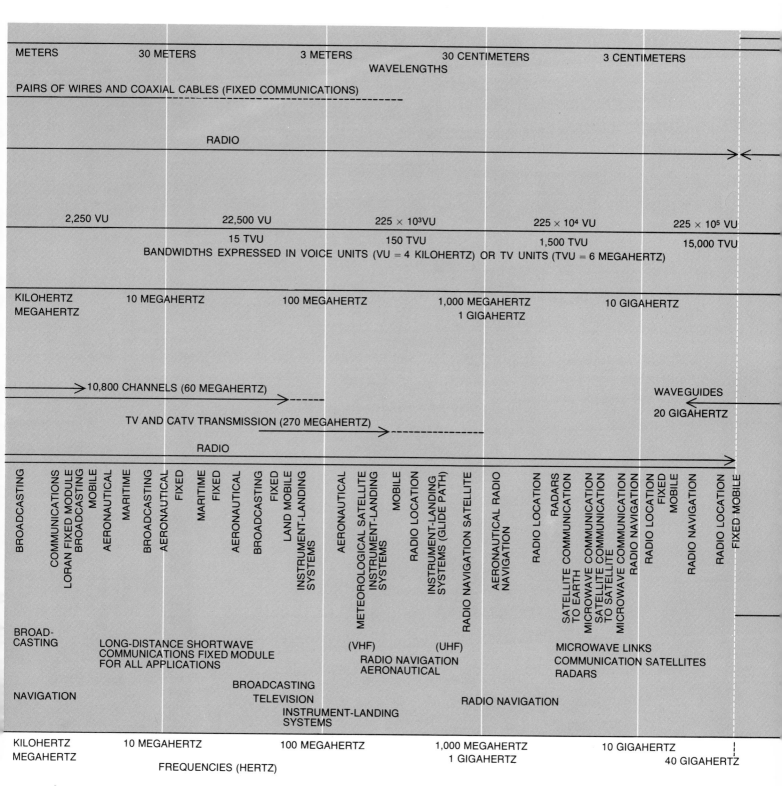

the spectrum is broadly designated "radio," communication channels at the lower end of the region are often supplied by material conductors: wire pairs and coaxial cables. An important feature of the frequency spectrum is that the information-handling capacity of a channel increases directly with frequency. The capacity of the channel is commonly expressed by the bandwidth, which is equivalent to the frequency. Thus a standard voice signal is assigned a bandwidth of four kilohertz, whereas a standard U.S. television signal is assigned a bandwidth 1,500 times greater (six megahertz). The number of voice units (VU) and television units (TVU) that could be potentially carried in each segment of the frequency spectrum are indicated in the upper portion of the illustration.

a signal, or the pulses can be used as a code to represent data bits. The big advantage of pulse code modulation is that trains of pulses can be regenerated almost perfectly by any number of repeaters over any distance, since the information is not related to the amplitude of the pulses. This advantage is exploited to reduce the effect of noise, which be-

low a certain level is not transmitted at all. In PCM transmission one pulse (or one bit) per second requires at least one cycle per second of bandwidth, but it is often advantageous to use several times as many cycles as bits.

In the 71 years since Guglielmo Marconi first demonstrated his transatlantic wireless telegraph, the useful radio

spectrum has been steadily expanded to include ever higher frequencies and has been divided and subdivided many times to provide space for dozens of new applications as they appeared [*see illustrations on this page and the preceding two pages*]. The propagation of radio waves in the atmosphere has turned out to be enormously complex, being influ-

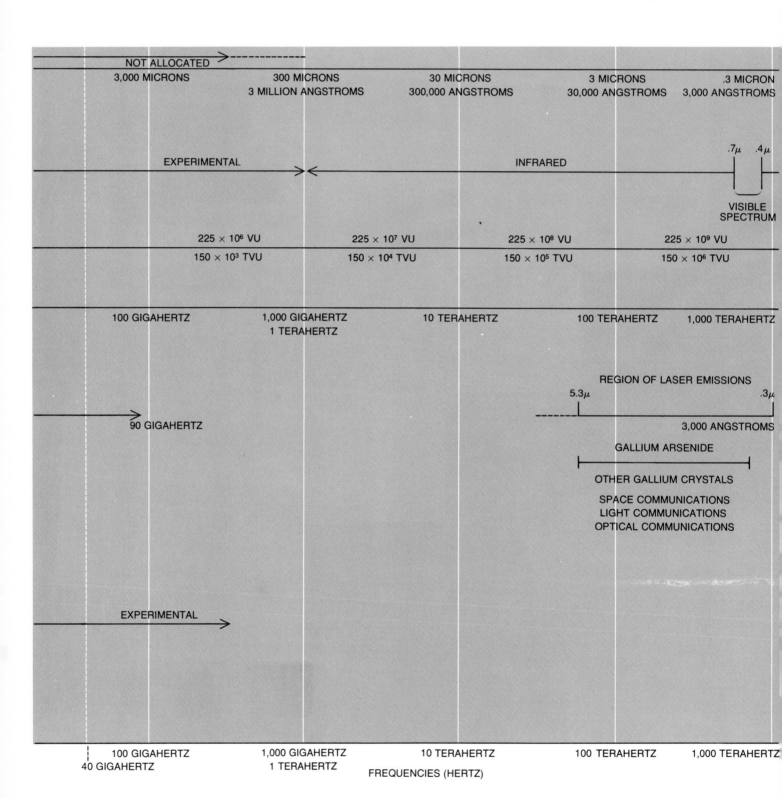

EXPERIMENTAL PART OF THE SPECTRUM embraces frequencies above 40 gigahertz and wavelengths shorter than about eight millimeters. It seems likely that communications technology will

skip much of the low-millimeter and submillimeter region and jump directly to optical wavelengths, which are readily generated by lasers and light-emitting diodes and carried by light pipes.

enced by the layers of the ionosphere, the presence of obstacles such as mountains and buildings, and the curvature of the earth. Each of these factors gives rise to different effects, depending on the wavelength of the electromagnetic radiation being propagated. In very general terms, as radio waves become shorter than a few tens of meters they increasingly resemble light in their tendency to travel in a straight line but unlike light they are little affected by rain, snow and clouds.

Radio broadcasting began with waves of medium length, corresponding to frequencies lying between 200 and 1,500 kilohertz. It was soon found, however, that for transoceanic communications much lower frequencies (from three to 30 kilohertz) were preferable because they can propagate long distances over the earth, assisted by the *D* layer of the ionosphere. Radio stations operating at these frequencies needed antennas many kilometers long and transmitters with hundreds of kilowatts of power. Moreover, the bandwidth was so narrow that only low-speed telegraphy could be transmitted. The first attempt to transmit voice messages across the Atlantic was made in 1923, using a frequency of 60 kilohertz and 200 kilowatts of power. Although the transmitter operated for several years, it was obviously not a solution for the future because it provided room for so few voice channels; in fact, only one channel across the Atlantic was ever used.

Subsequently frequencies above 1,500 kilohertz were found to propagate much farther than had been expected because they were reflected once or several times by the *E* and *F* layers of the ionosphere. Finally it was discovered that "shortwave" frequencies (from three to 30 megahertz) can travel halfway around the earth and more by being repeatedly reflected between the *F* layer and the earth. A fair amount of bandwidth was available at these frequencies to communicate by voice or telegraph over intercontinental distances and to communicate with ships on the high seas. Unfortunately the connections were subject to fading, and the frequencies of transmission had to be changed periodically because the sun not only creates the characteristics of the ionospheric layers but also alters them, depending on the hour of the day or night and on the level of sunspot activity. In spite of these drawbacks shortwave radio flourished from 1926 into the 1960's, when submarine cables and then satellites provided more satisfactory transmission and

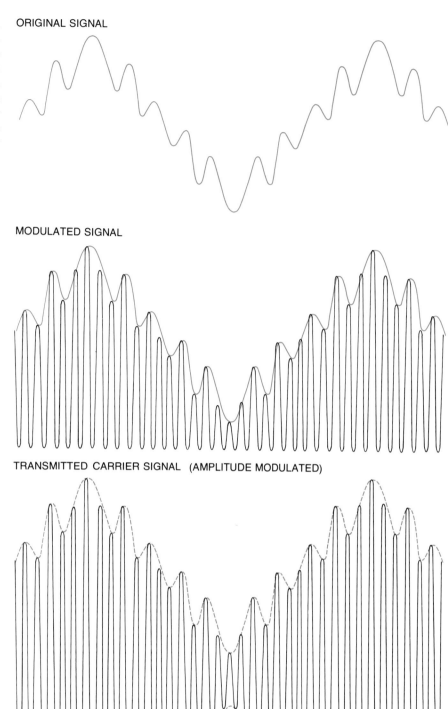

ORIGINAL SIGNAL

MODULATED SIGNAL

TRANSMITTED CARRIER SIGNAL (AMPLITUDE MODULATED)

AMPLITUDE MODULATION (AM) is the method most commonly used for modulating radio signals in commercial broadcasting. In AM the amplitude of the original wave (*top*) directly modulates the amplitude of a carrier wave of uniform frequency (*middle*), producing a transmitted carrier signal (*bottom*). At the radio receiver a rectifier, or detector, reproduces the solid envelope (*middle*), which, deprived of alternating-current component, represents the wave form of the original signal. This wave form actuates a loudspeaker.

ORIGINAL SIGNAL

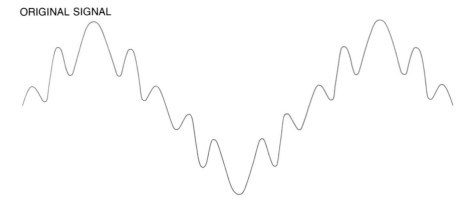

TRANSMITTED CARRIER SIGNAL (FREQUENCY MODULATED)

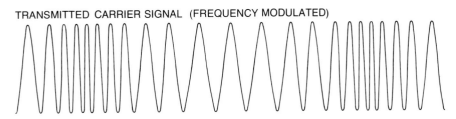

FREQUENCY MODULATION (FM) was introduced some 40 years ago by Edwin H. Armstrong to improve the quality of radio transmission. In FM the amplitude of the original wave (*top*) is translated so that it alters the frequency of a carrier wave of constant amplitude. At the receiver the original wave form is recovered from the FM carrier signal.

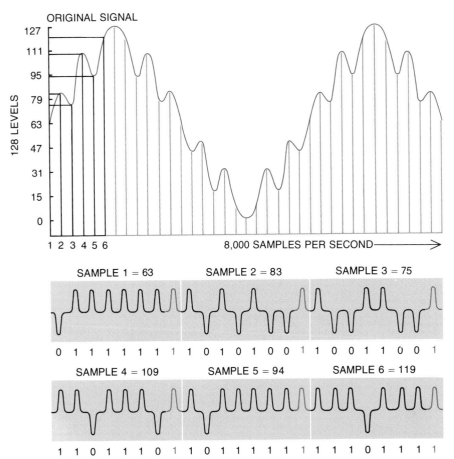

PULSE CODE MODULATION (PCM) was invented in 1939 by Alec H. Reeves of Britain to provide a signal highly resistant to noise. When PCM is used to transmit a voice signal, the amplitude of the original wave is sampled 8,000 times per second and the sampled values are translated into binary code groups consisting of 1's and 0's (positive and negative pulses). Code groups seven bits long make it possible to measure the instantaneous amplitude of original wave to an accuracy of one part in 127. An extra digit (*color*) is added to each group of seven for signaling and other functions, making the total number of pulses 64,000 per second. At receiver sequence of pulses is decoded to obtain original signal.

a veritable explosion in the number of channels.

Over the past 50 years certain regions of the radio spectrum have acquired distinctive labels [*see illustration on page 65*]. For example, the region between three and 30 kilohertz is designated very low frequency (VLF) and the region between three and 30 megahertz is designated high frequency (HF). The region between 30 and 300 megahertz is designated very high frequency (VHF); it is used for FM and television broadcasting and for aviation and other mobile communications. The region between 300 and 3,000 megahertz is designated ultrahigh frequency (UHF); it provides even more television channels than the VHF region and is used for such services as aeronautical and mobile communications, microwave relays, meteorological satellites and radio-location systems. Microwave radio links operating in the superhigh-frequency (SHF) region (from three to 30 gigahertz) make available large bandwidths for carrying thousands of voice channels. Because gigahertz waves require line-of-sight pathways and because the earth is round, relay towers have to be installed every 30 or 40 kilometers, depending on the terrain. Since microwave beams can be focused in a beam as sharp as one or two degrees, the same frequencies can be used again and again in neighboring systems, although limits are already being reached in densely populated areas.

A somewhat exotic form of microwave transmission is known as tropospheric-scatter transmission or over-the-horizon transmission. It has proved useful for military and civilian applications in remote regions such as the Arctic, where the terrain makes the installation of line-of-sight relay towers difficult and costly. Microwave transmitters with 1,000 times the output power of conventional relay transmitters are used to beam radiation into the troposphere, where the radiation is scattered earthward so that it can be received over the horizon at distances of 200 or 300 kilometers. The capacity of such systems is limited to a few hundred voice channels.

By all odds the most dramatic advance in long-distance communication began with the successful placement of the satellite Syncom III in synchronous orbit over the South Pacific in 1964, in time to relay live-television pictures of the Tokyo Olympics. Since then four types of communication satellite, Intelsat I (Early Bird) through Intelsat IV, have been launched, each type at two or three different longitudes. Some eight satellites of the more advanced types are

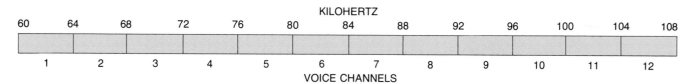

FREQUENCY-DIVISION MULTIPLEXING is the most widely used method for assembling tens, hundreds or thousands of voice signals for transmission over a single medium. Here 12 voice channels each with a bandwidth of four kilohertz are transposed up- ward in frequency to occupy 12 adjacent bands, each four kilohertz wide, lying between 60 and 108 kilohertz. The 48-kilohertz composite signal is then transmitted over the conducting medium. At the receiver the signal is demodulated into its 12 components.

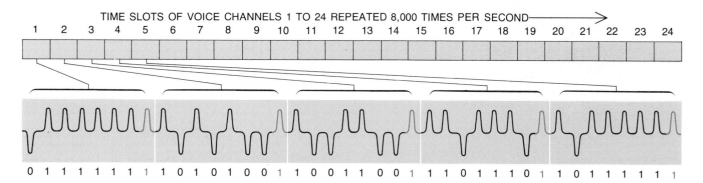

TIME-DIVISION MULTIPLEXING combines the noise-resistant properties of PCM with the economies of solid-state digital circuits. Here 24 voice channels are sampled in sequence 8,000 times a second and the amplitude of each sample is represented in binary form, as in PCM. The binary values of the samples are interleaved and transmitted as a succession of 1's and 0's. Twenty-four time slots of eight digits (192 digits) plus a spare (193) are repeated 8,000 times per second, for a total of 1,544,000 digits per second.

now in operation over the South Atlantic, the South Pacific and the Indian Ocean, with several older types in reserve. Intelsat I had a capacity of 240 voice channels or one television channel. The latest Intelsat has a capacity of 5,000 voice channels or 12 television channels, or various combinations of voice and television channels adding up to the same bandwidth. This fruitful application of space technology has linked together more countries with more channels at far lower cost than would have been possible by any other means. Regional satellite systems are now being planned for the U.S., Canada, Australia, New Zealand and Europe.

Submarine cables nevertheless continue to play a very important role. For example, the communication traffic across the North Atlantic represents 80 percent

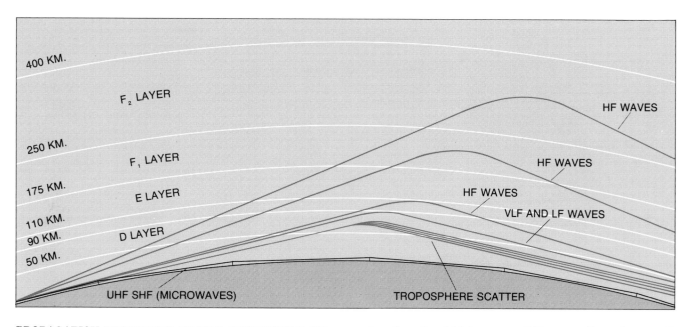

PROPAGATION PROPERTIES OF THE ATMOSPHERE differ markedly according to the frequency of the radiation being transmitted. The atmosphere has a series of ionized layers designated D, E, F_1 and F_2 that are created by sunlight and that have the ability to reflect waves of particular frequencies. The D layer primarily reflects or guides very-low-frequency (VLF) and low-frequency (LF) waves (from three to 300 kilohertz). The E, F_1 and F_2 layers primarily reflect high-frequency (HF) waves (from three to 30 megahertz). Waves of still higher frequency (VHF, UHF and SHF) follow line-of-sight pathways and hence must be relayed from tower to tower for transmission over long distances. UHF waves can be transmitted over the horizon by the tropospheric-scatter technique, in which signals radiated at high power into the troposphere are scattered so that a useful sample returns to the earth.

MICROWAVE-RELAY SYSTEMS provide most of the "bandwidth miles" for carrying television, telephone conversations and business data over transcontinental routes. A typical radio relay tower such as the one in this photograph is equipped with two pairs of horn-shaped antennas. One horn in each pair acts as a receiving antenna, the other as a transmitting antenna. The received signal is amplified by a repeater at the base of the tower before it is sent to the next tower, which is usually 30 or 40 kilometers away. Present transmission frequencies lie between two and 12 gigahertz. Beams of highest frequency can accommodate two high-quality television signals or as many as 2,700 voice channels. Up to 16 beams of adjacent frequency can share the same horn antenna.

of all international communications, and a large part of it is advantageously carried by submarine cables. Indeed, the number of channel-miles supplied by cables tripled in the five-year period 1965–1970, and it continues to increase rapidly. It is recognized that the competition from satellites has stimulated the rate of progress in cable technology. For example, the submarine cable linking Lisbon, Portugal, with Capetown, South Africa, a distance of 5,873 nautical miles, provides 360 telephone circuits with the aid of 624 repeaters and 50 equalizers. Cables being designed for the late 1970's and the 1980's will have capacities ranging from 4,000 to 10,000 voice channels, and one cable is under development with 30,000 channels.

For the more distant future developments in optical-fiber transmission could lead to new kinds of underground and submarine cables with virtually unlimited capacity. The light source for optical-fiber transmission can be either a laser or a light-emitting diode. In the early experimental fiber transmission systems light was attenuated so rapidly that in actual practice repeaters would have been needed every few hundred meters. Recently fibers a fraction of a millimeter in diameter have been improved to the point that the attenuation of laser light is only about 20 decibels per kilometer; in other words, 1 percent of the original light emerges after traveling one kilometer. With an attenuation of 20 decibels per kilometer repeaters could be spaced between two and six kilometers apart. That is about the same spacing as is now used in the repeaters for large coaxial cables. Although light can be conducted through carefully fabricated pipes a centimeter or so in diameter with an attenuation of only a few decibels per kilometer, thus needing fewer repeaters, light pipes have the drawback that they must either be perfectly straight or be provided with optical means for bending the rays wherever the pipe bends.

The bandwidth capacities of optical fibers are truly extraordinary: millions of voice channels or thousands of television channels on a single beam, when suitable light sources, modulators, light repeaters and sensitive receivers are developed. It is difficult to predict whether practical components will be available in 10 years or 20, but it seems likely that the systems will be ready before the need for millions of voice channels arrives. Meanwhile, perhaps still in the 1970's, one can expect to see the construction of light communication sys-

tems with more modest, but still enormous, bandwidths: 20,000 to 50,000 voice channels.

It is important to emphasize that whenever the technology changes in one area of telecommunications, such as the potential use of optical fibers to provide abundant channel capacity at relatively low cost, it is necessary to rethink the technology used in other parts of the total system. There is, for example, a close relation between channel costs and switching costs. If one user wants to correspond with another user frequently and on an exclusive basis, it makes sense to set up a "dedicated" channel between the two. It is obvious, however, that dedicated channels cannot be provided to connect all users of a public communication service. The alternative is to create an "on demand" connecting, or switching, system [see "Communication Networks," by Hiroshi Inose, page 77]. The first telephone switching systems were actuated by human operators; today the job is done automatically by means of a dial or "Touch-Tone" terminal on the user's telephone.

Originally an electromechanical operation, switching has become increasingly electronic and has been placed under computer control. The switching is done at one location or many, depending chiefly on the distance separating the two users. In order to connect switching centers many channels of communication are needed. It is clear that the cheaper the channels of communication become, the more direct channels can be provided between cities, with a consequent reduction in the number of intermediate switching points.

A new direction in communication channels is the progressive development of coaxial cable television. This system was originally introduced to bring television to viewers in remote or hilly regions, where UHF and VHF radio waves do not reach rooftop antennas. A tall community antenna is erected on a line of sight with one or more television transmitters, and the received signals are distributed by a coaxial cable system to homeowners. Similar systems were later installed within cities, where buildings often block a direct signal and give rise to "ghost" images, which are particularly objectionable in color television. Pictures supplied by cable are usually much better. In the next stage of development the cable concept was extended to distribute programs that serve educational and other purposes.

The latest development in that field is "interactive" television, which enables the viewer to participate in a program by answering questions or actually expressing his views. Such systems are being tested, using several types of terminal for returning signals. Genuine audience participation is probably not feasible unless the number of viewers involved in the exchange is limited to no more than perhaps 30 people in different locations. Any program worth showing at all, however, would presumably stimulate the response of hundreds of people if not thousands. Programs of regional interest could easily generate response from tens of thousands. In such cases the viewer's contribution would have to be limited to an indirect response, by means of a special terminal that will transmit coded signals to a center where they can be recorded, decoded and analyzed.

Other kinds of interactive terminal are clearly evolving for the purposes of banking, shopping and securing information from some central source, for example a library. It should not be long before important letters are sent as electrical messages, not simply in teletype form but as documents having the appearance of ordinary typed letters. They will be transmitted from desk to desk (perhaps telephone to telephone) in a matter of minutes; documents that need to be transmitted only within a few hours can be reserved for transmission at night.

Since such developments will tend to accumulate large amounts of information, steps will have to be taken to eliminate information that has become obsolete. The decisions to be made as we move into a new era of high-speed, high-volume information traffic will be difficult and require much thought and care.

There is in addition the important matter of preserving privacy.

Although some parts of the radiofrequency spectrum are already crowded, there will be no shortage of communication channels as far ahead as anyone can see. We can also expect new inventions to relieve the heavily loaded parts of the spectrum. From now on radio will be reserved mostly for satellites, mobile services (particularly air-traffic control), navigation and radar systems, space and military needs, and radio and television broadcasting, in short, for those applications where radio is indispensable. There will be unlimited capacity for communication through coaxial cables, waveguides and optical fibers. Their expanded use will require negligible amounts of energy, create no problems of pollution and place few, if any, strains on the environment.

7

COMMUNICATION NETWORKS

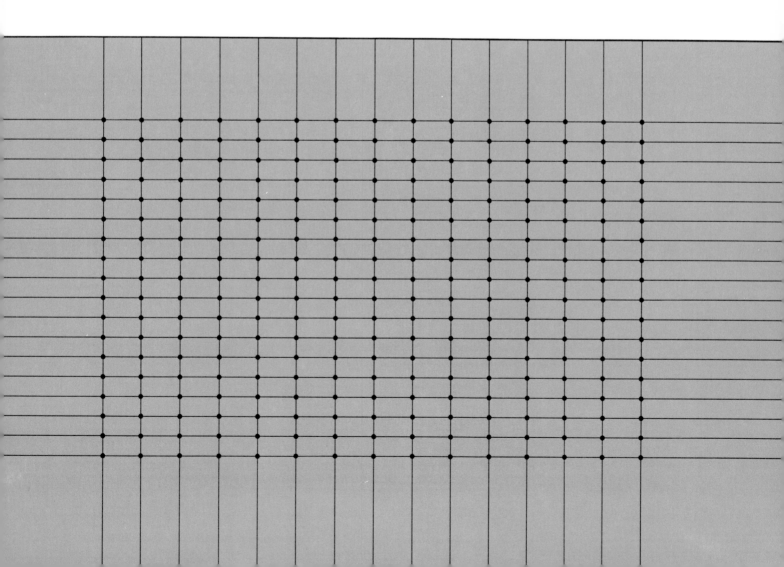

Communication Networks

HIROSHI INOSE

A channel with many sources and many destinations forms a network. Effective networks call for good switching and resourceful design to minimize the number of branches and to maximize their capacity.

The complex social and economic activities of a modern society are organized, developed and supported by three major networks: the transportation network, the power network and the communication network. The flow of passengers and freight, the flow of energy in the form of electricity and the flow of information provided by these networks combine the actions of individuals in diverse locations into an integrated whole. The communication network is probably the most vital. It clearly plays an indispensable role in almost all aspects of social and economic activity, including the regulation of the transportation and power networks. Today some 250 million telephone sets scattered around the world can be connected arbitrarily and almost instantaneously through the worldwide telephone network, which includes ocean cables and communication satellites. The radio and television broadcasting networks provide the people of the world with on-the-spot news reports, entertainment and educational programs through a billion radio and television receivers. The world is densely covered with an enormous invisible net by which each citizen is constantly exposed to information.

There has been remarkable progress in communication technology since the invention of the telegraph by Samuel F. B. Morse in 1837 and the invention of the telephone by Alexander Graham Bell in 1876. The communication network was born right after the invention of telephony. The conveniences provided by the network have stimulated the rapid growth of complex social and economic activities, which in turn have placed ever increasing demands on the network. This positive-feedback process will be intensified in the years ahead. To choose only one example, the demand for toll telephones is estimated to increase by at least 15 percent per year. Taking into account the rapid growth of data communication and other communication demands, the present communication network may double in less than five years and quadruple in less than 10. The growth rate of intercontinental telephone calls is estimated to be even greater. If the present annual growth of 30 percent continues, the intercontinental communication network may double in three years and quadruple in six.

Not only is the communication network expanding; it is also advancing qualitatively through innovations in technology. Many of these innovations have had dramatic effects. The transistor, which was invented in 1948 at the Bell Telephone Laboratories, opened a new area of solid-state electronic technology. As a result it is now possible to switch telephone connections electronically rather than electromechanically (with relays), and therefore to switch them faster and more efficiently. Communication by satellite has become a reality, and in general the communication network has been made more eco-nomical and reliable. Similarly, broadcasting has established a leading position in mass communication, supported by (among other things) a flood of transistorized radio and television receivers. At the same time the invention of the transistor led to a revolution in information processing by bringing the electronic computer into practical and reliable existence.

The rise of the telephone network stimulated research into the theory of networks in order to provide the most efficient way of organizing and utilizing the network. The direct connection of each telephone set to every other set in the network was inefficient and economically prohibitive. It was much more satisfactory to have a switching center with access to each telephone set; the connection between the sets was made by an operator in response to the request of the subscribers. The link between a telephone set and a switching center is known as a subscriber line. When a connection was required between telephone sets in different locations that were geographically far apart, it was found to be more convenient to set up a switching center called a local office in each of a number of areas and to connect the local offices by means of a second type of link called a trunk. Still another type of switching center, the toll office, was later introduced to connect the trunks for network economy. A modern telephone network therefore consists of a large number of terminals (telephone sets) interconnected by a large hierarchy of links and nodes between them.

Automatic electromechanical systems are used extensively in most switching centers, although manual switchboards still exist in some smaller remote communities. Electronic switching systems, which are controlled by special-

PART OF A PRIMITIVE COMMUNICATION NETWORK appears in the photograph on the opposite page, which shows a festoon of telephone wires at Broadway and Cortlandt Street in New York around 1883. Later poles were as much as 90 feet high and carried 30 crossarms supporting 300 wires. There were similar scenes in large cities in the U.S. and other countries, reflecting the rapid growth of the telephone network. The wires were unsightly in good weather and dangerous in storms; they were often blown down by high winds, dragging the poles with them. After turn of the century wires were laid underground.

purpose electronic computers, are rapidly replacing electromechanical systems, first in the local offices and then in the toll offices. A typical electronic switching system consists of two major parts: the switching network (which corresponds to the switchboard in the manual system) and the common control (which corresponds to the operator). The electronic switching system differs substantially from the manual system, however, in that it is much more than a simple combination of jacks and plugs, and the common control can handle several thousand connections simultaneously.

The switching network is a combination of a large number of contacts or their electronic equivalent that provide a path between an inlet and an outlet; the connection might be between two subscriber lines or a subscriber line and a trunk. The object of such a design is to reduce the number of crosspoints as much as possible. Consider a simplified model of a switching network in which N incoming lines are connected to N outgoing lines. The simplest way to organize the network would be to use an N-by-N matrix in which every line would cross every other line and a contact would be placed at each of the crosspoints. The number of crosspoint switch-

es in this single-stage configuration is N^2, and the number quickly gets out of hand for larger values of N.

The number of crosspoints can be considerably reduced by employing a more sophisticated arrangement called a **multistage network** [*see illustration on page 81*]. In a three-stage network, for example, the first stage consists of n matrixes each having $m = N/n$ inlets and l outlets; the N incoming lines are connected to the inlets. Similarly, the third stage of the network consists of n matrixes each having l inlets and $m = N/n$ outlets; the N outgoing lines are connected to the outlets. The second, or middle, stage of the network consists of l matrixes each having n inlets and n outlets. The connections between stages are made in such a way that the n inlets of each of the second-stage matrixes are connected to each of the n first-stage matrixes, and the n outlets of each of the second-stage matrixes are connected to each of the n third-stage matrixes. The number of crosspoints in this configuration is $2lmn + lm^2$. If for the sake of simplicity we assume $l = m = n = \sqrt{N}$, the number becomes $3N\sqrt{N}$, which is obviously smaller than N^2. The saving becomes significant for larger values of N. If N is 10,000, the single-stage net-

work requires 100 million crosspoints and the three-stage network requires only three million. The number of crosspoints can be reduced even further with a larger number of stages in the switching network; six-stage and eight-stage networks are commonly employed in a large switching system.

In exchange for the economy gained the multistage network has an inherent problem called internal blocking. Let us assume that an incoming line in one of the first-stage matrixes is to be connected to an outgoing line in one of the third-stage matrixes. The congestion is worst when the rest of the incoming lines of the first-stage matrix and the outgoing lines of the third-stage matrix are using connections in different second-stage matrixes. The number of second-stage matrixes engaged is $2(m - 1)$; in order to make the connection at least $2(m - 1) + 1$ second-stage matrixes are needed. If the number of second-stage matrixes is less than this, the switching network cannot always connect any given incoming line with any given outgoing line. A switching network free of internal blocking is called a nonblocking network. The principle of such networks is interesting, but they generally require a larger number of crosspoints than networks with internal blocking. In the preceding example, where $l = m = n = \sqrt{N}$, the nonblocking three-stage network needs $2\sqrt{N} - 1$ second-stage matrixes. The required number of crosspoints is $6N\sqrt{N} - 3N$; if N is 10,000, the number of crosspoints is 5.97 million. A way of drastically reducing the number of crosspoints in switching systems is time-division switching, to which I shall return.

One of the functions of the common control of an electronic switching network is to detect the request for service or the termination of any randomly occurring call. A scanner sequentially monitors the subscriber lines and trunks for changes of current. When it detects a request for service, a signal-distributor sends a dial tone to the calling subscriber. When the subscriber dials, the scanner checks his line more frequently and obtains the dial information, that is, the directory number. The directory number is translated into an equipment number that indicates the physical location of the line to the person who was called. If, for example, the called subscriber belongs to the same local office, the switching network searches for a path that will connect the two lines. When the path is found, the signal-distributor sends electrical signals to ring the telephone of the

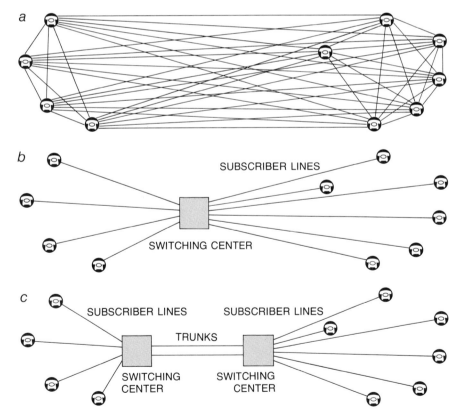

DIRECT CONNECTION between all the telephones of a communication network requires a large number of telephone lines. For example, 10 telephones linked in this way would require 45 lines (*a*). A switching office installed between them reduces the number of lines to 10 (*b*). If the telephones are separated by some distance, trunks connecting the local switching offices reduce the length of each of the individual subscriber lines (*c*).

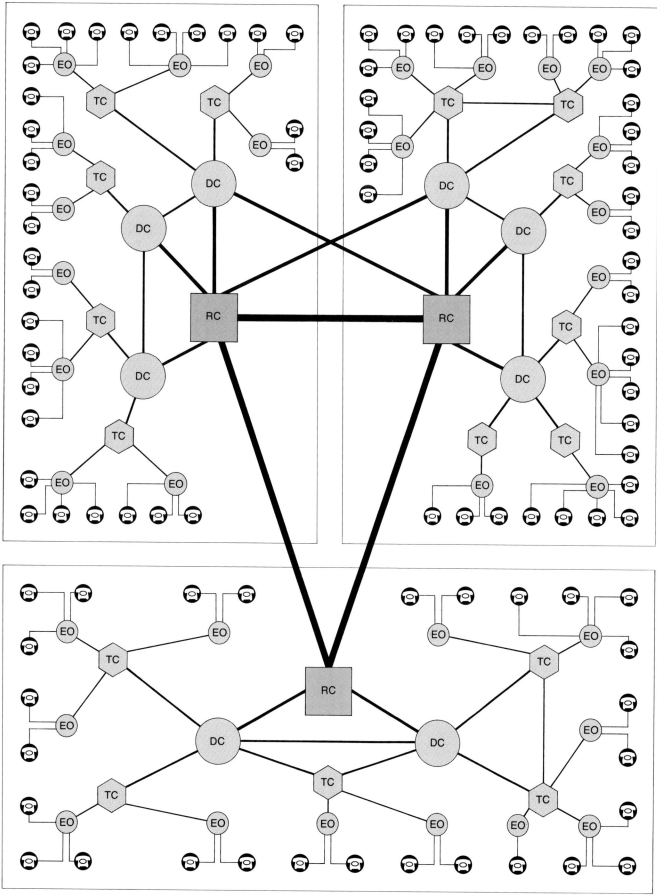

COMMUNICATION NETWORK consists of a hierarchical arrangement of terminals with many links and nodes. In the case of the telephone network the terminals are telephone sets. A node is a switching center for routing telephone calls. A link is a number of twisted wire pairs or coaxial tubes in the form of a cable or a microwave-relay station. The end office (*EO*) is of the lowest eche-

lon in the hierarchy, working as a local office; the toll offices range from toll centers (*TC*) to district centers (*DC*) to regional centers (*RC*) depending on each office's scope and responsibility. This same basic pattern of a communication network is found in broadcasting; the terminals are television or radio receivers, the nodes are broadcasting stations and the links are the radio waves.

called subscriber and sends ringback tones to the caller. The path is held during conversation; when the scanner detects the termination of the call, the path is traced in the switching network and the contacts are disconnected. In the event that no path is found or the called subscriber is talking with someone else, a busy signal is sent to the caller.

All these operations are performed under the control of a special-purpose computer with two kinds of memory: a temporary store and a semipermanent store. The temporary store is a ferrite core memory or its equivalent and is used for processing the call. The semipermanent store is a read-only memory for storing programs and translation. Magnetic drums are used in some systems. The processing of a call generally requires several thousand computer steps to set up the connection and release it.

In the telephone network the subscriber lines and some of the lower-echelon links consist of a pair of twisted wires that transmit speech signals in both directions. Higher-echelon links employ coaxial cables and microwave relays that can transmit many speech signals simultaneously. In order for speech to sound reasonably natural and well articulated the telephone network has to be able to handle signals covering a band of frequencies from 300 hertz (cycles per second) to 3,400 hertz.

The pair of twisted wires generally has a bandwidth of more than 100 kilohertz (100,000 hertz) and a coaxial cable a bandwidth of more than 100 megahertz (100 million hertz). Repeaters are provided along the transmission line to compensate for the attenuation and distortion of the signal introduced by the characteristics of the line itself.

In order to accommodate a number of speech signals on one line, frequency-division multiplexing was developed and has been used extensively. The technique takes advantage of the fact that speech signals have a bandwidth of roughly four kilohertz whereas the twisted wires on which they may be transmitted have a bandwidth 25 times larger. By means of modulators each speech signal is assigned to a channel of a certain frequency that is four kilohertz from the frequency of the next channel, and all the signals are sent simultaneously. At the receiving end demodulators bring back the individual speech signals at their original frequencies.

A second method of sending a number of speech signals over a common transmission medium is called time-division multiplexing. A pair of switches, one at each end of the transmission line, rotate synchronously across 24 contacts. At the transmitting end 24 different speech signals are fed to the contact; as the switch rotates, the 24 signals are chopped, and the signal fragments are sent successive-

ly over the common transmission line. At the receiving end the second switch, if it is properly synchronized with the first, rotates across its 24 contacts and separates the signals. The process is called sampling; if the switches rotate faster than 6,800 revolutions per second, a speech signal with an upper frequency of 3,400 hertz can be completely recovered. In practice the sampling rate is 8,000 revolutions per second, and each signal is sampled once every 125 microseconds. The sampled speech signal appears as a pulse, the amplitude of which is proportional to the amplitude of the speech signal at the instant it was sampled. The amplitude of the pulse, however, is subject to distortion and noise as it is transmitted. The situation can be improved if this single pulse is converted into a train of on-off pulses of uniform amplitude by an analogue-to-digital converter; the train of pulses contains the necessary information about the original signal—its amplitude and position—in coded digital form. Digital signals are immune to distortion and noise in the transmission line if repeaters are provided along their path to reshape and retime the train of pulses, so that the presence or absence of pulses in proper timing can be identified at the receiving end. When the coded pulses are received, they are converted back into an analogue speech signal by means of a digital-to-analogue converter. The T1 carrier of the Bell Telephone System, which multiplexes 24 speech signals, is a typical example of a pulse-code-modulation (PCM) system [see "Communication Terminals," by Ernest R. Kretzmer, page 91].

The frequency-division and time-division techniques both call for modulators, demodulators and amplifiers, which are inherently unidirectional devices. Two separate paths, one for transmitting signals in each direction, must be provided in order to set up a telephone conversation. Such an arrangement is called a four-wire link because it requires the physical equivalent of two pairs of wires. The links typically represented by the subscriber lines have no unidirectional devices attached and can therefore transmit information in both directions; these links are called two-wire links. Because there is no amplifier in two-wire transmission to compensate for attenuation of the signal, the length of the link is restricted. Four-wire transmission is required for longer-distance links.

A matter of prime importance in a telephone-switching network is the elimination of as many contacts as possible.

COMMON CONTROL electronic switching system for local telephone offices consists of two major parts: a switching network (*gray*) and a common control (*light color*). A scanner sequentially monitors the subscriber lines and trunks for changes in electric current. When it detects a request for service, a signal-distributor sends a dial tone to the calling subscriber. When the subscriber dials, the scanner checks his line more frequently to obtain the directory number, which indicates the physical location of the line to the person who was called. The switching network searches for a path that will connect the two lines. When the path is found, the signal-distributor sends electrical signals to ring the telephone of the called subscriber. These operations are performed under the control of a special-purpose computer (*central control*) with two kinds of memory: a temporary store for processing the call and a semipermanent store for storing programs and translation.

Either the frequency-division technique or the time-division technique can be applied to switching systems to allow a multiplex use of the contacts. The system must have the capacity, however, to make individual speech signals occupy specified locations either in frequency or in time. The frequency-division technique requires that modulation, demodulation and filtering processes be accomplished in a variable and arbitrary manner; hence it is economically prohibitive. The time-division technique requires that only the sampling time be variable, which can be achieved simply by controlling the timing and gating of the signal in the switching network. Additional gains in economy can be obtained by employing pulse code modulation to integrate the functions of switching and transmission. Such integration prevents the quality of the speech signal from being degraded, no matter how many links and nodes there are in its path.

Switching based on both time-division multiplexing and pulse code modulation emerged in the late 1950's along with a new concept: the integrated communication system. In this system speech signals are coded and decoded only at the points of origin and termination of the path, and the signals flow through the network in coded form. Time-division gates are provided at the crosspoints of time-division links in the system, each of which allows the coded signals to pass in specific time slots as directed by the central control. This basic configuration suffers from internal blocking, since there is no guaranty that the correct sequence of idle time slots will be available for any given speech signal traveling between the subscribers during their conversation. The system can be made nonblocking by providing variable-delay devices that allow the use of different time slots for any given speech signal.

In order for the switching system to work properly and to ensure that contacts will be ready when the signal arrives, the operations of the system must be synchronized. It is necessary to establish a unique clock frequency throughout the network so that events occur at identical time intervals, called frames, instead of at random. One way of establishing the clock frequency would be to provide a master clock in one of the switching centers that would synchronize slave clocks at the rest of the nodes in the network. Although this is satisfactory for local switching centers, it is not adequate for a larger network in-

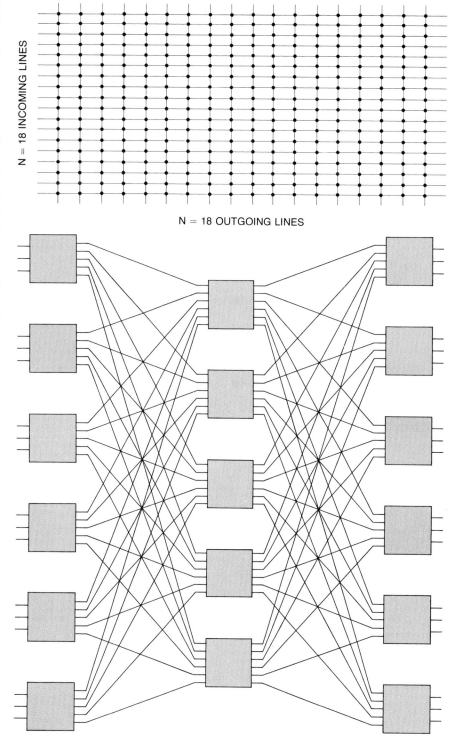

SWITCHING NETWORK is a combination of a large number of electrical contacts that provide a path between an inlet and an outlet. The simplest way to connect any number of N incoming lines to N outgoing lines would be to use an N-by-N matrix in which every line would cross every other line and a contact would be placed at each of the crosspoints (*top*). The number of crosspoint switches in such a single-stage configuration is N^2; in the example, where $N = 18$ incoming lines are joined with 18 outgoing lines, the number of crosspoints is 324. The number can be considerably reduced by employing a multistage network. In the example of a three-stage network (*bottom*) the first stage consists of $n = 6$ matrixes, each having $m = N/n = 3$ inlets and $l = 5$ outlets. Similarly, the third stage of the network consists of six matrixes, each having five inlets and three outlets, and the 18 incoming lines are connected to the outlets. The connections between stages are made in such a way that the six inlets of each of the second-stage matrixes are connected to each of the six first-stage matrixes, and the six outlets of each of the second-stage matrixes are connected to each of the six third-stage matrixes. The number of crosspoints in this configuration is $2lmn + lm^2$ or 225 for the example, a saving of nearly 100 contacts over the N-by-N matrix. This three-stage network is nonblocking; any incoming line is guaranteed to be connected to any unused outgoing line regardless of traffic in between.

cluding a number of switching centers because of the complicated procedure involved in assigning one of the slave clocks to take control if the master clock fails. One prospective solution is to set up a mutual synchronization system whereby phase locked oscillators would be set up in each switching center and would be allowed to interact with one another. The electric-power network already has such a system, in which a number of synchronous generators interact with one another and maintain a unique power frequency of 60 cycles per second. Since there is no hierarchy in this system, as there is with the master and slave clocks, it is more reliable for larger networks in case of a failure with the master clock.

The intercontinental communication network consists of ocean cables and communication satellites with associated switching centers and stations on land. An ocean cable generally consists of a single coaxial tube with a number of highly reliable submarine repeaters. The cable can carry between 48 and 720 speech signals in both directions by means of frequency-division multiplexing. Newer systems under development will be able to carry 3,600 speech signals or more. A sophisticated technique called TASI (time-assignment speech interpolation) has increased the number of speech signals that can be carried by existing cable systems. The TASI system takes advantage of the fact that a subscriber talks less than 50 percent of the

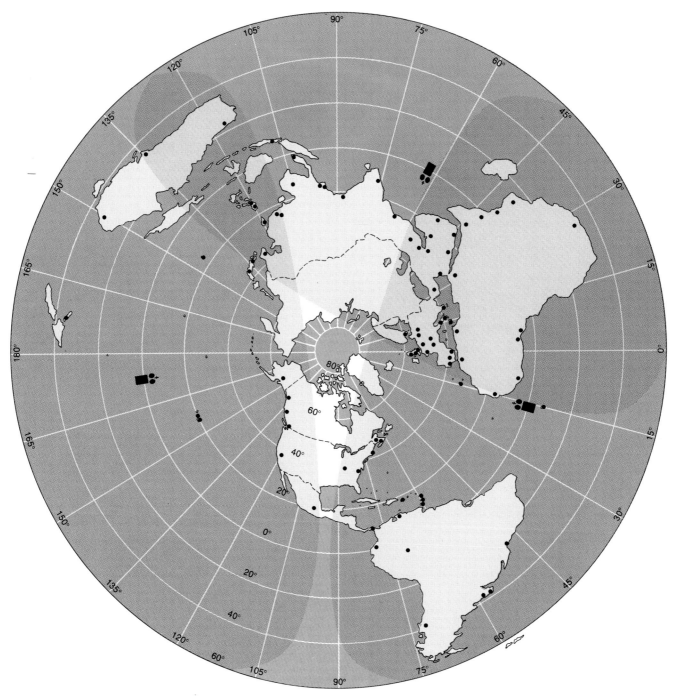

SATELLITES AND CABLES link the continents in an international communication network. Three satellites in synchronous orbit around the earth would be sufficient to provide adequate communication coverage (gray at left) for major land areas. There are currently three Intelsat III and three Intelsat IV communication satellites in orbit distributed over the Atlantic, Pacific and Indian oceans. They are managed by the International Telecommunications Satellite Consortium, comprising a partnership of telecommunications organizations in 82 nations. Intelsat ground stations (dots) are owned by the agencies or authorities in the countries

time spent in a telephone conversation. The speech of another subscriber can be temporarily inserted into this pause, allowing for a greater number of simultaneous conversations. The cost of TASI is small compared with the cost of the ocean-cable system, and it is made up by the number of additional subscribers who can use the cable at any one time.

Communication satellites transmit to and from stations on the earth at microwave frequencies (4,000 and 6,000 megahertz). Commercial communication satellites are synchronous satellites: they have an orbital period equal to the earth's period of rotation and hence are stationary with respect to the earth. Three synchronous satellites can essentially cover the entire surface of the earth. The number of speech signals that could be simultaneously carried by the satellite Intelsat III was 1,200. Five satellites of this type were launched: two over the Atlantic, one over the Pacific and two over the Indian Ocean.

Intelsat IV can carry more than 5,000 speech signals in 12 groups, each occupying a bandwidth of 36 megahertz; two such satellites are currently over the Atlantic and one over the Pacific. So far communication has only been from ground to satellite to ground. Satellite-to-satellite communication is also being planned to widen the effective coverage of the individual satellites. The link between satellites will possibly operate on frequencies above 20,000 megahertz, which would be attenuated

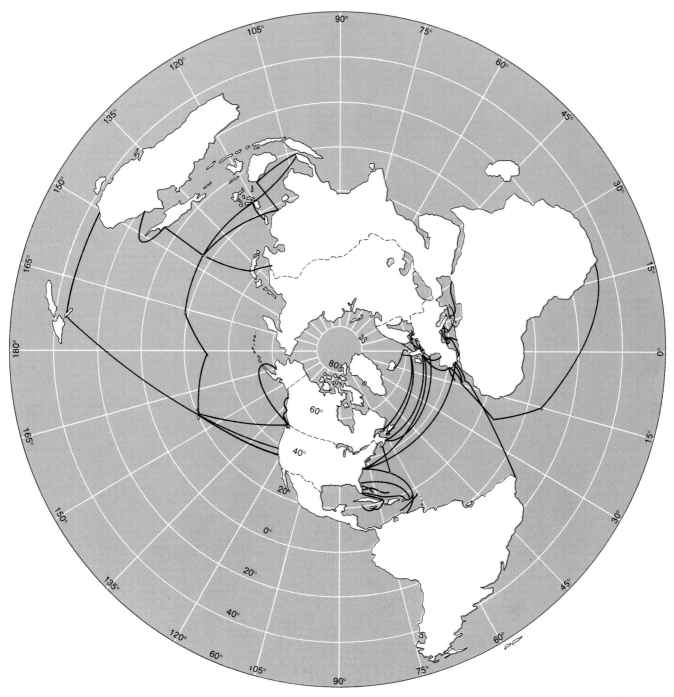

in which they are located. Submarine-cable systems (*black lines at right*) are a natural complement to communication satellites. Most major countries are now linked by cables. The latest generation of transistorized repeater cable systems can carry up to 1,840 two-way channels. One such cable will be installed between Britain and Canada in 1974; it will provide double the channel capacity available from all six transatlantic cables currently in operation. Scale of the map precludes showing every cable in existence; for example, there are nearly 20 cables between England and continental Europe. The map shows only half of them.

by the atmosphere if they were used on the ground.

The speech channels relayed by a satellite can be subdivided on a frequency-division basis, with each frequency pre-assigned to the respective earth stations. It may be preferable, however, to assign as many speech stations to the satellite as are required to handle the traffic without pairing each channel with a station on the earth. This system, named Multiple Access Demand Assignment, employs the techniques of frequency division, time division and space division. In the frequency division as many as 800 speech signals coded in pulses are aligned in channels each with a bandwidth of 45 kilohertz. An earth station can basically seize any one of these channels as the demand arises. The system is considered suitable for an area with a large number of earth stations having light traffic. In the time division as many as 700 speech channels contained in a frame of 125 microseconds are divided into subframes, each of which is assigned to an earth station according to the demand. Since the transmissions from the individual earth stations are not always exactly synchronized, a "guard time" is provided between the subframes to prevent the overlapping of signals.

The system is considered most suitable for an area with a small number of earth stations having heavier traffic. Speech channels can also be assigned by space division: installing on the satellite several antennas that can concentrate energy sharply. The satellite can thereby communicate with a number of earth stations by directional beam without interference, and it can switch the narrow beams in accordance with the demand for transmission and reception. Space division can be combined with frequency division or time division for further economy.

Ocean cables and communication satellites can serve in parallel because of their complementary features. A typical ocean-cable system may cost $150 million, but it is very reliable and its useful life may be longer than 20 years. A modern satellite costs $30 million for construction and launching, but it is usually less reliable and its useful life is estimated to be seven years. Moreover, virtually any number of ocean cables can be laid on the ocean floor, but if there are too many satellites in one area, they will interfere with one another.

An elementary feature of intercontinental communication is the difference in local time in various areas of the world. When it is midnight in New York, it is daytime in Tokyo and Sydney. The traffic between Tokyo and Sydney can therefore be routed through New York instead of providing many direct links between the two cities. The assignment of signals and numbers for each telephone on the earth is the major problem in realizing intercontinental direct long-distance dialing. Signaling methods and the assignment of national number codes are now being standardized, however. For example, if you want to call *Scientific American* from outside the U.S., you dial 01-1-212-688-3900. The two-digit code (01) is the international prefix indicating that the call is going outside the country and the third digit (1) is the national code for the U.S.

I have described the communication network with particular reference to telephone traffic. The telephone network is still the largest communication network. Part of it, however, is used for telegraphy and radio and television programs as well as voice calls.

In the telephone network information flows from terminal to terminal simultaneously in both directions. To ensure strictly simultaneous conversation no appreciable delay is allowed in the bidirectional path. The function of a telephone switching center is to set up a path between two terminals as if it were a single metallic line. This type of switching is therefore called line switching.

Strict simultaneity in the bidirectional path is not usually required, however, by traffic in data. In the system used by airlines to reserve seats for passengers it does not discommode the customer if he has to wait a few seconds to get a seat reservation made and confirmed. The information flows between a terminal and the reservation center in two directions successively rather than in two directions simultaneously. When someone sends a telegram, he is satisfied if the message is delivered within a few hours or, in the case of a night letter, even the next morning. The telegraph information flows unidirectionally from terminal to terminal with considerable delay.

The time needed for a center to respond to an input event is called the response time or the turnaround time. The permissable response time ranges from a fraction of a second to several hours or more depending on the purpose of the system. In any data system a certain amount of delay is allowed as long as it is not an appreciable hazard to the user's activities, and this slack time is employed for information-han-

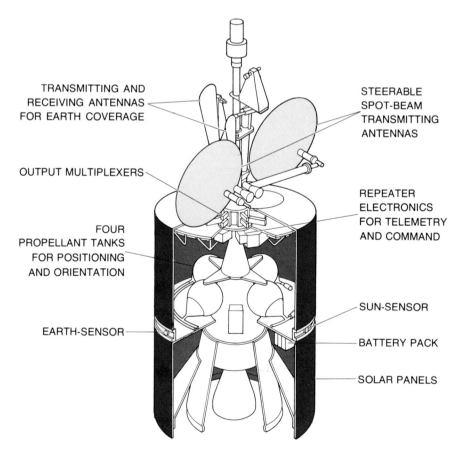

TRANSMITTING AND RECEIVING ANTENNAS FOR EARTH COVERAGE

STEERABLE SPOT-BEAM TRANSMITTING ANTENNAS

OUTPUT MULTIPLEXERS

FOUR PROPELLANT TANKS FOR POSITIONING AND ORIENTATION

REPEATER ELECTRONICS FOR TELEMETRY AND COMMAND

EARTH-SENSOR

SUN-SENSOR

BATTERY PACK

SOLAR PANELS

INTELSAT IV SATELLITE is one of the six Intelsat communication satellites in orbit around the earth. The satellite has 12 repeaters, each with a bandwidth of 36 megahertz; all together they can handle some 9,000 telephone circuits. Lifetime of satellite is seven years.

SATELLITE-TRACKING ANTENNA 97 feet in diameter at James-burg, Calif., transmits and receives high-speed data from the Intel-sat satellite over the Pacific. It can handle multichannel telephone, teletypewriter and black-and-white and color television signals.

dling. The information from a terminal is stored temporarily in a data-switching center either before, during or after the processing to increase the usage of the processor as well as the transmission paths. The arrangement is called message-switching, or store-and-forward switching. The term message-switching comes from the practice in traditional automatic telegraph switching, where messages are temporarily stored on punched paper tape before being transmitted.

In broadcasting the information is disseminated unidirectionally from a broadcasting center to a large number of terminals. This pattern is not restricted to radio and television broadcasting; it is typical of the information flow in all mass communications. It includes newspaper and magazine delivery, although of course such deliveries are handled in part by the transportation network rather than by the communication network.

In actual communication networks the flow of information may be a mixture of all these basic patterns. In broadcasting the response to a question or opinion program can be fed back to the center by telephone. An advanced cable-television system can provide specific programs for individual subscribers at the request of the subscriber. A telephone switching center can retrieve a recently changed telephone number on a customer's inquiry and then answer by synthetic speech after a delay of a few seconds. A data-processing center can respond to inquiries, provide message-switching and occasionally broadcast data. A telemetry surveillance center can send alarm signals to a number of control points when, for example, pollution exceeds a predetermined threshold.

The advent of data communication has opened a new epoch for communication networks. Information for machine communication is now being handled as well as information for human communication. Information-processing, an entirely new service, is being added to the traditional functions of transmission and switching. The evolution of computer systems and the development of diversified types of data terminal will doubtless bring about larger and more sophisticated data-communication systems in coming years.

The basic configuration of a typical data-communication system consists of a data center, a communication network and a number of terminals on the subscriber's premises. Since the telephone network transmits an alternating-current signal, modulator-demodulators (modem's) are needed at the interfaces between the communication network and the terminals and the data-center equipment to convert the binary signal into the alternating-current signal and vice versa. Low-speed data terminals with a great deal of traffic or high-speed terminals generally employ leased lines that are permanently connected to the data center. With terminals that are used infrequently the data center can be called by dialing, and the transmission path is established and maintained through the switching centers until the conversation with the computer is finished. The path established by dialing was originally designed for telephone conversation; such paths can pass low-speed data (up to 2,000 bits per second) with a bandwidth less than or equal to the bandwidth of speech. Low-speed data terminals include teletypewriters, paper-tape readers and paper-tape punches. High-speed leased lines provide a data speed of 48 to 240 kilobits per second. Typical high-speed data terminals are magnetic tapes, line printers and cathode-ray-tube displays.

A data center generally includes a large-scale computer system consisting of several central processing units, a main memory and peripheral devices (such as magnetic drums, magnetic disks, magnetic tapes and line printers) that are connected to the main memory through selector channels. The data center also has communication-control units that forward data from terminals to the computer and back again. Communication-control units accommodating several low-speed terminals are connected to the main memory through multiplexer channels; the units dealing with high-speed terminals are connected to the main memory through selector channels. The role of the communication-control unit varies with the system. It can act essentially as a computer and perform several functions, including routing commands and messages, checking errors and converting one data format to another. The unit is often called a front-end processor or a communication processor.

One example of a communication-control unit is the interface message processor (IMP) used in the computer network set up by the Advanced Research Projects Agency (ARPA) of the Department of Defense. The ARPA Network is one of the more interesting computer networks being organized. It connects different types of computers located at various universities and other institutions by means of IMP's and leased lines capable of transmitting information at 50 kilobits per second. The objective of the computer network is to utilize all the computers making up the network in common so that the resources of various institutions are shared. An

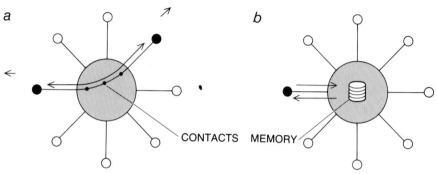

a TERMINAL AND TERMINAL
BIDIRECTIONAL AND SIMULTANEOUS

b TERMINAL AND CENTER
BIDIRECTIONAL WITH DELAY

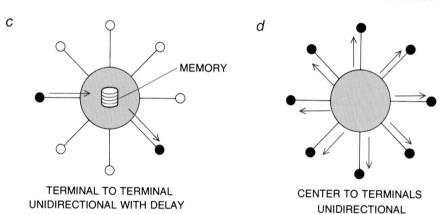

c TERMINAL TO TERMINAL
UNIDIRECTIONAL WITH DELAY

d CENTER TO TERMINALS
UNIDIRECTIONAL

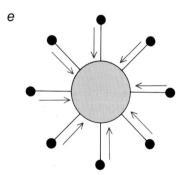

e TERMINALS TO CENTER
UNIDIRECTIONAL

INFORMATION FLOWS in a number of different patterns depending on the medium of communication. Telephone conversations are bidirectional and simultaneous between two terminals (a). A computer inquiry system, such as the seat-reservation system airlines employ, is bidirectional communication between a terminal and a center with some delay (b). Telegraph communication is unidirectional from terminal to terminal with considerable delay; this pattern is essentially the same as the traditional pattern of letter delivery (c). In broadcasting the information flows unidirectionally from center to terminals with no delay. Newspapers and magazines follow the same pattern with a delay for delivery (d). Telemetry from pollution devices or rain-gauge meters or communication from any outpost stations to a central monitor is a case of the terminal-to-center flow of information (e).

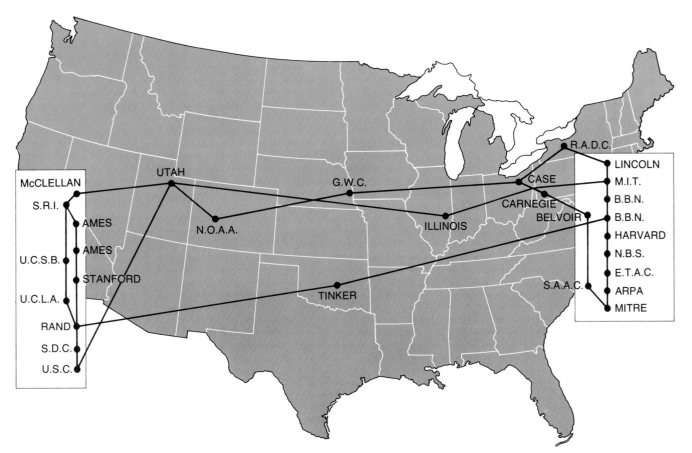

ARPA NETWORK, operated by the Advanced Research Projects Agency of the Department of Defense, is one of several emerging computer networks connecting various educational and research institutions over the country. Each dot indicates the location of an interface message processor (IMP) that gives access to the "host" computers of the network. The hosts are joined by leased lines capable of handling data at a rate of 50 kilobits per second. The network configuration allows the data to travel from terminal to terminal by alternate routes. "McClellan" is McClellan Air Force Base in Sacramento, Calif.; "S.R.I.," Stanford Research Institute in Menlo Park, Calif.; "Ames," Ames Research Center at Moffett Field, Calif. (two IMP's); "Stanford," Stanford University; "U.C.S.B.," University of California at Santa Barbara; "U.C.L.A.," University of California at Los Angeles; "Rand," Rand Corporation in Santa Monica, Calif.; "S.D.C.," System Development Corporation in Santa Monica, Calif.; "U.S.C.," University of Southern California in Los Angeles, Calif.; "Utah," University of Utah in Salt Lake City; "N.O.A.A.," National Oceanographic and Atmospheric Agency in Boulder, Col.; "G.W.C.," Global Weather Central at Offutt Air Force Base in Omaha, Neb.; "Tinker," Tinker Air Force Base in Oklahoma City, Okla.; "Illinois," University of Illinois in Urbana, Ill.; "Case," Case-Western Reserve University in Cleveland; "Carnegie," Carnegie-Mellon University in Pittsburgh; "Belvoir," Fort Belvoir, Va.; "S.A.A.C.," Seismic Array Analysis Center in Alexandria, Va.; "R.A.D.C.," Rome Air Development Center at Griffiss Air Force Base in Rome, N.Y.; "Lincoln," Lincoln Laboratory in Lexington, Mass.; "M.I.T.," Massachusetts Institute of Technology in Cambridge, Mass.; "B.B.N.," Bolt Beranek and Newman Inc., Cambridge, Mass. (two IMP's); "Harvard," Harvard University; "N.B.S.," National Bureau of Standards in Washington; "E.T.A.C.," Environment Technical Applications Center in Washington; "ARPA," Advanced Research Projects Agency in Washington; "MITRE," MITRE Corporation in Washington. Map shows the ARPA Network as of July, 1972.

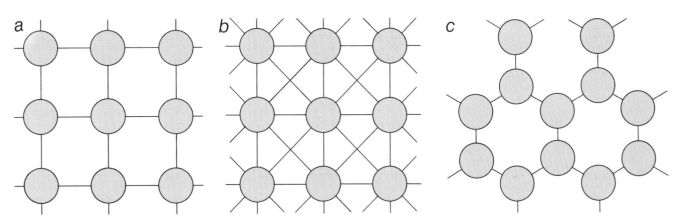

DISTRIBUTED NETWORKS consist of a mesh of links connecting the nodes of the network in a nonhierarchical structure. Signals traveling through the network from one node to another can take a number of alternate routes to arrive at their destination; therefore even if the individual links and nodes are somewhat unreliable, the overall form of the network ensures a highly reliable connection. Three different varieties of distributed networks are the grid network (a), the polygrid network (b) and the honeycomb network (c). The AUTOVON telephone network operated by the Department of Defense employs the polygrid configuration.

IMP receives messages in blocks of less than 8,096 bits from its "host" computer. It reads the address of the host computer that is to receive the message and transmits one block after another over the links connecting the two hosts. As each message block arrives the IMP of the receiving host sends back a request for the next block until the entire message has been transmitted.

Another data network of much interest is the ALOHA system developed at the University of Hawaii. The system provides a time-sharing computer service for terminals on four of the Hawaiian Islands by means of a single ultrahigh-frequency radio channel. The communication-control unit transmits and receives messages in blocks of 704 bits at a speed of 24 kilobits per second. The terminals transmit their messages without coordination, so that blocks from individual terminals may interfere with one another. For protection against such interference a cyclic error-detecting code is used; the terminals repeat their transmissions until no error is detected.

One of the major technical problems in organizing an efficient data-communication system is that the existing communication network has been oriented mainly toward speech communication. The links between stations are plagued with impulsive noise and instantaneous interruptions. Such disturbances cause no appreciable degradation in the quality of speech, but they may result in serious errors in transmitted data if no measures for detecting or correcting them are provided. The bandwidths of the existing links are satisfactory for transmitting a basic group of 12 speech channels, but quite a few terminals operate at data speeds ranging from five to 20 kilobits per second, which is too fast for a speech channel and too slow to make full use of the bandwidth of the basic group of 12 channels. The time required to set up a connection by dialing through the switching centers can be as much as 10 seconds, which is too long for data transmission that typically takes a few seconds or less. Above all, a communication network based on frequency-division multiplexing is inefficient for transmitting digital data compared with a network based on time-division multiplexing. For example, a speech channel that is frequency-divided can provide a data speed of only up to 9.6 kilobits per second, whereas a time-divided speech channel can transmit eight bits of data 8,000 times per second, that is, it can provide a data speed of 64 kilobits per second.

It is conceivable that a new communication network will be built in which the transmission, switching and processing of speech, data and other information are all performed digitally. Progress in large-scale integrated-circuit technology is drastically cutting the cost of digital hardware. Extremely broad-band (although rather noisy) transmission media such as millimeter-wavelength waveguides and laser systems are now available and match the characteristics of digital transmission. Pulse-code-modulation transmission systems are rapidly becoming popular; pulse-code-modulation switching is almost ready for service. All these factors support the concept of digital networks. One of the conveniences of a digital time-division-multiplexing system is that it provides a wide variety of transmission speeds. Digital techniques can also provide for a more efficient use of telephone sub-scriber lines, which have been the least efficient part of the telephone network, in their capacity for transmitting data and visual patterns as well as speech. If subscriber lines of wider bandwidth become available, it will be possible to integrate into the network a cable-television system with individual two-way transmission. One of the obvious advantages of cable television is that the very-high-frequency and ultrahigh-frequency radio bands taken up by television broadcasting can be devoted to mobile communication and other purposes. Up to now such a shift has not been at all popular in spite of the enormous potential demand because of the lack of frequencies available for mobile communication.

As the communication network evolves and integrates human activities ever more tightly, its social role gains ever more weight. Society can ill afford unreliable communication networks, so that now and in the future there must be much emphasis on reliability. A modern electronic switching system is designed with dual computers for emergencies; it is estimated that its total time out of service for repairs over a period of 40 years will be only a few hours. Such a network is also organized to be nonblocking and to provide alternate routes for messages. Networks having no hierarchy of connections can be made quite reliable with a large number of possible routes, even if unreliable low-cost links and nodes are used. All these advances will surely enhance the benefits the human species gains from closer interaction.

8

COMMUNICATION TERMINALS

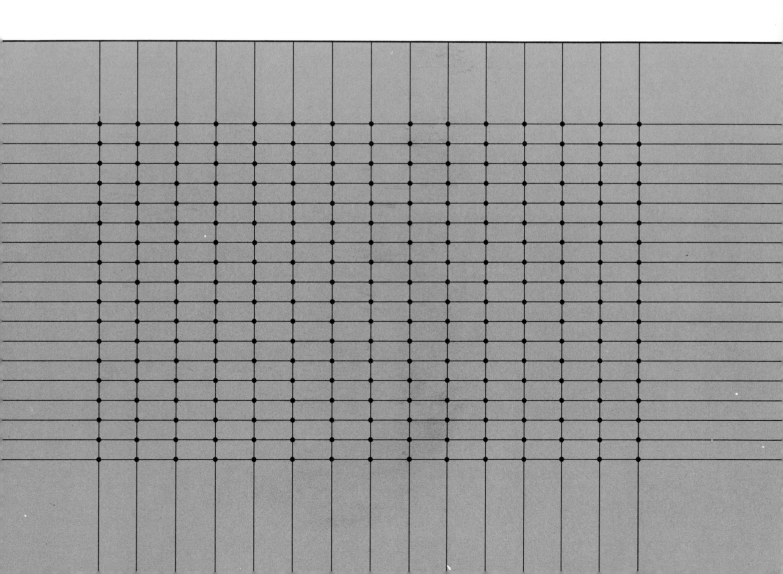

Communication Terminals

ERNEST R. KRETZMER

They convert the message from a source into a form well adapted to a communication channel. At the end of the line other terminals convert the signal into a form suitable for ultimate consumption.

Communication signals are of many distinctive types, depending on the channel used for transmission and on the kind of information being carried. In every case a communication terminal is needed at the source to convert the message into a signal well adapted for its intended channel; at the other end of the channel another terminal converts the signal into a form well adapted for its intended recipient. In the classical model of a communication system the first terminal, which receives the message from the source and tailors it to fit the channel, is called an encoder; the terminal at the end of the channel, which recovers the message for delivery to its destination (or information sink), is called a decoder.

In his celebrated paper "The Mathematical Theory of Communication" Claude E. Shannon some 25 years ago defined and quantified the key parameters of communication systems. He distinguished between the continuous channel (the conventional type normally used for audio, video and other analogue signals) and the discrete channel (for digital data or digitized analogue signals). In both cases the information flow, expressed in bits per second, can approach an upper limit known as the channel capacity, provided that the proper encoding is found and used. A surprising theorem states that with such encoding the discrete channel can function up to capacity with vanishingly small probability of output error, in spite of the inevitable noise disturbances that are present in all communication systems. This finding lent impetus to a successful search for efficient error-detecting and error-correcting codes, which are increasingly employed in today's digital terminals used for data communication. In the case of analogue signals one of the earliest methods for combating noise was the substitution of wide-swing frequency modulation (FM) for simple amplitude modulation (AM). In general the terminal designer striving for the best performance possible within the allowable cost can select from a wide range of signal-processing stratagems.

Long before the advent of electrical telecommunication, of course, the human sensory and vocal organs served as communication terminals with extraordinary capabilities, in concert with the ultimate information sink: the brain. The vocal cords in combination with the variably resonant oral cavity serve as the principal human transmitting terminal. It generates an acoustic signal well matched to the transmission medium: air. Of the five human receiving terminals (the eye, the ear and the organs of touch, smell and taste) the eye has by far the highest capacity and seems to be capable of the most subtle discriminations. In a young person the eye's elastic lens can alter the eye's focal distance from a few inches to infinity as fast as the gaze can be shifted; changes in aperture together with slower chemical changes in the retinal receptors provide vision over enormous variations in the level of light; the organization of the retina combines high acuity in the central field with simultaneous peripheral perception; receptors with peak response in three regions of the visible spectrum deal with images in tens of thousands of discriminable hues. Finally, the two eyes working together produce a three-dimensional view of the world.

A rigorous definition of a communication terminal is somewhat elusive. A typical communication system, whether biological or man-made, consists of a chain of several terminals and channels; a typical terminal converts the signal appropriate to one channel to another signal appropriate to the next channel, while preserving the signal's information content. For example, a message may originate in a human brain, be transmitted to the fingers, pass into a teletypewriter, then travel over a wire line to a radio transmitter, journey through space to a radio receiver, be typed out onto a sheet of paper, be scanned by a pair of eyes and finally enter another human brain. The communication engineer is likely to regard as a terminal any apparatus at either end of a discrete electromagnetic channel, but perhaps more commonly a terminal is viewed as an apparatus designed to convert a visual, acoustic or tactile signal into an electrical signal, or vice versa.

Some of the most ingenious terminals devised by man are those intended for television, consisting of a television camera and a transmitter at one end of the channel and a television receiver and a picture tube at the other. The television camera converts the variable light intensity of an image into a modulated electric current: the video signal. Stated more abstractly, the camera transforms a two-dimensional space function, an im-

COLOR-TELEVISION COMPUTER TERMINAL presents the computer model of a highway intersection shown on the opposite page. The model, produced by a computer graphic system developed by the Electronics Laboratory of the General Electric Company, shows an actual intersection on highway Interstate 90 near Albany, N.Y. On command any full-color perspective view of the highway can be computed and displayed on the terminal in seconds. With time-lapse photography the dynamic conditions of an actual drive along the highway can be reproduced. Such models are helpful in testing designs before construction.

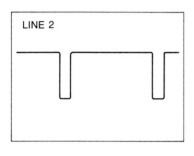

LINE 2

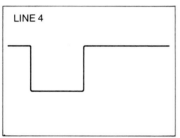

LINE 4

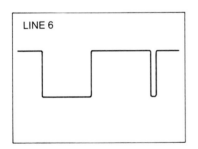

LINE 6

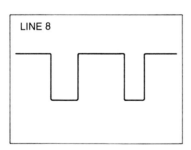

LINE 8

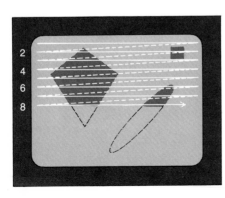

TELEVISION TERMINALS consist of a camera that converts a two-dimensional optical image into a one-dimensional electrical signal varying in time, and a receiver that performs a reverse operation, assisted by the persistence of vision. In the camera a visual scene is focused on a light-sensitive surface (*top*) that is scanned line by line by an electron beam. Successive horizontal scans yield a modulated electric current: the video signal. Upward and downward excursions in the signal trace for each line correspond respectively to bright and dark picture elements. In U.S. television the scanning beam sweeps across a line in about 60 microseconds. The U.S. picture has 525 horizontal lines, repeated 30 times per second.

age formed by a lens, into a one-dimensional time function. This transformation is accomplished by focusing a visual scene onto a light-sensitive surface that is systematically scanned by an electron beam. The scanning pattern, or raster, is a sequence of 525 horizontal lines, each one below the preceding one, composing a complete "frame" in just under a thirtieth of a second. (In actuality every other line is scanned in just under a sixtieth of a second and the missing lines are interlaced in the next sixtieth of a second.) Since 30 complete frames are generated in a second, the successive images create an acceptable illusion of motion at the receiver. Here another electron beam, whose intensity is modulated by the received video signal, traces out the same raster on the phosphor-sensitized face of the picture tube [*see illustration at left*]. The television receiver also performs the function of selecting one of many incoming signals on channels of various frequencies, amplifying it and stripping off the information needed to synchronize the re-created lines and frames with those at the transmitting terminal.

The process becomes still more intricate if the image is transmitted and received in full color. The transmitting terminal now has three cameras, one sensitive to each of the primary colors: red, green and blue. It also incorporates an encoder that "piggybacks" the color information onto the video signal. The face of the picture tube most commonly used in the color receiver is coated with three kinds of light-emitting phosphor, one for each of the primary colors, interspersed as thousands of carefully positioned dots. The received signal is decoded into its components and used to modulate three independent electron beams, each of which is allowed to strike only the red, green or blue phosphor dots through the interposition of an ac-

curately perforated sheet known as a shadow mask.

As owners of television sets are well aware, television terminals must be coupled to television channels through antennas (except when the signal is sent by cable). At the transmitter electromagnetic radiation carrying the video signal is launched from a phased array of dipoles or similar elements on top of a tall building or tower. The phasing acts to concentrate, or focus, the main radiation toward the horizon, forming a beamlike pattern of radiation. The antenna gain achieved in this way is usually equivalent to at least a tenfold magnification of power. Thus the transmitter might need to furnish only 10 kilowatts to yield an "effective radiated power" of 100 kilowatts.

Receiving antennas vary in design from a simple whip, often adequate in strong-signal areas, to the complex structures seen on roofs in areas where the signal is weak. In still more remote areas, where rooftops are no longer within the line of sight of the transmitting antenna, community antennas can be mounted on high towers. Antenna gain at the receiving end is accomplished by using phased elements to achieve directivity horizontally as well as vertically and simply pointing the array at the signal source.

In comparison with a color television receiver the telephone on one's desk is a remarkably simple terminal. Unlike the television receiver, however, it is capable of activating hundreds or thousands of intermediate terminals when one places a call to another city or another country. These highly sophisticated terminals are largely hidden from view in telephone offices, underground and, most recently, in satellites 22,300 miles above the Equator.

Some of the most complex terminals in the telephone system are those that combine dozens, hundreds or thousands of voice signals for transmission over a medium such as a coaxial cable or a microwave beam. These terminals are usually embedded in a hierarchical network in which channels of lesser capacity converge into one channel of high capacity for long-distance transmission [see "Communication Networks," by Hiroshi Inose, page 77]. The combining of many signals is called multiplexing, and it can be accomplished in either of two principal ways: frequency division or time division.

In frequency-division multiplexing different signals are assigned to different frequency bands to which they are usually translated by single side-band modulation. They are then all transmitted simultaneously; at the receiving terminal the signals are individually demodulated. In time-division multiplexing different signals are chopped into brief segments that are interleaved and transmitted sequentially; at the destination all the segments belonging to each individual message are extracted and reassembled. Although the two techniques are totally different, they are fully equivalent in what they accomplish [*see top illustrations on page 71*].

An example of advanced frequency-division multiplexing is found in undersea telephone cables. The first transatlantic telephone cable, in service since 1956, accommodates 48 voice signals in what

was called the SB system. A more recent cable, employing the SF system, has a capacity of 845 two-way conversations.

Before such a large number of signals can be dispatched from a land terminal to an ocean cable they must be processed in several major steps. The typical telephone signal has a bandwidth of approximately three kilohertz (3,000 cycles per second). In the first multiplexing step 16 signals are combined into a "group" by modulating the individual three-kilohertz signals into adjacent frequency bands. In the next step most of these groups are combined, five at a time, to form "supergroups" of 80 conversations each. Originally nine such supergroups were adjoined to form a nearly contin-

uous frequency band of 720 voice channels, requiring a band some 2,200 kilohertz wide. Subsequently another 125 channels were squeezed in, with the result that the frequency spectrum extends from below 400 kilohertz to nearly 3,000 kilohertz for transmission in one direction; in the other direction the band extends from roughly 3,600 kilohertz to about 6,100. (By way of comparison the AM broadcast band extends from about 550 kilohertz to 1,600 and is divided into 106 radio channels.)

Each of the broad-band spectra includes some supervisory signals to monitor the system for proper operation. Such signals are used, for example, to prevent outages due to equipment fail-

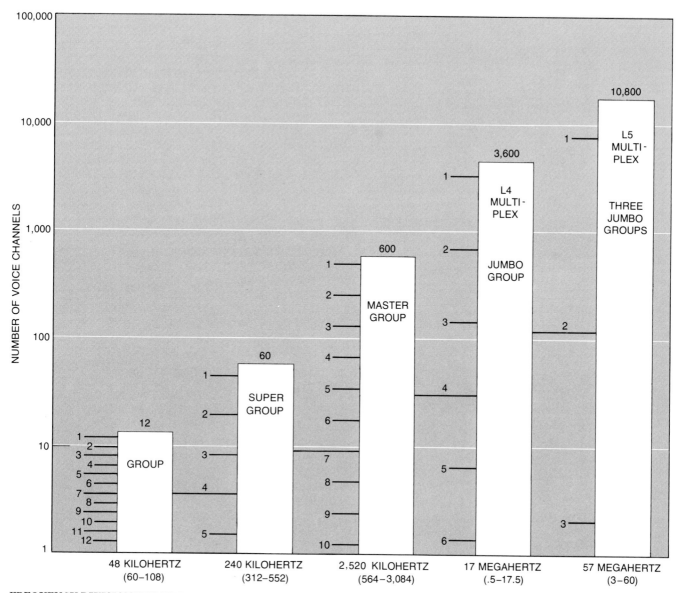

FREQUENCY-DIVISION-MULTIPLEXING TERMINALS used in the telephone system assemble many individual voice channels into a hierarchy of composite signals of increasing bandwidth. The basic voice channel occupies a bandwidth of three kilohertz (3,000 cycles per second). In the first stage of multiplexing 12 voice channels, each centered in a band four kilohertz wide, form a "group" with a bandwidth of 48 kilohertz. The transmission frequency lies between 60 and 108 kilohertz. Five groups form a "supergroup" with a bandwidth of 240 kilohertz transmitted at a frequency of between 312 and 552 kilohertz. Ten supergroups form a "mastergroup" with a bandwidth of 2,520 kilohertz. In the Bell System's L4 multiplex system six mastergroups are assembled into a "jumbo group" for transmission through a single coaxial cable at a frequency of between .5 and 17.5 megahertz. The still more advanced L5 system will be able to transmit three jumbo groups in a single coaxial cable at a frequency of between three and 60 megahertz.

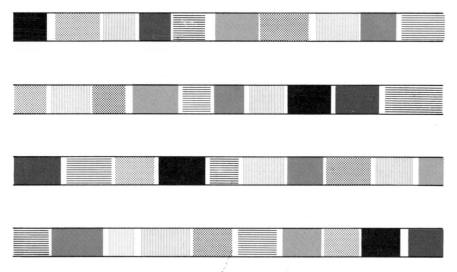

TIME-ASSIGNMENT SPEECH INTERPOLATION (TASI) uses terminals that exploit the brief silences in ordinary conversation to reduce by at least a half the number of costly overseas channels needed to carry a given volume of traffic. In this simplified diagram 10 speakers compete for time on four voice channels. Whenever a speaker pauses, the channel is taken away from him and assigned to an active speaker. The latest TASI terminals are able to shuttle as many as 235 conversations among 96 overseas telephone channels.

ure. To ensure the required dependability the terminal equipment for each supergroup is completely duplicated; the standby terminal can be automatically switched into service in response to a supervisory signal.

Still other functions are performed by the terminal. In addition to the voice signals it must transmit direct-current power into the cable in order to run the amplifiers that are located every 10 miles along the transoceanic route. The transmitter also shapes the composite signal spectrum prior to transmission in each direction in order to ensure a uniform signal-to-noise ratio across each frequency band.

Many such cables have been installed within the past decade, connecting the U.S. with the islands of the Caribbean, Britain, Japan, the Philippines, France and Spain. There are now a total of six cables spanning the Atlantic between North America and Europe; new systems are in the making with individual capacities more than four times greater than the largest in existence.

Communication terminals of a similar kind also serve for long-distance overland cable transmission. They are installed in a wide range of sizes, depending on where they fit into the hierarchy of the ubiquitous telephone network. Near the bottom of the hierarchy are the short-haul systems that connect, for example, switching offices perhaps 15 miles apart across a large city or in different cities more than 100 miles apart. The channel between such offices typically carries one or two groups of 12

voice conversations each. Such systems were introduced in the 1940's.

At the top of the hierarchy are the long-haul systems, designed for distances of up to 4,000 miles, with capacities of thousands of voice channels organized at the terminals into groups, supergroups, "mastergroups" and "jumbo groups" [see illustration on preceding page]. The individual voice channels are spaced at four kilohertz instead of three, thus allowing only 12 channels per group instead of the 16 found in ocean-cable systems. The overland systems also differ from the undersea systems in that the cable and amplifiers along the route are more accessible for maintenance; in addition, intermediate terminals can be installed as desired to terminate some of the channels in cities along the route. The first of these systems, designated L1, was installed in 1941. The typical L1 system had a capacity of 1,800 two-way voice channels provided by three pairs of coaxial cables, each pair carrying a mastergroup of 600 voice channels. In 1953 the L1 system was superseded by the L3 system, in which the capacity of each cable was tripled. The still more recent L4 system, first installed between Washington and Miami in 1967, accommodates 3,600 two-way conversations in just one pair of 3/8-inch coaxial cables; nine such pairs can carry a total of 32,400 conversations. This capacity will again be more than tripled by the introduction of the L5 system.

In the early 1950's a television terminal was developed for transmitting on the L3 coaxial system a single video signal in a frequency band that would nor-

mally carry two mastergroups, or 1,200 voice channels. The bandwidth thus made available was 4,500 kilohertz (4.5 megahertz), which is ample for high-quality broadcast television, including color signals. The L3 system provided one of the early potential means for the television industry to distribute its programs nationwide. Instead, however, microwave-carrier, or radio-relay, systems took over as the prevailing method for coast-to-coast distribution.

Indeed, it was the mounting distribution requirements of the television industry in the late 1940's that stimulated the development of the first commercial microwave radio-relay system, designated TD2. Today the terminals and relay towers of the TD2 system, and of its successor, the TD3 system, dot the countryside. Except for local and short-haul facilities, the microwave-relay system provides a greater volume of "bandwidth miles" than all other facilities combined. Although coaxial-cable systems could have been designed to meet the needs of television, radio relay was said to carry "the lure of lower first cost," even though it called for many more technological innovations and more difficult design choices.

One such choice involved the selection of antennas, the most visible working parts of each radio tower. The original towers were equipped with antennas incorporating what was called a delay lens. In the mid-1950's the delay lenses were replaced by horn reflectors having much sharper directivity; their great power gain (upward of 10,000) helps to prevent interference among neighboring microwave channels. They also handle two directions of polarization (vertical and horizontal) and accommodate a broader range of frequencies in anticipation of expanding needs.

The frequency commonly used in the TD microwave systems is in the neighborhood of four gigahertz (4,000 megahertz), which corresponds to a wavelength of about 7.5 centimeters. (Later terminals designated TH operate at about six gigahertz and others at 11 gigahertz.) The microwave beam carries a single high-quality television signal or as many as 1,800 voice channels in the six-gigahertz band. More than a dozen such beams can be superimposed, operating on adjacent frequency bands but sharing antennas, to achieve capacities exceeding 22,000 voice channels.

Microwave technology calls for terminals that are distinctly different from those in coaxial-cable systems. For example, in order to conduct high-frequency energy from the terminals at ground level to the horns on top of the towers it is necessary to use carefully fabricated waveguides with a rectangular cross section. Whereas coaxial systems had used single side-band modulation, which is akin to AM, FM was chosen from the outset for modulating the microwave carrier by the composite voice signals transmitted over the microwave system. One reason is that the frequency of microwave sources can be varied in linear fashion with comparative ease. In addition FM is more effective than AM in resisting variations in amplitude under conditions that cause the signal to fade.

The electronic circuitry of both the high-capacity cable terminals and the radio terminals was originally based entirely on vacuum tubes, many of them specially developed to meet extremely exacting requirements: uncommon reliability, low noise level and great bandwidth. In the past decade solid-state technology has largely taken over, with dramatic reductions in size and power consumption combined with significant improvements in performance.

One vacuum-tube component that made the original TD2 terminal possible was not replaced in the otherwise solid-state TD3 terminal: the traveling-wave high-frequency amplifier. The steady increase in the channel capacity of microwave systems is attributable to the constant improvements in terminal technology. The combination of increased transmitter power with reduced noise contribution from receiver amplifiers has led to significant improvements in the signal-to-noise ratio. This improvement can be traded off for less deviation in the FM frequency swing, thus allowing more channels in the same bandwidth.

A still more sophisticated microwave terminal is the one required by earth stations for communication satellites. The first one, built for Project Telstar, was completed at Andover, Me., in 1962. In July of that year transatlantic television transmission by satellite was accomplished for the first time. Today, only 10 years later, satellites are capable of beaming television signals to virtually every inhabited point on the globe.

Unlike the more recent communica-

tion satellites, which occupy "fixed" stations high above the Equator by virtue of completing an orbit every 24 hours, the Telstar satellites were much lower and circled the earth once every several hours. This meant that the antennas on the earth had to be movable and capable of tracking the satellite with a pointing accuracy of better than four minutes of arc, equivalent to holding a dime in the sight of a gun at 50 feet, no mean feat when the "gun" weighs 380 tons. The antennas were of the horn type, similar to those installed on radio-relay towers but much bigger, having an aperture of 3,600 square feet. The antenna's beam width was 10 minutes of arc, giving it a power gain of about a million (slightly more at its transmitting wavelength of five centimeters, or six gigahertz, and a little less at its receiving wavelength of 7.5 centimeters, or four gigahertz).

Several exotic electronic techniques, both new and old, were crucial to the powerful transmitter and the supersensitive receiver of the Telstar earth stations. The transmitter's signal power of 2,000 watts was achieved by a specially designed traveling-wave-tube amplifier: a

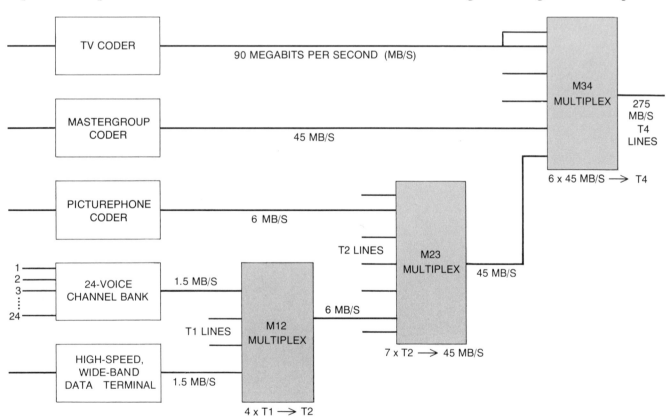

DIGITAL ENCODING TERMINALS are being developed to provide time-division multiplexing in a still evolving hierarchy. All incoming signals, unless they are already in digital form, will first be translated by pulse code modulation into strings of uniform pulses and spaces representing bits, or binary digits (0 and 1). The bits representing several signals are interleaved to produce a composite signal that is unscrambled at the end of its journey. Thus 24 voice channels can be combined by a "channel bank" to produce a signal of 1.5 megabits (1.5 million bits) per second, which can be carried by a T1 wire pair. Four T1 signals can be multiplexed into a T2 signal of six megabits per second and fed into an M23 multiplexer capable of combining seven such signals into one signal of about 45 megabits per second. Each six-megabit T1 pulse stream is capable of carrying 96 voice signals or one "Picturephone" signal. The M34 multiplexer will be able to combine three television signals, or their equivalent, into one signal of 275 megabits per second. Because of the addition of extra "housekeeping" bits, the composite signals exceed simple multiples of the input signals.

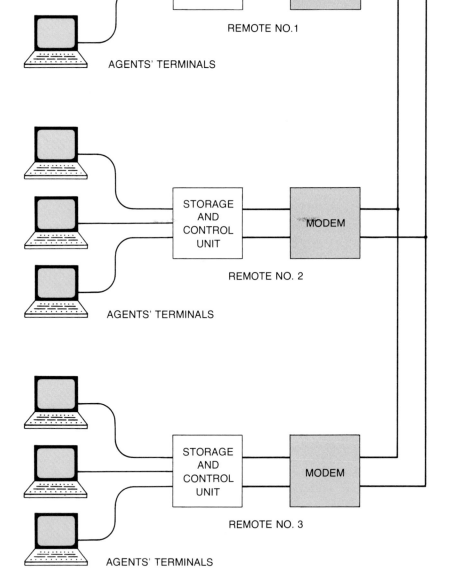

CENTRAL COMPUTER AND STORE

MODEM

MULTIPOINT
PRIVATE LINE

STORAGE
AND
CONTROL
UNIT

MODEM

REMOTE NO.1

AGENTS' TERMINALS

STORAGE
AND
CONTROL
UNIT

MODEM

REMOTE NO. 2

AGENTS' TERMINALS

STORAGE
AND
CONTROL
UNIT

MODEM

REMOTE NO. 3

AGENTS' TERMINALS

MULTIPLE TERMINALS linked to a central computer and memory store are used by airlines to handle reservation requests and to keep a single up-to-the-second centralized record. "Modem" is a contraction of modulator-demodulator. Modems, also known as data sets, adapt alphanumeric information (letters and numerals) for transmission over standard voice channels. Questions and answers, or requests and acknowledgements, flow in rapid message bursts from agents' terminals to the central computer and back again. Control units provide buffering, editing, code conversion, error control and other functions.

four-foot structure with a cathode at one end and a collector at the other and a large electromagnet surrounding the midsection. As a matter of historic interest, it was Rudolf Kompfner's work on the traveling-wave concept more than a decade earlier that had led to his being invited to join the Bell Telephone Laboratories by John R. Pierce. Subsequently, and prior to the launching of the first artificial satellite by the U.S.S.R., Pierce made the first mathematically supported proposal that artificial satellites be used for global communication. When the output of Kompfner's 2,000-watt traveling-wave tube was fed into the Andover horn antenna, the effective radiated power beamed to Telstar was two billion watts.

The receiving portion of the Telstar earth terminal made use of a technique known as FM feedback, invented in the early 1930's but never before harnessed, to attain the equivalent of a threefold enhancement of the received signal power. The wide-deviation FM signal transmitted or received by the terminal is subject to a well-defined power threshold, below which reception deteriorates drastically. FM feedback operates to reduce the threshold. The greatest contributor, however, to the receiver's ability to handle Telstar's faint signals (about 10^{-12} watt) was a maser amplifier that combined very high gain with extremely low noise.

In present-day satellite-communication terminals the maser amplifier has given way to the cooled parametric amplifier, which combines low-noise performance with an even wider bandwidth. These new terminals handle ever increasing numbers of voice and video channels. A single Intelsat IV satellite can relay 12 television signals or upward of 6,000 voice signals. The ground terminals have become steadily simpler and more compact, as is indicated by the portable unit equipped with a dish antenna that preceded President Nixon to China earlier this year. The rapid progress has resulted from notable technical contributions by a large number of individuals and organizations.

Costly communication links such as the ones I have been describing can justify extraordinary signal processing at the terminal if their traffic capacity can thus be materially increased. One such signal-processing adjunct, called time-assignment speech interpolation (TASI), capitalizes on the brief silences in normal conversation to achieve channel savings of more than two to one. The silences are simply not transmitted; when the speaker pauses, the channel is taken away from him and assigned to an active speaker. With this stratagem 96 overseas telephone channels can carry 235 simultaneous conversations spread over 274 trunk lines.

In a two-way conversation the average speaker is actually talking somewhat less than 40 percent of the time. TASI monitors each speaker's line and compares its signal 25,000 times per second against five distinct reference levels; the speaker is assigned a channel only when he is judged to be active [*see illustration on page 94*]. In general a speaker will retain a channel for the second or so taken up by a word or group of syllables. Only after a pause of a fourth of a second is the channel taken away from him; when he resumes speaking, he is likely to be assigned a different channel.

Other functions performed by the latest TASI terminal include the automatic testing and restoration of lost overseas circuits. For example, the 96 channels handled by the terminal can be subdivided among separate communication links: 32 for satellite transmission, 32 for one submarine cable and 32 for another cable. The 96 channels, with TASI working below its capacity, can readily serve 175 telephone trunks. If either of the cables on the satellite is interrupted, the terminal will immediately start juggling the 175 trunks through the remaining 64 channels without audible loss of quality. Although terminals with these capabilities have been built and operated, those in actual service are more modest earlier designs developed for transoceanic-cable systems.

The idea of time-sharing a channel among many users is not unique to TASI. One of the most rapidly growing classes of terminals is based on time-division multiplexing: the orderly sequential interspersal of successive snatches of different signals. With TASI the time-sharing is of a random nature, depending on the demand, and the time scale is on the order of a second. With terminals based on time-division multiplexing the time scale is much shorter. The sound waves of speech, for example, are typically sampled 8,000 times per second; each sample conveys a numerical value corresponding to the amplitude of the signal at a single point in time.

In such systems the numerical value of the signal at each point in time is translated into a binary code and transmitted as a group of pulses. Since the pulses represent binary digits (0 or 1), such a signal is termed digital, distinguishing it from its original analogue format. Since computers, teletypewriters and other

BELL SYSTEM MODEM converts digital data from business machines and computers to an analogue signal well adapted for traveling over a telephone voice channel. The modem is the oblong box in the foreground; in the background is part of the computer. In this modem the phase of a carrier wave is rotated by one of eight allowed amounts, thus tripling the channel bit rate over the rate provided when only two phase changes are used. An adaptive filter automatically compensates for the "pulse-smearing," or dispersion, that the signal may suffer in transmission. The modem operates at the rate of 4,800 bits per second.

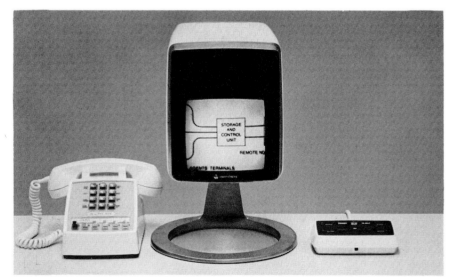

PICTUREPHONE SET, developed by the Bell Telephone Laboratories, provides a picture 5½ inches wide and five inches high that can be "zoomed" over a range of 2.5 to one. It can transmit documentary material at a magnification of .85. The picture is made up of 267 horizontal lines and is scanned at the rate of 30 frames per second. The Picturephone signal requires a bandwidth of one megahertz, or the equivalent of some 300 voice channels. A standard television signal occupies the equivalent of more than 1,000 voice channels. The picture on the screen in this picture is part of the illustration on the opposite page.

machines naturally originate information in digital form, digital coding has important advantages for data transmission.

The fastest-growing digital system is the Bell System's "T1 carrier." Its transmission medium is the standard 22-gauge twisted-wire pair used as an analogue voice trunk between central offices. The digital terminals, with regularly spaced regenerative repeaters placed in manholes, convert the wire pair into a digital channel capable of transmitting 1.5 megabits (1.5 million binary digits) per second. The channel can provide 24 telephone voice channels when the total stream is divided into 24 substreams of 64 kilobits per second. Each substream is processed by a "channel bank," part of the T1 terminal housed at a central office.

The processing includes the analogue-to-digital (A/D) conversion before transmission and the inverse digital-to-analogue (D/A) conversion after transmission. The terminal also performs important associated functions such as "companding." This function is a quasi-logarithmic compression of the analogue signal before or concurrent with A/D conversion and a corresponding ex-pansion after or concurrent with D/A conversion; its purpose is the handling of the large dynamic range of diverse speakers without sacrificing the overall signal-to-noise ratio for those who speak softly. The terminal must also interleave and sort out the pulse sequences belonging to each voice channel and the individual pulses within each sequence.

The first T1 carrier systems for voice transmission were installed more than a decade ago. Today the number of T1-based voice channels, which are designed to be no more than 50 miles long, exceeds 1.25 million. This figure means that throughout the U.S. there are more than 100,000 terminals sending and receiving impulses at the rate of 1.5 megabits per second. They constitute the first step in a carefully planned hierarchy of digital channels. In the years to come the top of the hierarchy will include terminals handling streams of nearly 300 megabits per second over coast-to-coast distances [see illustration on page 95].

As the hardware implementation of the hierarchy of T carriers is evolving, a variety of competitive digital channels and networks are in the making, primarily aimed at handling the type of traffic most naturally suited to them, namely digital data. In this application no A/D or D/A conversion is needed because the data are digital to start with. Of the most immediate interest is a terminal for frequency-multiplexing a 1.5-megabit-per-second digital stream with the analogue telephone signals already being carried by existing microwave systems. It will enable the 1.5-megabit T1-carrier stream to be extended across the country for wide accessibility to consumers of alpha-numeric business data.

The next step in the hierarchy of purely digital channels is the T2 carrier now coming into service. It has a capacity of six megabits per second, the equivalent of four T1 streams. With time-division-multiplexing terminals at appropriate telephone offices, each bit stream is interleaved into the stream of the next-highest speed. The fastest stream now being designed will transmit about 275 megabits per second. These bit rates and still higher ones will require advanced technology to implement both the terminals and the channels.

The terminal technology will depend in large measure on the transmission media selected for future channels. For example, coaxial cables can carry the bit stream directly at "baseband," that is, without modulation of a carrier signal, and thus they will be attractive for metropolitan service. Microwave radio relay operating in the 18-gigahertz region (a wavelength of about 17 millimeters) will be able to accommodate six streams of 275 megabits per second in adjacent frequency bands. A new entry, circular waveguides carrying waves measured in millimeters, can handle the staggering total of 60 streams of 275 megabits in each direction, the equivalent of 250,000 two-way voice channels. Millimeter waveguide, based on a technology originally developed during World War II for radar, has been waiting in the wings while the traffic projections are gradually edging up to its capabilities and while circuit techniques, including all-solid-state designs, are making it more attractive. The terminal technology for waveguides is similar to that for microwave radio except that here the wavelengths are much shorter, ranging from about seven millimeters to less than three millimeters, corresponding to a spectrum of between 40 and 110 gigahertz.

Beyond millimeter waveguide, with still higher capacity, lies a new world of optical communications harnessing laser-generated or diode-generated light beams in free space or guided through light pipes or fibers made of glass or filled with liquid. This exciting and still evolving technology appears to be the

CATHODE-RAY-TUBE PICTURE of portions of DNA, the molecule that embodies the genetic code, is typical of displays that can be produced by terminals attached to large computers. The picture shows an electron-density contour map of guanine and cytosine, two of the four bases in which the code is written in the molecule. The computer model was devised at San Jose, Calif., laboratory of International Business Machines Corporation.

HIGH-SPEED PRINTER built by the Control Data Corporation is a special kind of terminal that handles alphanumeric data gener- **ated by a source such as a computer or a magnetic tape. The terminal shown can print 1,600 lines 136 characters wide in a minute.**

logical choice for filling the superhigh-capacity communication needs of the long-term future. Present applications are limited to special situations, such as interconnecting high-speed computer equipment in neighboring buildings by sending optical beams through the open air. The terminals for such optical systems can be surprisingly simple: the transmitter is a light-emitting solid-state diode (modulated by the signal source) and the receiver is a light-sensitive transistor. The light beam is directed, collimated and collected by ordinary optical reflectors and lenses.

Although the explosive growth of data transmission has hastened the evolution of digital terminals, such terminals will not be used only for data. The dominant "passengers" will for some time continue to be groups of pulses representing samples of speech, transmitted at the rate of 64 kilobits per second per voice channel. "Picturephone" signals for intercity transmission will require a bit rate near-

ly 100 times higher: six megabits per second. A broadcast-quality color-television signal in digital code calls for 90 megabits per second.

The general use of the Picturephone set still lies in the future. The most widely available interactive communication terminal in the world remains the ordinary telephone. There are more than 120 million telephones in the U.S. and 130 million more in other countries. The telephone exploits a basic electro-acoustic technology that is difficult to improve on, given very tight economic bounds. Simple as this terminal is, it acquires enormous power by virtue of the network to which it provides access. That network embraces more than 200 countries and territories, making it possible for virtually any pair of telephones among the more than 270 million to be interconnected on command.

The versatility and ubiquity of the worldwide telephone network make it attractive for the transmission of ana-

logue signals other than speech by means of specialized terminals. For example, a simple attachment to the telephone handset makes it possible to transmit a patient's heart signals to the office of a physician, where the signals are reproduced on a cardiograph. Other analogue terminals mediate the low-speed transmission of pictures, weather maps or other graphic material.

Among nonvoice terminals the fastest-growing group is the digital terminals designed to handle alphanumeric information. Such terminals are called data sets or "modems," a contraction of modulator-demodulator. Among specialists in computer communications the word "terminal" is actually reserved for something else: the keyboard machine, tape reader or other device that feeds data into a modem; or the printer, tape recorder or computer that accepts the output of a modem.

Rather slow and intermittent transmission is required for a keyboard machine such as an on-line teletypewriter or the "Touch-Tone" telephone (when that instrument doubles as a simple terminal for sending numerals). A much more complex terminal is represented by the apparatus at an airline reservation desk. When you telephone the reservation clerk to ask if there is a seat on flight such-and-such, he punches the information into his keyboard. The terminal is not on line but dumps the information (preceded by his identity code) into an electronic memory that is fed by dozens of other agents for the same airline [*see illustration on page 96*]. Every second or so a central computer, possibly hundreds of miles away, "polls" (interrogates) the memory store; the accumulated questions, if any, are sped to the computer. The computer consults its master memory and returns the answer to the desk of the appropriate agent, where it is displayed on a cathode ray tube. When you order your reservation, the clerk types in the required data and the computer updates its master memory so that the next caller cannot get the same seat. The computer also confirms the transac-

tion with a message that shows up on the agent's display tube.

During peak hours messages are going back and forth at a fast clip. In early installations the data-flow rate was usually 2,400 bits per second; in newer systems the rate is likely to be twice as high. The messages tend to be brief, generally no more than a few hundred bits, so that the receivers must be ready to "listen" all the time. Hence in this application and similar ones the terminals are tied together on a full-time basis through leased or private lines. Since modems associated with high-speed polling systems must operate reliably at 4,800 bits per second over voice channels, they are reasonably complex pieces of equipment [*see top illustration on page 97*]. They must encode the data efficiently into a signal well suited not only to the typical voice channel but also to the "worst case" channel. This calls for a modulation-demodulation scheme capable of accurate synchronization and of compensating for distortions introduced by the channel. In some cases the compensation is achieved automatically by internal error-sensing and feedback control.

Proliferation without end seems to characterize the evolution of terminals, particularly those that serve as the "tentacles" of a computer. In the business world more and more input-output devices perform such functions as the reading of credit cards, the updating of bank accounts and the issuing of tickets. Additional data-handling applications are found in brokerage, health care, inventory management, computer-aided education, police information retrieval and off-track betting. Character-recognition systems, which now constitute an important class of terminals, identify account numbers on checks, help with the composition of newspapers and magazines and promise the automatic sorting of mail. High-speed printers and cathode-ray-tube displays have become increasingly familiar as visual-output terminals.

Various forms of facsimile terminal have been in use for decades, particularly for the transmission of the "wirephotos" often seen in newspapers. Techniques such as electronic scanning and xerography have helped to broaden the potential usefulness of facsimile transmission. Inexpensive lasers, aided by ingenious new light-deflectors, promise to be key elements in scanning and printing terminals with excellent resolving power. Futurists predict that a "fax" terminal in the home or business office may someday supplement or even replace the mail carrier.

Keyboard terminals are widely found in the engineering and scientific communities for the purpose of utilizing remote computers. Such terminals enable many users to "talk" with a single large computer. The centralized computer may itself be thought of as a versatile terminal, programmable and capable of consulting a memory store and of executing logic functions. Aided by suitable peripheral devices, its capacities can assume astonishing proportions. The computer can do a literature search in a library of microfilms or magnetic tapes or it can generate complex graphs or drawings on the cathode-ray-tube display of a remote user. After feeding in a sufficiently definitive description of a three-dimensional object, for example, an architect may command a true-perspective view of the object from any desired angle or distance and then make modifications as desired.

Clearly there is no end in sight to the continuing evolution of communication terminals. A wealth of technological means is at hand; economic factors will determine the speed of progress.

EDITING AND PROOFING TERMINAL built by the Harris-Intertype Corporation is representative of an extensive family of computer terminals that combine a keyboard with a pictorial display. The terminal is designed to be the primary means of correcting, editing and proofreading text prior to typesetting. It can accept data from a computer or paper tape at the rate of 1,200 characters per second. Once the copy has been edited the terminal can produce a tape output or transmit the text to a computer for subsequent typesetting.

9

COMMUNICATION AND
THE COMMUNITY

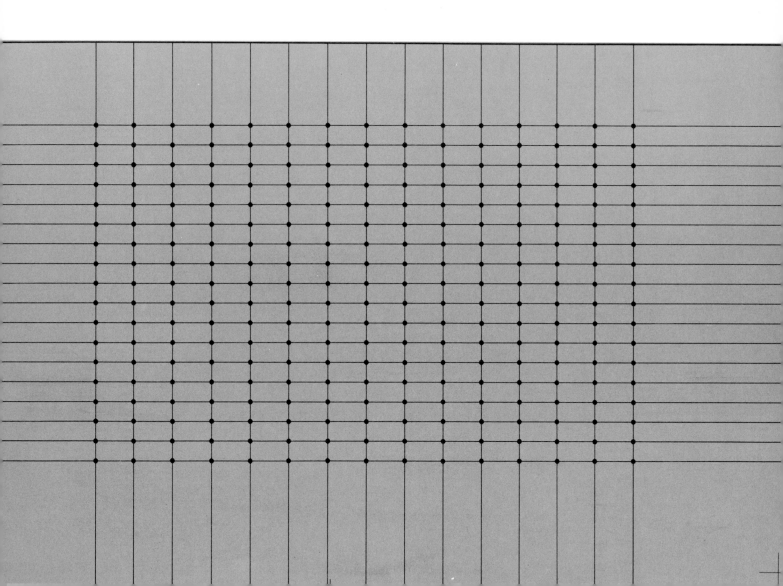

Communication and the Community

PETER C. GOLDMARK

*Cities exist largely because they enhance communication.
Modern telecommunication systems provide a means for
extending the web of urban communication and
improving the quality of urban life.*

In human terms the rapid advance of communication technology during the past few decades has greatly extended the connections between individuals and has bound men much more closely. By telephone, radio, leased wire and links with computers one can communicate with someone else almost anywhere in the world; buy, sell, obtain credit and salary; conduct business with a bank; make reservations for transportation and hotel space; send and receive data in numerous forms, and in many other ways link oneself to other parts of the human community without leaving one's home or office. By print, radio, television and satellite one can receive information and entertainment from all parts of the world, often as the event is happening. With tape and other forms of recording one has access to the memorable sights and sounds of the recent past.

These achievements are impressive and would doubtless strike the people of past centuries as marvels. Nonetheless, in many respects the things that can be done by communication today represent only a fraction of what could be done to improve the quality of life for everyone if communication systems were more carefully planned and if the full potential of certain technologies were exploited. The point can be made by picturing someone who, while driving through a suburban or rural area where he is a stranger, sees a building on fire and wants to report it. He does not know where to find a public telephone or an alarm box. He does not know what fire department to call. If he finds a tele-

phone and resorts to the expedient of dialing "Operator," the operator must ascertain where the caller is in order to alert the right fire department, and the traveler may not know exactly where he is. By the time the right connection is made the fire may be well advanced.

The technology is at hand for solving such problems. The traveler could have as part of his automobile radio a two-way link with a nearby computer that would ascertain his location and direct him to the nearest public telephone or alarm box. Once there he would dial a universal emergency number (such as the 911 now used in New York and other large, centralized jurisdictions). An automatic locating arrangement that was part of the telephone system would identify the source of the call, so that the dispatcher would know at once the approximate location of the fire and what fire department to send.

My purpose in this article is to suggest a number of ways in which new applications of communication technology could make communication more useful to people as individuals or to entire communities. My remarks reflect closely the findings in a report, *Communications Technology for Urban Improvement,* presented recently by a panel on urban communications established by the National Academy of Engineering. The panel, of which I was chairman, undertook the study at the request of a number of Federal agencies, which sought advice on (1) the possibilities for better application of telecommunication technology to city functions in order to im-

prove city living and (2) the potential of such applications for stimulating valuable patterns of regional development.

Our panel reported to the Committee on Telecommunications of the National Academy of Engineering. That committee has defined telecommunication as "any transmission, emission or reception of signs, signals, written images and sounds or intelligence of any nature by wire, radio, visual or other electromagnetic systems including any intervening processing and storage." The definition encompasses signal processing and storage by computers, sensors and transducers. A signal does not have to be transmitted to a distant point to be included under the definition.

As a basis for discussing the potential of various telecommunication systems it will be helpful if I describe briefly the present status of the principal systems. The telephone is certainly the major vehicle for personal communication, having almost totally replaced the telegram and taken up also a good deal of the communicating that once would have been done by mail. More than 90 percent of the homes in the U.S. contain at least one telephone. The 30 largest urban centers have 37 million telephones, and the usage is high everywhere; for example, the five million telephones in New York City generate more than 30 million calls each business day.

The telephone network is engineered to optimize selective, private communication between two people. Therefore it is of low suitability for broadcasting or its opposite: simultaneous data-gathering from a number of points. It is suitable, however, for transmitting all forms of data between two points, often over leased lines. The business community has applied this capability widely, employing telephone lines to transmit data

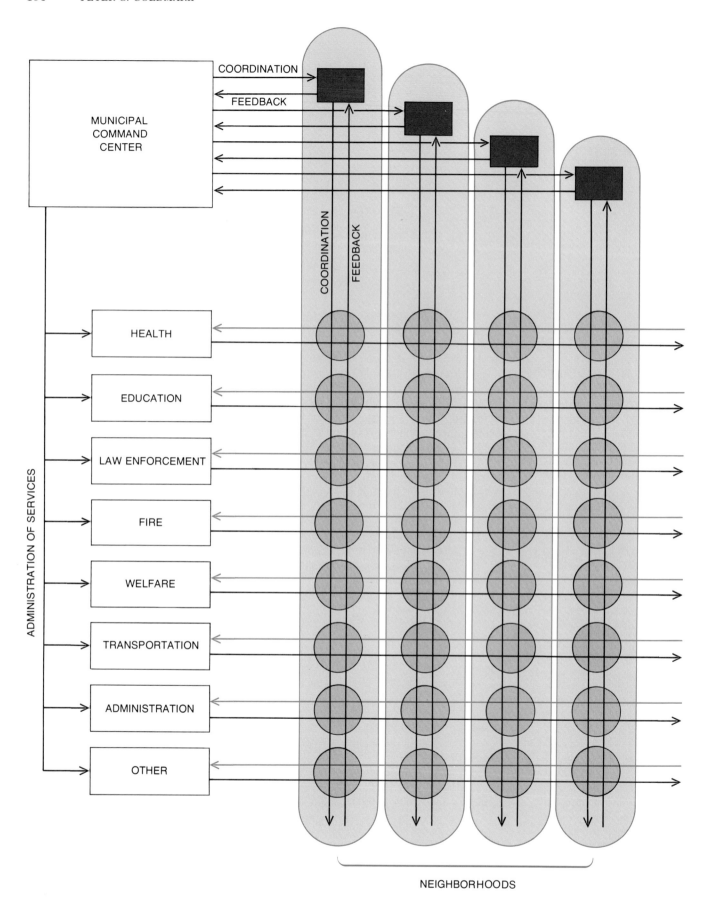

FUTURE NETWORK of communication in a city is depicted schematically. The emphasis of the system is on giving city officials more direct means of communication with residents and on giving residents better ways of finding out about municipal services and conditions and of reaching public officials. Each neighborhood (*light color*) would have a community information center (*black boxes*) that would include a computer programmed to provide information about services and conditions. Neighborhoods and regions within a neighborhood (*gray circles*) would be able to voice needs (*color*) to municipal departments and obtain services (*black*).

from computer to computer, keyboard to keyboard, card to tape, human to computer and so on.

I need not dwell on the elaborateness of the web of radio and television communication or on the number of people making up the radio and television audience. The figures speak for themselves: the U.S. has more than 6,500 commercial radio stations and 700 television stations; an audience of 55 million people is watching 37 million television sets at any given moment in prime time. The pervasiveness of mobile radio is less widely recognized, since its applications are mostly in public safety, transportation and industrial activity.

The major development of the past 20 years has been what is usually called cable television, although the name broad-band communication networks (BCN) is coming increasingly into play as being more descriptive of what the system can do. The growth of the system has been remarkable, from zero in 1949 to more than 2,500 systems and 5.5 million subscribers now. The technology has also advanced rapidly, beginning with an arrangement whereby a single well-placed antenna in a community brought in television signals that were then delivered by cable to the homes of subscribers who otherwise would receive no signals or poor ones, and extending now to a multiplicity of services that could be made available but in general have not been.

Cable service can have a frequency bandwidth of 300 million cycles per second with the possibility of limited return communication. (Telephone service into the home has a frequency bandwidth of 3,500 cycles.) Through technical developments in the past few years it is now possible and economically sound to furnish 20 or more television channels to each cable subscriber. Indeed, this capacity has been built into most systems that have been organized since 1970.

With the limited two-way feature added to a cable system that is also linked to a centrally located digital computer, a system could do any or all of the following things: (1) enable the subscriber to select any one of 12 or more television channels, including local and distant broadcast signals, locally originated nonbroadcast programs and perhaps cable programs distributed nationally by way of domestic satellites; (2) provide channels for groups with specific communicative needs, such as physicians and public officials; (3) enable subscribers to order products; (4) enable viewers to take part in public-opinion polls, with the responder's identity concealed if that

is desirable; (5) provide warning at an appropriate responding point of fire or burglary in the home or of a medical emergency in the family; (6) offer educational channels with an option for response by the student; (7) provide statistical data on the opinions of viewers about the television programs being offered; (8) offer a service whereby lights, heat, warning systems and other devices would be turned on or off in a home according to the owner's instructions; (9) read light, gas and water meters, send the reading to the utility's computer and return the bill to the user; (10) provide copies of printed material in the subscriber's home; (11) offer a "frame-grabber" facility whereby the subscriber could obtain and store for continuous display single pictures from a television program or a slide presentation; (12) provide channels for programs offered by individuals or groups, and (13) offer access to premium programming with better color and resolution than the commercial standard.

This list does not exhaust the possibilities; indeed, they are limited only by imagination and the strictures of the marketplace. As an example let us consider interactive home terminals, which will be made possible by the advances that can be foreseen over the next few years in the technology of integrated circuits, displays, communication and magnetic recording. By these means a neighborhood information center or a home could be provided with access to a vast amount of information from computer memories and libraries.

One can envision an interactive home terminal consisting of a television receiver, a voice-response computer and various combinations of keyboards, light pens, printers and electronic logic and storage. Through the return cable signal the subscriber is connected to the computer. Data from the computer would be received and converted to any of several formats for display on the television screen.

A simple but effective way of presenting information with this system entails a process akin to choosing from a menu. With each incoming frame the user is asked to choose one of several alternatives (up to 10) to define more precisely the information he wants. For example, if he were seeking travel information, he would with the first frame indicate whether he wanted to go by airplane, train, bus or taxicab. The second frame (if he chose, say, air travel) would enable him to specify what airport he would use. The process would continue

until the user had before him on his television screen the schedule of all airline flights of interest.

In exploring the possibilities for improving cities by improving their communication it is helpful to regard a city as a large information-processing system in which much of the work going on involves obtaining, processing and exchanging information. The aim, therefore, is to improve the city's capacity to move information rather than people and materials. In this way one sees the city as a confederation of neighborhoods sharing facilities and services.

At present the framework of the city's information-processing system is a variety of networks that provide a means for management, service, coordination and feedback. They include the network of streets and public transportation, the telephone network, the two-way radio networks employed by police, fire, street-maintenance and emergency-service groups and finally the one-way informational network of radio and television broadcasting. These networks are vital to the city as a nerve system is vital to the body.

Beyond them, however, lie several major opportunities for improving the flow of information through telecommunications. It is helpful to describe them in terms of four basic telecommunication networks. Although I must necessarily describe the networks separately, the reader should bear in mind that they will be interrelated and in some instances combined physically.

The primary network already exists but should be encouraged to expand. It is the telephone network: a full, two-way, random-access network that can accommodate voice, data and (at present only to a limited extent) pictures. The basic attribute of the network is its ability to put anyone in personal touch with anyone else quickly and reliably. With the advent of data processing this network could provide a similar random access between man and machines or between machines. It can be looked on as providing a pipeline into every home, office and library through which one can not only converse but also transmit written materials and pictures.

A second network, which would be based on present or future cable-television systems, would take over the task of distributing information in bulk from central facilities to offices and homes. It would, in effect, be an alternative way of receiving the information that now comes through books, records, broadcasting and so on. The network is envi-

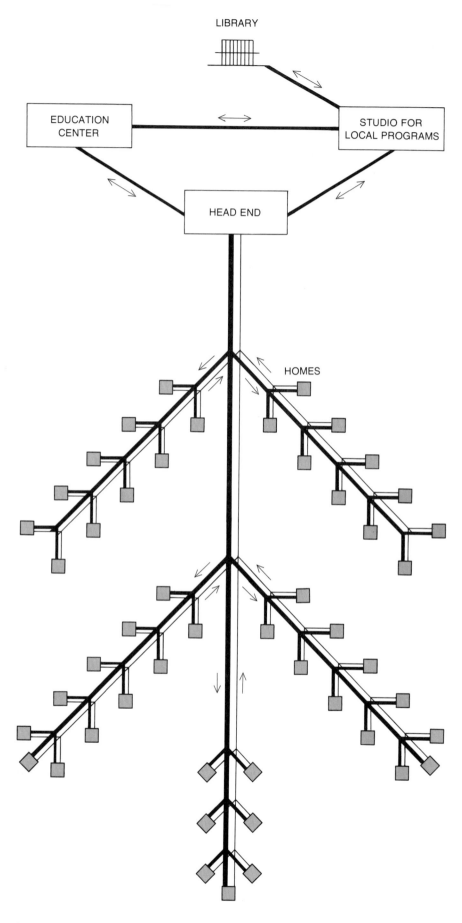

LIBRARY

EDUCATION CENTER

STUDIO FOR LOCAL PROGRAMS

HEAD END

HOMES

BROAD-BAND COMMUNICATION NETWORK is envisioned as an evolution of present cable-television systems. Its main task would be distributing information in bulk from central facilities to homes and offices. The network would also have limited facilities for information and queries going the other way and so could be used for polling and for various inquiries from subscribers. "Head end" is the operating center of the cable system.

sioned as a broad-band, two-way information pipe with a capacity equivalent to 30 or more television channels. It would be arranged to provide limited-address, narrow-band call-back for polling or making requests. If the network were organized with subcenters at the neighborhood level (between, say, 3,000 and 15,000 homes), it would be possible for a neighborhood to cater to its own programming requirements.

The third network would be another broad-band "pipe" carrying the equivalent of 30 television channels in both directions. It would interconnect the major public institutions of the city, such as the health, educational or emergency services. Some of the institutions would be interconnected permanently; others would be patched in as needed.

The fourth network would represent the city's sensory nerves. It would be a commonly owned network to provide information to appropriate centers on such matters as weather, pollution, traffic, the location of emergency vehicles and the status of public transportation. Some of this information is carried now on telephone lines, but under the fourth-network concept the process, using cable-television facilities, would be greatly expanded and much better coordinated than it is now.

In a city having these four networks the amenities of life could be greatly improved. The nature of the improvement is suggested by a number of pilot projects that our committee commended to the attention of interested institutions and agencies. I shall describe examples in five fields: municipal administration, education, health, pollution and transportation.

In the field of municipal administration I am thinking not only about the problems faced by the government in dealing with the citizens but also about the problems faced by the citizens in dealing with the government. From the government's point of view there are surprisingly few effective channels of communication between officials and the community. Moreover, since they are mostly one-way channels, as represented by newspapers and the broadcasting enterprises, the opportunities for city officials to obtain feedback from the public about city projects are limited. From the citizen's point of view the effort to communicate with the government is often frustrating, involving waiting lines, slow responses and seemingly harried or bored officials.

A response to this problem is to establish several community information centers. Our pilot project calls for such a center to be set up and operated in a typical city. The center would have as its primary function a referral service that would tell any citizen where to go or call to obtain the information or service he wants. The center might also undertake to provide forms, brochures and the like. The telecommunication base of the center would be the telephone system, manned around the clock by trained operators, and a small computer with stored information of the type the operators would be likely to need.

In education the goal of any program should be to increase the attractiveness and relevance of the curriculum and its availability to the educationally deprived. Another aim is to make education more available to all people. Communication technology offers vast opportunities in this field through the computer and cable television and, perhaps more important, the willingness of teachers to make them work.

Three applications of this technology to education seem promising: interactive instructional television, interactive community information retrieval and computer-assisted instruction. The distinctive feature of interactive instructional television is that it is two-way, whereas the instructional television offered until now has been one-way. A degree of student interaction can be added to television instruction by such expedients as having a small studio audience that serves as proxy for a larger audience in asking questions and providing feedback to the instructor or making arrangements for responses from students after they have seen the television material.

Recent trends in education have emphasized the importance of student interaction on a more continuous basis. Instructional television with audio return channels offers the opportunity for students in remote classrooms to ask questions and to join in the discussion on almost the same basis as students in the classroom. Similarly, recent developments in subscriber-response systems for cable television offer large groups a way to interact on a limited but more or less continuous basis throughout an instructional television program. All viewers see the same picture, and each viewer has a 12-button response pad with which he can respond to questions posed by the instructor. A computer polls the students every 10 seconds or so to pick up their responses. The system engages the attention of the students and also provides feedback to the instructor.

With such a system university courses

and continuing adult-education classes could be offered to thousands of students in their homes simultaneously. In the same way high school teachers offering material of interest to only a few students in one high school could provide simultaneous classes for students in all the high schools of a region. Moreover, classes could be offered through interactive television to people interested in furthering professional careers.

The aim of the interactive community information-retrieval system, which is distinct from the transportation-information scheme I shall describe below, is to make available in one place such information as television and motion-picture schedules, sports schedules, vacation and travel information, data on welfare and social security, certain classes of product information, political information and even bibliographic data. In the long run it might be possible to employ the system to provide information from the public library, although the problems of indexing and storing such large amounts of data are so severe that for the time being the system will be confined to information that is likely to change fairly rapidly.

The technology of the system is available today. It entails making alphanumeric (letter and number) information available to the cable-television subscriber on his television screen. The subscriber calls for information through his response pad. A computer at the head end (the cable-television center) extracts the information from its memory and transmits it to the subscriber over a regular cable channel that is time-shared with a number of other subscribers. Among 10,000 subscribers perhaps 300 might want to use the service at any given time. Since a single television frame contains all the information desired at one time by a subscriber and can be transmitted in 1/30 second, one channel shared among 300 users would provide each subscriber with access to a new frame every 10 seconds.

Computer-assisted instruction has been available for some time and has evoked mixed reactions because it is costly and some teachers are doubtful of its educational value. The cost appears likely to come down in the near future, and with good curriculum planning that takes computer-assisted instruction beyond the drill-and-practice stage the educational value should rise. For example, the computer can play a role in developing critical thinking skills through game-playing techniques. An example is the game of nim, in which the computer displays nine sticks on a television screen

and instructs the student: "Take turns with me, taking away 1 or 2 or 3 sticks at a time. The one who takes away the last stick loses." The program is designed so that the computer always goes first, randomly removing one, two or three sticks. If the student thinks ahead, he is in a position to win, although the computer is programmed to try to win after the student's first move.

It is possible to foresee systems delivering computer-assisted instruction through two-way cable-television arrangements. At present, however, the economics of the matter suggest that the interaction will take place through one-way television with students responding by teletypewriter.

In the health field the major problems that seem open to improvement through telecommunications are the limited number of physicians, particularly in rural areas, the uneven geographical distribution of physicians even in urban areas and the fact that the time of physicians is not always optimally employed. It is widely agreed that the strategy for improving the system is to extend the services of individual physicians, both geographically and in terms of the number of patients each one can serve, and to rely more extensively on medical assistants. Telecommunication technology can play an important role in the development of innovative systems for delivering medical care.

One scheme is to have a number of satellite clinics that would be linked to one or more physicians by various forms of communication. The clinics would be in such places as neighborhood buildings, schools, prisons and nursing homes and would be staffed by medically trained people such as nurses and physicians' assistants. The clinic staff would make preliminary examinations and carry out certain tests. If the staff felt that consultation with a physician was necessary, it could be done by telephone or point-to-point television. It has already been demonstrated that a physician can obtain an adequate medical history, perform a significant part of the physical examination, read electrocardiograms, examine X rays and so on by means of a television link.

The role of the computer in health care appears likely to grow [see "The Delivery of Medical Care," by Sidney R. Garfield; SCIENTIFIC AMERICAN, April, 1970]. Computers already are extensively involved in the record-keeping of hospitals. Computer-aided diagnosis in busy outpatient clinics may soon reach a similar degree of acceptance. Centralized maintenance of patients' histories in computer data banks, with remote access from the physician's office, appears to offer important benefits, but the system would require safeguards to ensure privacy and to control the right to add to or delete from the records.

The effectiveness of moves to control pollution depends to a large extent on the development of systems that can obtain information on the presence and the amount of pollutants. The problem here is not in processing or transferring data but in developing inexpensive and reliable sensing devices, some of which would operate at remote, unattended sites, transmitting their data to central monitoring stations, and some of which would enable officials in vehicles to make spot checks. A promising physical principle for measuring air pollution is the absorption and scattering of infrared radiation by the atmosphere. Every molecule has a specific signature in the infrared spectrum, and so in principle spectral measurements (of emission, scattering or absorption of radiation) can identify the type and concentration of various pollutants.

Each of the three measuring techniques requires a reliable and stable infrared source of narrow bandwidth, together with a sensitive detector. Laser technology can meet the requirement. One strategy would be to employ a heterodyne method using a carbon dioxide laser generating frequencies close to the desired one. Another possibility would be a tunable laser that could be placed on the precise frequency desired. Experimental work on each method is in progress.

In the transportation field telecommunication can be employed much more extensively than it is now to monitor and guide the flow of traffic and to improve the efficiency of mass-transit systems. Anyone familiar with the effort of traveling by bus in New York and other large cities, where only the regular riders know what route a bus will follow, will perceive the value of a system that would provide information at every bus stop about routes, schedules, transfer points, the current passenger load and the estimated time of arrival of the next bus. The technology is available. Probably at first the information would have to be sought and delivered by telephone, but ultimately the system would require a computerized operation that kept track of the location of each vehicle and of the situation along each route with respect to the number of passengers waiting, boarding and leaving.

From the rider's viewpoint the system would provide an information box at the bus stop. By means of push buttons the rider could ask for such information as the route followed by each bus serving the stop and the estimated time of arrival of the next bus going his way. The information would be displayed on a screen. Indeed, by way of an interactive television terminal one could receive the same kind of information at home.

Another transportation project that merits trial is a fringe parking lot adjacent to one or more transit lines and supplied with much more in the way of facilities than are available in the lots of this type now in existence. One facility would enable the driver to go directly to an empty parking space near the transit line he intended to ride. The system would include a sensor at each parking slot, telecommunication lines linking each sensor to a computer and display screens to show the driver where to go. Another facility would make it possible to prepay the parking fee quickly, by means of a credit card if the driver wished. The terminal would also be equipped with the transit-information boxes I have described for bus stops.

Regarded together, the various systems I have discussed depict what has been described as the "wired city." The achievement of such a concept would rest on communication technology. The aim, however, would be to help the community function more efficiently and humanely.

Our panel also considered the application of communication technology to a broader improvement of life in the U.S. Some 80 percent of the people live in crowded urban areas, which occupy less than 10 percent of the land. Problems of pollution, crime, health and education have caused city life to deteriorate for most people and particularly for the poor.

We have investigated ways of enabling more of the population to live in attractive rural environments and to combine that mode of life with some of the amenities offered by large cities. Employment, improved health and educational services, cultural and entertainment opportunities and so on could be provided for every part of the country through the imaginative application of telecommunication technology. The U.S. Department of Housing and Urban Development has provided money for study of a specific project that our panel proposed. The project, which is called the "New Rural Society," is centered in Connecticut, but the findings of our study there will have national significance.

10

COMMUNICATION AND
THE SOCIAL ENVIRONMENT

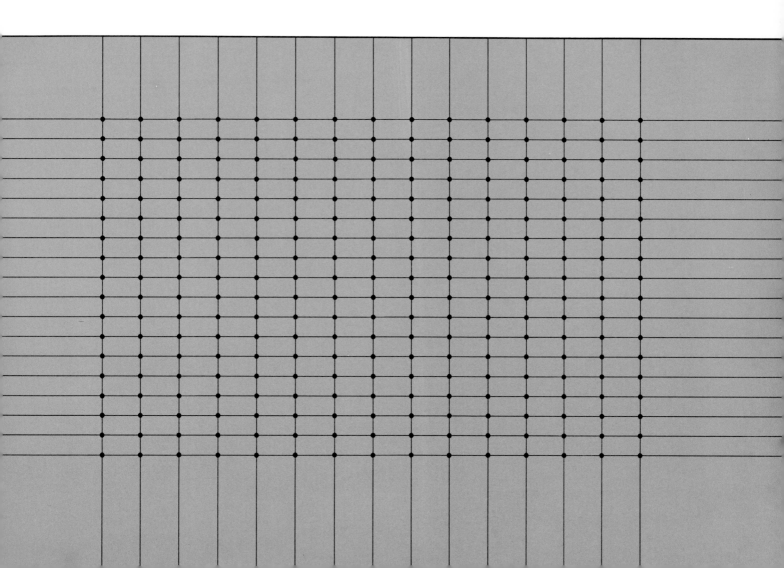

Communication and Social Environment

GEORGE GERBNER

*Messages are the medium in which human beings exist.
Precisely how human behavior and attitudes are shaped
by the multifarious forms of mass communication
is now beginning to be investigated.*

The ways in which people reflect on things and relate to one another are rooted in the human ability to compose images, produce messages and employ complex systems of symbols. A change in these processes transforms the nature of human affairs. We are in the midst of such a transformation. It stems from the mass production of symbols and messages, which represents a revolution in information and popular culture. Of all the changes in what has come to be called the quality of life, none has had a larger direct impact on human consciousness and social behavior than the rise of communication technology.

Long ago the development of writing freed memory of much of its burden and shifted control over the accumulation of knowledge from storytellers to makers and keepers of records. The spread of literacy broke that monopoly and prepared the ground for the mobility of ideas and people that is so important in modern industry. Printing sped ideas and commands to all who could read. Today satellites fly and spy overhead, and we are wired together so tightly that a short circuit can fry us all. A "hot line" is needed to make sure that if humankind seems about to exterminate itself, the deed is purposeful rather than the result of error. When most people can be exposed to the same sources of power at the same time, the shape and pace of history have changed.

The Scottish patriot Andrew Fletcher once said: "If a man were permitted to write all the ballads, he need not care who should make the laws of the nation." The mass production of all the ballads is at the heart of the cultural transformation now in progress. The ballads of an age are powerful myths depicting its visions of the invisible forces of life, society and the universe. They are blends of fact and fiction designed to reveal how things are or ought to be. They compel attention for their own sake. They inform as they entertain. They make entertainment—the celebration of conventional morality—the only collective drill in which most members of a culture engage with pleasure. Today's popular entertainment in news, drama and fiction has become the universal source of public acculturation.

Developments in communication not only have extended the human ability to exchange messages but also have transformed the symbolic environment of human consciousness and are continuing to alter it. Perhaps the most profound human dilemma is this: Just as knowledge can be said to confer power, so power generates and uses knowledge for its own purposes. Social and institutional structures (the Government, the broadcasting networks, the publishing houses and the educational institutions) have a steadily increasing role in shaping the symbolic environment.

Self-government can no longer be supposed to follow from the assumption that the press and other communication agencies are free. In a highly centralized mass-production structure of the kind characterizing modern communication, "freedom" is the right of the managers of the media to decide what the public will be told. The question is whether enlightenment through communication can lead to liberation from the shackles of mind and body that still oppress mankind or whether only liberation from those shackles can lead to further enlightenment through communication.

The simplest organisms take energy from their immediate surroundings. They need little information except what is contained in a fixed hereditary code. Higher organisms have specialized senses to receive information and complex brains to process and store it. They can reach out, search a larger area, pick up signals from a distance, accumulate impressions over a period of time, relate to one another, assume different roles and engage in behavior based on a sharing of learned significance. Only man, however, acts primarily in terms of symbol systems.

Symbolic context gives an act its human significance. Meanings do not reside within people any more than breathing resides only in the lungs. Meanings are the product of an exchange between the brain and the symbolic environment, which is to the brain what air is to the lungs. The exchange is the reason one can say that although all organisms behave, only humans act. Action is behavior that derives its distinctively human meaning from the symbolic context in which it is embedded or to which it is related.

The exchange by means of the symbolic environment is what I define as communication. It is interaction through messages. Even when people interact face to face, they usually do it partly or wholly through the patterned exchange of messages. By messages I mean formally coded symbolic or representational patterns of some shared significance

TELEVISION CONTROL ROOM is one of many linkages in the complex system that creates the communicative environment of the U.S. The control room on the opposite page is one of those operated by the Columbia Broadcasting System in New York. When a "live" program is being broadcast, the monitor screens show what each one of several cameras is picking up. The director can cut from one camera to another to synthesize the program.

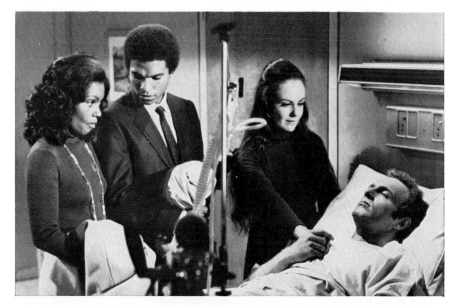

DRAMATIC SCENES from television programs and motion pictures are employed by the author's group at the Annenberg School of Communications of the University of Pennsylvania to test the influence of the media on the perceptions that viewers form of people, life and society. Pictures such as these are shown without identification to respondents, who are asked such questions as what the characters are saying, what might happen next and whether the characters are strangers or people who have known each other for some time.

in a culture. Indeed, culture itself can be regarded broadly as a system in which messages cultivate and regulate the relations between people. In one form or another such processes appear in all types of life and in all social systems, but it is in human culture and in the conduct of human life and society that communication plays its most complex and distinctive part.

Even the most primitive peoples have employed shapes and images for symbolic and representational purposes and have erected imposing symbolic structures of religion, statecraft and play. Through communication they have performed elaborate rituals, observed intricate kinship systems and conducted the affairs of the tribe or nation. Today systems of messages that can be recorded and widely transported enable man to bridge vast reaches of space and time and to cultivate values of collective survival. They also facilitate spasms of mass destruction, a distinctively human trait.

A change in the relation of people to the common culture marks the transition from one epoch to another in the way that members of our species are "humanized." The increasing rate of this change and the lengthening span of life mean that different generations living side by side can now be humanized in different ways, so that they live in essentially different (but overlapping) cultural epochs. Distant storytellers mass-produce new tales steadily and can tell them to millions of children, parents and grandparents simultaneously. As a result the traditional process of socialization has been altered. Never before have so many people in so many places shared so much of a common system of messages and images—and the assumptions about life, society and the world that the system embodies—while having so little to do with creating the system. In sum, the fabric of popular culture that relates the elements of existence to one another and shapes the common consciousness of what is, what is important, what is right and what is related to what else is now largely a manufactured product.

The experiments in self-government that brought to an end the era of absolute monarchs were based on a new conception of popular culture, namely that reason confronts reality on terms made available by the culture. It was thought that popular self-government consisted in citizens' collectively creating alternatives of policy rather than simply responding to them. A great deal has happened since these assumptions found expression in revolutionary documents of societies at a time when public communications were mostly hand-crafted by individuals speaking for diverse publics. Now that public communications have become commodities manufactured by powerful agencies of the industrial society for sale to heterogeneous audiences, the perspective of the communications reflects institutional organization and control.

The organs of mass communication—printing, television and radio—provide the means of selecting, recording, viewing and sharing man's notions of what is, what is important, what is right and what is related to what else. The media are the cultural arms of the industrial order from which they spring. They bring into existence and then cultivate a new form of common consciousness: modern mass publics.

The significance of mass communication does not stem from the numbers of people involved. Large groups of people were reached by other forms of communication long before the advent of the modern forms. The modern concept of masses is groups so large and dispersed that only methods of mass production and distribution can reach them with the same message in a short period of time. The significance of the mass media therefore lies in their ability to mass-produce messages that create mass publics: heterogeneous social aggregates that never meet face to face and may have nothing in common except the messages they share. The biggest of the mass media form the only common bond among all the groups in an otherwise fragmented society. As an official of a broadcast network said recently, television is "the only mass entertainment and information medium that does not disfranchise the rural and urban poor." They are therefore the first poor people in history who share much of the culture of the rich, designed by and for the more affluent—a function that only the church served in earlier times.

Such "public-making" is the chief instrument of modern social cohesion. When rebels take over a radio station or candidates demand equal time or advertisers buy space or time, what is fought for or bought is not time or space but the chief product of the modern media: access to the publics they have created.

These publics are maintained through continued publication, by which I mean the output of all the organs of mass communication. The publics are supplied

STANDARD PHOTOGRAPHS, which are of people at the University of Pennsylvania, are also shown in tests of the influence of the mass media. Respondents are asked such questions as which person is probably not American, who is most likely to be friendly with whom and who would win if X got into a fight with Y. The answers of viewers of different television programs or different types of motion picture are compared with one another and with those of nonviewers to determine the effects of types of content on perceptions.

with selections of information and entertainment that are regarded by the selectors as important in terms of the perspectives to be cultivated. Publication therefore is the selection of shared ways of viewing events and aspects of life.

Publication is thus the basis of community consciousness among diverse groups of people too numerous or dispersed to interact face to face or in any other personally mediated way. The great significance of publication is its ability to form new bases for collective thought and action quickly, continuously and pervasively across boundaries of time, space and class. That is why the organs of public communication have a special place in all modern states, which through legal or economic mechanisms confer the right to control large presses, motion-picture and television studios and postal and wireless communications on government agencies or on private holders of licenses, patents, franchises or properties.

Selectivity and control, which are inherent in any communication, dominate the mass-communication process. The right to acculturate a nation and to shape the public agenda has never been open to all; it is one of the most carefully guarded powers in any society. The real question is not whether the organs of mass communication are free but rather: By whom, how, for what purposes and with what consequences are the inevitable controls exercised?

A few programs of research in mass communication, mostly affiliated with the universities, have begun to ask this question. The development is fairly recent. Until the late 1950's such research was under the influence of the marketplace. The methods of the behavioral sciences were applied mainly in an attempt to control, influence or manipulate behavior on behalf of clients rather than to understand communication as a crucial element of the social environment.

For more than 40 years various governmental and private bodies have called for some kind of surveillance of the organs of mass communication. None of the proposals, however, specified how the surveillance might be done or limited the scope to manageable proportions. As a result there is probably no area of important social policy in which far-reaching decisions are made with as little reliable, systematic, cumulative and comparable information about trends and the state of affairs as the area of the mass production and distribution of the most broadly shared messages of our culture. Little is known about trends in the composition and structure of the mass-produced systems of messages that define life in urbanized societies, and no more is known about the institutional processes that compose and structure those systems. Much of the standard research on how people respond in various situations lacks insight into the dynamics of the common cultural context.

Other reasons can be cited for pursuing the university-based programs of research in communication. One is to look for evidence of cultural trends. Citizens concerned with such issues as health, education, delinquency, aging, generational conflict, drugs and violence often point to cultural "trends" to support their case, but there is no convincing evidence to support any case.

Moreover, educators wonder increasingly about the consequences inherent in the commercial compulsion to present life in salable packages. Corporate, technological and other processes of producing messages short-circuit former networks of social communication and superimpose their own forms of collective consciousness—their own publics—on other social relations, harnessing acculturation to consumer markets. The new programs of academic research in mass communication are designed to monitor the elements of the system of generating and using bodies of broadly shared messages that are most relevant to social issues and to issues of public policy.

Much of what I say about these research programs is based on my own work, first at the University of Illinois and later at the University of Pennsylvania. My colleagues and I have studied such subjects as popular conceptions of mental illness; ideological perspectives inherent in news reporting; the portrayal of teachers, schools and education in the mass-produced cultures of several countries; the image of the film hero in American and foreign movies, and the social functions of symbolic violence as presented in television drama. With these studies we have developed the areas and terms of analysis for examining modern communication.

I have defined communication as interaction through messages bearing man's notions of existence, priorities, values and relations. Codes of symbolic significance conveyed through modes of expression form the currency of social relations. Institutions package, media compose and technologies distribute message systems to heterogeneous mass publics.

How is this massive flow managed?

How does it fit into or alter the existing cultural context? What perspectives on life and the world does it express and cultivate? How does it vary across times, societies and cultures? How does its cultivation of collective assumptions relate to the conduct of public affairs and vice versa?

The questions suggest three areas of analysis: institutional processes, message systems and cultivation. The first area involves questions of how the organs of mass communication make decisions, compose message systems and relate to other institutions. In examining message systems one asks how large bodies of messages can be observed as dynamic systems with symbolic functions that have social consequences. Cultivation analysis asks what common assumptions, points of view, images and associations the message systems tend to cultivate in large and heterogeneous communities and what the implications are for public policy.

Every decision to communicate certain things is at the same time a decision to suppress other things. What comes out is a result of competitive pressure breaking through structured inhibitions. When only a fragment of all available and plausible messages can be selected for transmission, an analysis cannot realistically focus on whether or not suppression is involved but must consider the question of what systems of pressures and inhibitions determine the patterns of selection by communicators.

How do media managers determine and perform the functions their institutions, clients and the social order require? What is the overall effect of corporate controls on symbolic output? What policy changes do in fact alter that output and how? These are the main questions for the analysis of institutional processes.

The policies of the mass media reflect not only a stage in industrial development and the general structure of social relations but also particular types of institutional powers and pressures. Mass communicators everywhere occupy sensitive and central positions in the social network. The groups that have a stake in shaping content and influence or power over it include the authorities who issue licenses and administer the laws; the patrons who invest in or subsidize the operation; organizations, institutions and loose aggregations of publics that require attention and cultivation; the managements that set policies and supervise operations; the auxiliary groups that provide services, raw materials and

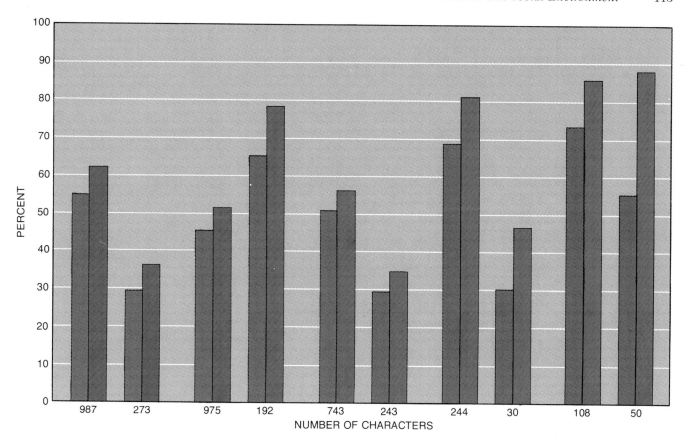

VIOLENCE AND VICTIMIZATION of leading characters in television drama are charted according to type and whether the character committed violence (*color*) or suffered it (*black*). The survey found victimization to be always more frequent than aggression. Each pair of bars represents the type of character identified in the corresponding single bars in illustration at bottom of page.

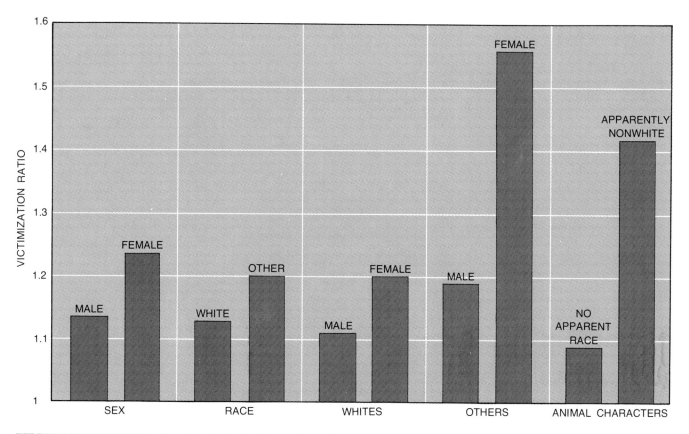

TELEVISION VIOLENCE is charted on the basis of an analysis of dramatic programs on the networks in the evening and on Saturday morning from 1967 to 1971. The bars show the type of victim and the ratio of victims per violent character. The author's group made the study in examining the social symbolism portrayed on television and its relation to real-life attitudes. The findings revealed a "pecking order" in which white males and animal characters of no apparent race were least likely to be victimized when they were involved in violence and nonwhite females and animal characters judged to represent nonwhites were most likely to be victimized.

protection; the creative talent, experts and technicians who actually form the symbolic content and transmit the signals, and the colleagues and competitors whose solidarity or innovation helps to set standards and maintain vigilance.

Our studies suggest that any message system produced by an institutional source has certain ideological orientations implicit in selection, emphasis and treatment. Other researchers have found that most newsmen respond more to the pressures and expectations of the newsroom than to any generalized concept of audience or public interest. One study of newsroom decisions concluded that three out of four publishers are active in directing news decisions, with their influence greatest in news of the immediate market area and in subjects that affect the revenue of the paper.

Our recent survey of how the content of television programs is regulated concludes, with regard to dramatic programming: "In a fictional world governed by the economics of the assembly line and the 'production values' of optimum appeal at least cost, symbolic action follows conventional rules of social morality. The requirements of wide acceptability and a suitable environment for the sponsor's message assure general adherence to consumer values and to common notions of justice and fair play. The issue is rarely in doubt; the action is typically a game of skill and power."

Intellectuals who assume that television can commit substantial resources to high-risk cultural productions have been talking past the issue. The basic role of television—the most massive communication medium of modern society—is to provide the symbolic functions formerly performed only by popular religions. The highly predictable scenarios of news, fiction, drama and "intimate" conversation watched by millions can easily pass for the rituals, cults, passion plays and myths of modern life.

Studies of the occupations in communication suggest that they may represent anachronistically upper-class standards of quality and autonomy, particularly in the news area. With new technological developments there may come such a proliferation and fragmentation of channels that the communication professional may give way to even more direct control by the business office and to a kind of populist commercialism that can be most easily programmed by technicians.

I turn now to the analysis of message systems, which observes the record of institutional behavior in mass-producing messages for entire communities. The observation reveals collective and common rather than individual and unique features of the process of forming and cultivating public images.

Our program of research in this area rests on two assumptions, one of which is that communication is the environment of social behavior rather than just specific acts, utterances and campaigns. The most profound effects of communication can be found not in making sales, getting votes, influencing opinions and changing attitudes but in the selective maintenance of relatively stable structures of images and associations that stem from institutional structures and policies and that define the common perspectives of a society. The difficulty (often failure) of any campaign designed to change views or attitudes indicates how powerful the currents that cultivate the prevailing outlooks are. Without knowing what these currents are, what they cultivate and how they change, neither social behavior nor public attitudes can be fully understood.

Our second assumption is that just as the effects of communication cannot be limited to specific messages or to attempts to change or control behavior, so the effects are not necessarily available to the conscious scrutiny of any of the parties involved in the communication. One always communicates more things—or other things—than one is aware of. Indeed, there are no failures of communication, only failures of intention and of understanding of what the message was in the first place. Many breakdowns in social and personal communication result because the recipient gets the message better and more accurately than the sender realizes and thus turns the sender and his message off.

Symbolic functions are the consequences that flow from a communication, regardless of intentions and pretensions. To investigate these functions one must analyze the symbolic environment and particular configurations of symbols in it. In this way one can obtain information about what the actual messages, rather than the presumed messages, might be. The next step is to form a hypothesis about what conceptions the particular symbolic functions might cultivate in an exchange with particular communicating parties. The human and social consequences of the communication can be explored by investigating the contributions that the symbolic functions and their cultivation of particular notions might make to thinking and behavior. These contributions are usually of a cultivating and reinforcing kind; that is what culture does.

Cultures also change, however, and from time to time real shifts in perspective become possible. Herein lies

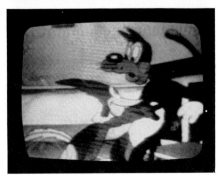

CARTOON SERIES shown on television indicates the violence that characterizes many cartoon programs. The photographs, which depict two anthropomorphic animals trying to stuff each other into an oven, are from a tape made by the Pennsylvania research group during a commercial television program. The group is exploring the hypothesis that fantasy figures and remote settings facilitate assimilation of messages that real settings may inhibit.

the subject matter of the analysis of cultivation.

The most distinctive characteristics of large groups of people are acquired through living in one culture rather than another. Individuals make their own selection of materials for cultivating personal images, tastes, views and preferences, and they seek to influence the materials available to their children. They cannot, however, cultivate what is not available, and they will seldom select what is scarcely available or not much emphasized. A culture cultivates not only patterns of conformity but also patterns of alienation and rebellion. The culture's affirmations pose the issues most likely to be the targets of symbolic provocation or protest.

The dominant agencies of communication produce the message systems that cultivate the dominant image patterns. They structure the public agenda of existence, priorities, values and relations. People use this agenda (some more selectively than others) to support their ideas and actions in ways that on the whole tend to match the general composition and structure of message systems, provided of course that there is also other environmental support for these choices and interpretations.

A significant change in this process takes place with a change in the technology, ownership, clientele or other institutional characteristics of the dominant communication agencies. Decisive cultural change does not occur in the symbolic field alone. When it occurs, it stems from a change in social relations that puts the old symbolic patterns out of step with the new order. In such a case the relative meanings and functions of the existing images and practices change before the images and practices themselves change. When the new cultural patterns are developed, they restore to public communication its basic function: the support and maintenance of the new order.

Cultivation analysis begins with the insights derived from the analyses of institutions and message systems. It goes on to investigate the contributions these systems and their symbolic functions make to the cultivation of common assumptions about life and the world. The study does not pay much attention to style of expression, quality of representation, artistic excellence or the nature of the individual's experience with mass culture. It focuses instead on the functions that large systems of messages perform regardless of what people think of them.

The main approaches taken in cultivation analysis are projective techniques (wherein respondents are presented with situations that tend to lead them to reveal views, expectations and values they may not be conscious of or might not talk about if they were asked directly), interviews in depth and periodic surveys of sample groups. We work with panels of adults and children. In all these activities the aim is to see how exposure to the mass media has influenced the thinking of the respondents about selected issues and aspects of real life.

Two areas are of particular concern in this study. One is the impact of television, since for most people television *is* culture. The other is the cultivation of social concepts among children, since the social symbolic patterns established in childhood are the ones most easily cultivated throughout life.

The cultural transformation resulting from mass communication has created societies whose parts increasingly relate to one another through distant communication. The more complex, specialized, extended and interrelated a system becomes, the more information it needs (and generates) to maintain stability. Moreover, self-governing social systems of high specialization and complexity require indicators that measure the trend of events in the intricate society. In recent years the effort to find such social indicators has gained mo-

FOREIGN COPY DESK of *The New York Times* is where foreign news is edited and the headline for each foreign news story is written. The processing includes choosing from a large volume of foreign news what will be published in the next day's *Times* and in what form. The work of the copy editors and the foreign-news editor clearly has a strong influence on what readers see in the paper.

mentum with the increasing speed of technological change, of which the developments in the space program are an example. The indicators would provide the society with information about its changing state while its methods of generating and using information are themselves being altered. When the symbolic environment is changing, the nature of social behavior and the usefulness of information relating to social policy can best be assessed if cultural winds and tides can be measured.

My colleague Larry P. Gross and I have recently launched a program at the University of Pennsylvania to collect and report such information. The program, which is sponsored on a pilot basis by the National Institute of Mental Health, is called Cultural Indicators. For the first time it will relate a long-term analysis of message systems (mostly television) to research on symbolic functions and how they cultivate popular notions about people and life.

Cultural indicators will trace people, topics and types of action represented in mass-produced cultures. They will touch on the history, geography, demography and ethnography of the symbolic worlds. The symbolic populations and their interpersonal and group relations will be observed. Themes of nature, science, politics, law, crime, business, education, art, health, peace, sex, love and friendship as well as violence will be noted. The roles, values and goals of the characters who populate the symbolic worlds will be related to the issues with which they grapple and to the fates to which they are destined.

We are developing tests of imagery to indicate the nature and extent of the contributions these elements of content and symbolic function make to the development and cultivation of basic concepts about people and life. Amid the clamor of commercial and political interests it may be helpful to have the third voice of social scientific inquiry keep a score of the functional significance of the deeper messages and points of view that capture public attention, occupy more time than any other activity and animate the collective imagination.

The inquiry will be the first step toward creating the conditions of cultural self-consciousness in the new symbolic environment. If it succeeds, it will help people to understand the impact of communication technology on the symbolic climate that affects all they think and do. We can then inquire into the institutional aspects of policy with a sharper awareness of the currents that tug at us all.

11

COMMUNICATION AND FREEDOM OF EXPRESSION

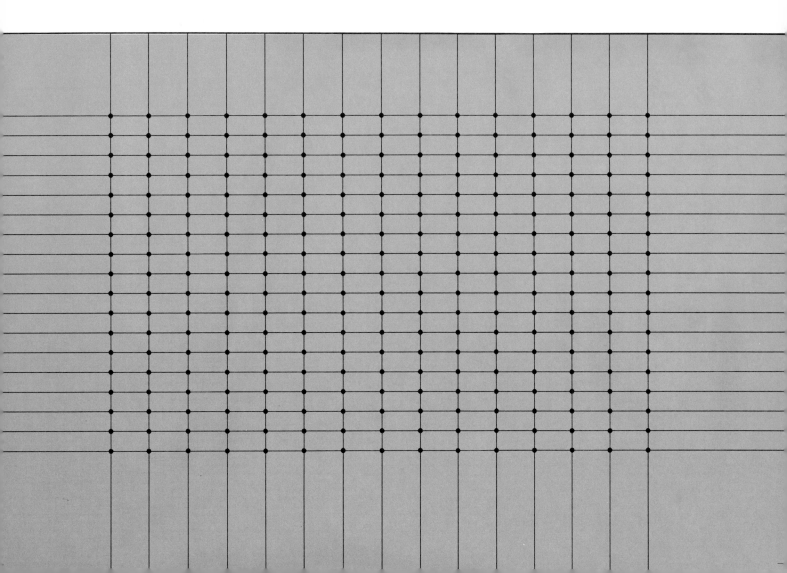

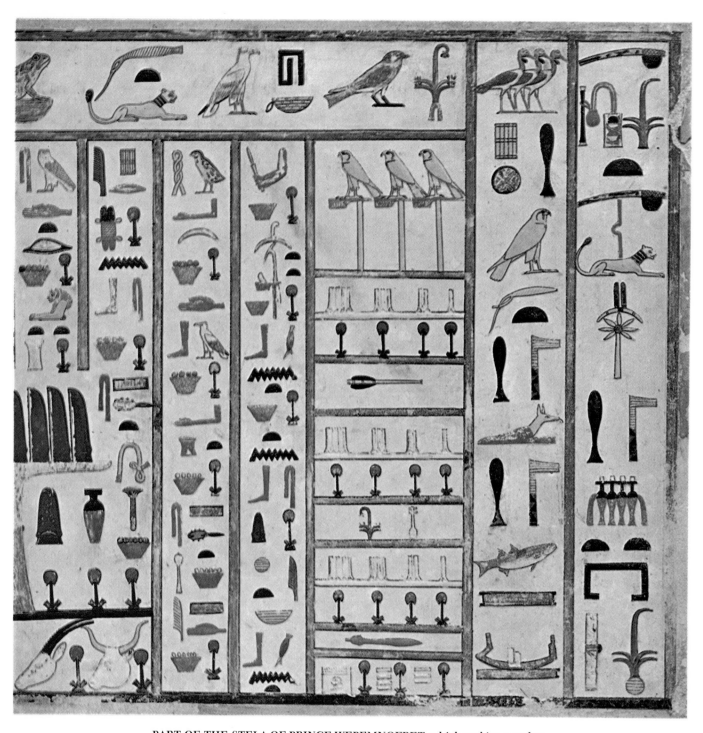

PART OF THE STELA OF PRINCE WEPEMNOFRET, a high-ranking member of the family of the Egyptian ruler Cheops, which dates back to the twenty-seventh century B.C. It is regarded as the best-preserved example of painted relief from the Old Kingdom of Egypt. Uncovered at Giza in 1905, it is now in the Robert H. Lowie Museum of Anthropology at the University of California, Berkeley.

Communication and Freedom of Expression
THOMAS I. EMERSON

Freedom of expression is a system of communication. The system defined by the First Amendment of the Constitution must now be adapted to the capabilities of modern communication technology.

The concept of freedom of expression rests on the proposition that certain kinds of communication are entitled to special protection by our laws and institutions. In large degree this special treatment consists of immunity from governmental restraint, but it also includes other forms of encouragement and support. The principal problems involved are not so much technical ones of method and efficiency in communication, or semantic ones of interpretation or meaning, as they are questions of political and social control over the effects of communication. Nevertheless, it is useful to consider the entire subject of freedom of expression as constituting a system, in almost the same sense as the term is used in other areas of communication theory.

The system of freedom of expression consists of a series of fundamental rights, constitutive principles, working rules and social institutions that have an overall unity and are designed to perform specific functions in our society. Basically the rights are those of the individual to communicate ideas, opinions, moods or information on any subject of interest to him, whether in the sphere of politics, religion, culture or otherwise, and through speech, writing, music, art or some other medium. In some degree the rights may be considered to embrace more than "communication" in a narrow sense. They include the right to form or hold beliefs and opinions (prior to communication). They also include certain rights to access to the means of communication, to receive communications from others and to obtain information on which to base decisions or engage in communication. Furthermore, whereas the rights are ultimately those of the individual, they embrace also the right to associate with other persons in order to obtain the means of communication or to magnify its impact.

These rights are embodied in constitutive principles—moral, philosophical or legal—that identify the right, suggest its justification and indicate its limitations. The principles are translated into working rules, mostly legal in nature, and are in turn put into operation through various social institutions designed to render the basic rights realizable in practice. The rights, principles, rules and institutions all work to achieve certain social goals, which will be described below.

The system of freedom of expression that prevails at present in the U.S. had its origins in the growth of constitutional liberalism in the 17th and 18th centuries; it was nurtured in the laissez-faire atmosphere of the 19th century, and it operates today in the modified capitalism of the 20th century. Yet the system is not bound to any particular form of economic, political or social structure. It could be adapted to any kind of society that is capable of affording its citizens the requisite degree of independence and autonomy.

It should be noted that a system of freedom of expression is by no means a common or usual feature of the social structure. On the contrary, most societies operate under what might be called a system of nonfreedom of expression. The natural tendency of governmental and other institutions seeking to organize the social order is to suppress, manipulate or otherwise control communication on most matters having any general import. A totalitarian society, of course, carries this process to its furthest limits. Other forms of social structure, however, exhibit the same tendency. On the introduction of printing in England the secular and ecclesiastical authorities established an elaborate system of censorship that not only required advance approval of any publication but also strictly limited the number of presses and printers. On the abandonment of this licensing system at the end of the 17th century the laws of treason and seditious libel were utilized to prohibit any expression criticizing the government or its officials. Similar forms of direct repression of communication exist in most countries today, and they are supplemented by indirect measures such as a denial of benefits or privileges to persons of unorthodox or "subversive" views. In addition, most governments control the mass media of communication, monopolize education and engage in pervasive expression themselves. Thus an effective system of free expression is a rare phenomenon, attainable only by the conscious efforts of a mature and sophisticated society.

No attempt will be made here to describe or to defend the philosophical or political premises of a system of freedom of expression. Rather this article will merely comment on some of its legal foundations. It is necessary first, however, to outline the major functions the system of free expression performs in our society, and to indicate some of the principles that are implicit in these goals.

The system of freedom of expression, as it has developed in the U.S., is designed to achieve four separate but related objectives. The first is individual self-fulfillment. Freedom of expression is essential to the realization of man's character and potential as a human being. Man lives, grows and finds meaning in life through self-expression and communication with his fellows. Expression is thus a vital part of his being and becoming. Conversely, suppression of thought or opinion contradicts the dignity and integrity of man.

From this it follows that the right to freedom of expression does not necessarily depend on whether or not the expression promotes other social goals. Expression is an end in itself, not necessarily subordinate to the other ends of the good society.

Second, to borrow John Stuart Mill's formulation, freedom of expression is essential to the attainment of "truth." A rational judgment is possible only by considering all facts and ideas, from whatever source, and testing one's conclusion against the onslaught of opposing opinions. This process demands that all points of view be heard, no matter how dangerous or "fraught with death" they may seem. All ideas are either true, in which case they ought to be accepted; partly true and partly false, in which case they add some element to the truth, or wholly false, in which case they serve the function of making us rethink and retest the accepted opinion and thereby understand it more fully.

The modern man may not agree with Mill's assumption that an objective truth exists, waiting to be discovered through the rational use of man's faculties. Nevertheless, the ultimate goal sought by Mill is still pursued. Today we may substitute "judgment" for Mill's "truth," and we acknowledge the part played by irrational factors. Yet freedom of expression remains an essential instrument for advancing knowledge and enabling an autonomous man to reach a considered decision.

From this function of freedom of expression, it follows that the right to express oneself does not depend on whether the communication is considered by the society to be true or false, good or bad, socially useful or harmful. No point of view ought to be suppressed.

Third, a system of freedom of expression is essential to popular decision-making in a democratic society. Under our theory of government the people are sovereign: the Government is the servant, not the master. As Alexander Meiklejohn has argued most forcefully, if the people are to perform their role and instruct their government, they must be able to hear all voices. Meiklejohn was concerned principally with the political process, but the same considerations apply to collective decision-making on any issue.

The implication of this line of thinking is that the Government has no authority to determine what may be said or heard by the citizens of the community. The servant cannot tell the master how to make up his mind.

Finally, a system of freedom of expression enables a society to find the proper balance between stability and change. The process of communication prevents stultification and encourages change. At the same time it promotes stability by permitting the testing of proposals in advance rather than through a process of trial and error. Most important, freedom of expression facilitates change without resort to violence. Open discussion gives legitimacy to change, whereas suppression substitutes force for reason and makes rational argument irrelevant.

The implication of these considerations is that the system is intended, in one sense, to encourage conflict. As Justice Brennan has said, expression often is "uninhibited, robust and wide open." The conflict, however, is contained within the system. There is a confrontation of ideas, not of force.

From these basic functions are derived the rights, principles, rules and institutions that make up the system of freedom of expression. Its form and status at any one time are the product of numerous forces in our society. Our economic and political structures, our educational practices, our religious institutions, our system of justice, our attitudes and philosophy are all significant factors in determining the shape and health of the system. Nevertheless, we rely on law and legal institutions for the most direct support of the system, and here we are chiefly concerned with that area.

The main legal principle that underlies the system of freedom of expression in the U.S. is set forth in the First Amendment to the Constitution. That provision, adopted as part of the Bill of Rights in 1791, reads: "Congress shall make no law respecting an establishment of religion, or prohibiting the free exercise thereof; or abridging the freedom of speech, or of the press; or the right of the people peaceably to assemble, and to petition the Government for a redress of grievances." Although the First Amendment refers specifically to freedom of conscience, speech, press, assembly and petition (the features of most interest to the draftsmen), the courts have interpreted the provision as embodying a general right to freedom of expression, in short, as broadly guaranteeing the system as a whole.

It is somewhat surprising to note that no major cases involving the First Amendment reached the Supreme Court for nearly 130 years. It was not until 1919, in a series of decisions growing out of the antisedition laws of World War I, that the Supreme Court began an intensive development of First Amendment doctrine. By the mid-1920's the court had ruled that the constitutional guaranty applied not only to the Federal Government but also to the states. In the past 50 years the legal foundations of the system have been expanded through literally hundreds of First Amendment cases.

The first task in developing workable rules of law from the First Amendment is to determine what forms of conduct fall within the ambit of that provision and are therefore entitled to its special protection. This calls for a definition of "expression," to be distinguished from conduct not covered by the First Amendment, which may be designated "action." The formulation of this definition is beset with difficulties. Clearly the core of the "expression" category consists of linguistic communication. Some verbal utterances, however, are the equivalent of action, such as a command by the leader of a riotous mob to his followers, or a false shout of "Fire!" in a crowded theatre. "Expression" must also include many forms of symbolic communication, such as the wearing of armbands or a silent vigil. Yet it is often difficult to separate the communicative element from the total context, as it is, for example, in a sit-in demonstration. Again, some conduct not on its face constituting "expression" is nevertheless necessary to convey the message, such as hiring a hall or publishing a newspaper. In addition, some aspects of collective "expression," such as organizing an association or collecting dues, may not in themselves constitute pure communication.

Nonetheless, the distinction between expression and action, difficult as it is to formulate in some cases, is fundamental to operation of the system and must be drawn as best it can be. The basic guides are derived from the functions performed by the system. In general, expression is conduct that conveys attitudes, ideas or information, and hence its protection is central to any system of freedom. Expression is also entitled to special treatment because by and large it is less directly harmful to the state or to other individuals than action. In fact, the state is usually concerned not directly with expression but with the ensuing action, and it can ordinarily achieve its proper goals through control of such action. The definition of expression is thus a functional one, based on the nature of the system and guided by the needs for effective administration.

Actually in most instances the question of whether conduct is to be classified as expression or action will be self-evident. More difficult problems will gradually be settled as the courts prick out the boundaries on a case-by-case basis. Although there will always remain a residue of borderline cases, it is entirely possible for the courts to resolve these in a manner that does not jeopardize the system as a whole.

Another approach to the solution of this initial problem has been suggested by Thomas M. Scanlon, Jr., a member of the philosophy department at Princeton University. He argues that it is a mistake to attempt to define expression and action, and that instead one should concentrate on the nature of the harm attributable to the communication. On his analysis, where the "harm" caused by the communication consists merely in affecting the beliefs or opinions of another person, the communication should be fully protected; otherwise its protection should depend on a balancing of various interests. Scanlon's proposal is interesting and deserves further exploration in the context of actual cases. It is doubtful, however, that his approach would afford adequate protection for many kinds of communication that need it, or that the balancing of harms, which would be necessary in most cases under his theory, could be reduced to workable legal rules.

The Supreme Court has so far tended to follow the expression-action analysis. Its development of the law in this crucial area, however, has been slow and sometimes retrogressive. Two lines of cases are particularly disturbing. Recently the court has held that such forms of conduct as parading, nonlabor picketing and wearing armbands constitute "speech plus" and are to be given a lesser degree of protection than "pure speech." Moreover, in the "symbolic speech" cases, involving mixed conduct such as burning a draft card, the court seems to have abandoned the effort to decide whether the conduct as a whole is predominantly expression, and therefore entitled to protection, or is predominantly action and hence not covered by the First Amendment. The court has ruled that the action element of the conduct can be prohibited, when the Government has a good reason to do so, even though the prohibitory regulation in practice totally suppresses the expression element. In both situations the court, by failing to draw a proper distinction between expression and action, has seriously impaired the system.

Once it has been determined that certain conduct is expression and hence within the coverage of the First Amendment, the remaining issues relate to what protection or support should be accorded such conduct. In order to maintain an effective system of free expression the law must provide rules for dealing with at least four major problems, along with a number of other less important but still significant questions.

The first major area embraces the rules for protection of expression against government interference. Traditionally this has been the principal concern of First Amendment doctrine, and most of the decided cases deal with it in one way or another. The problems break down into two sets: government regulations that attempt to control the content of expression and government regulations that relate to the time, place and manner of expression.

As to content, the starting point is that the nature of the governmental interference is not decisive. Whether governmental power is exerted through a criminal penalty, a civil proceeding (such as an injunction), the denial of a benefit or privilege, the summoning of a witness by a legislative committee or some other measure having a "chilling effect" is immaterial. As long as the Government's conduct has a substantial impact on expression, it is subject to the limitations of the First Amendment.

A second point of departure, essential to any worthwhile system of free expression, is that in general expression must be protected from government interference because of content. This proposition holds whether the expression is critical of any government policy or official, whether it embarrasses the Government or impairs the effectiveness of any government enterprise, whether it represents the accepted opinion or a despised opinion, whether it is temperate or militant, whether it is true or false or in between, or whether it is deemed to have social value or not. The presumption is that expression will be uninhibited.

Beyond this point the issue becomes whether any exceptions or qualifications to these two initial propositions are to be recognized. A strong argument can be made for the rule that all conduct classified as expression should receive full protection against any form of governmental restriction imposed because of the content of the expression. As I have noted, conduct that falls short of action normally causes no direct harm, and the Government has sufficient power and resources to secure its legitimate goals through controlling action. Moreover, the full-protection rule is relatively simple to understand and easy to apply. It therefore affords courts, prosecutors, police and citizens a reasonably definite guide to their respective rights and obligations.

The Supreme Court, however, has never adopted the full-protection rule. Only Justices Black and Douglas have accepted that position, and Justice Black has coupled it with a very narrow definition of "expression." The court as a whole, although it is unable to agree on any comprehensive theory, has from the beginning made certain flat exceptions and imposed certain broad qualifications.

The principal exceptions have been obscenity, libel and "fighting words." At an early point in the development of First Amendment doctrine the Supreme Court announced that conduct falling into these categories was not entitled to any protection under the First Amendment. Since that time the court has softened its position. Only "hard-core pornography," having no "redeeming social value," is subject to governmental suppression under the rubric of obscenity. Defamatory language concerning "public figures" and dealing with "public issues" is now protected unless it is false and uttered with knowledge of its falsity or with reckless disregard of whether it is false or not. The "fighting words" exception is largely limited to insulting epithets delivered face to face.

More wide-ranging qualifications have, however, been consistently recognized by the Supreme Court. The main controversy has centered around issues of whether or not expression that advocates violation of law, particularly the use of force or violence, should receive the protection of the First Amendment. The Supreme Court has at different times employed different tests for resolving these issues. In its earlier decisions the court applied the test of a "clear and present danger," holding that expression could be suppressed when it created a clear and present danger of a substantive evil the Government had a right to prevent. Later the court adopted a balancing test, in which it balanced the interests the Government was seeking to protect against the interests in freedom of expression. In its latest decision on the subject the court ruled that advocacy of force or of law violation was permissible "except where such advocacy is directed to inciting or producing imminent lawless action and is likely to incite or produce such action." All these tests cut off expression at a point well before it has become an integral part of action.

The rules for dealing with expression of this character are crucial in a system of free expression. Most militant political movements operate on the edge of violence. Their adherents are likely to feel that the laws are stacked against them and that it is necessary to break out of the legal structure that entraps them. Hence their political analysis and their language, at least the language of their more extreme adherents, are apt to include some appeal to violation of law. Yet such a political movement is ordinarily expressing grievances that society should deal with. Further, prosecution of militants for their expression affects many other persons, chills associations, arouses public hysteria and dampens the entire political process. The test of the openness of a society and the health of its system of freedom of expression is likely to be found in its tolerance for militant rhetoric.

Pressures on the system of freedom of expression also tend to be severe where expression is seen as a threat to "national security," and demands for qualification of the basic rules may be expected to occur in this sector too. As far as the threat is caused by advocacy of violation of law the issues are the same as those just discussed. In time of war or crisis, however, government efforts to control expression have extended further. Recently, in the "Pentagon papers" case, the Government contended that *The New York Times, The Washington Post* and other newspapers should be enjoined from publishing material that it claimed threatened a "grave and irreparable injury" to "national security." The Supreme Court rejected the Government's request for an injunction but only three members of the court definitely repudiated the Government's theory. The Government has also contended that widespread surveillance by the Federal Bureau of Investigation and other agencies, including wiretapping, is justifiable in "national security" cases without a search warrant or any kind of statutory authority. The Supreme Court rebuffed this claim as to wiretapping, but it refused to intervene with respect to surveillance of civilian activities by the military. Curtailment of expression in the name of "national security" can readily undermine the entire system. Once freedom of expression is subordinated to the vague demands of "national security" there is no end to the chain of restrictive measures that are certain to follow.

Government regulation of the time, place and manner of expression raises quite different issues. In some situations this form of government control is necessary in order to allocate scarce facilities for expression among different users, as in the case of licensing radio and television stations. Here the regulation operates entirely within the system of freedom of expression and provides the order necessary to ensure maximum use of the facilities for expression. In other situations government regulation of time, place and manner is essential to allocate physical facilities between different uses, as in the case of a decision whether to use New York's Fifth Avenue for a parade or for automobile travel. In both situations the function of the Government is one of traffic regulation and the applicable principle is one of fair accommodation between different users or uses. Rules to effectuate this purpose are entirely manageable and, if they are nondiscriminatory, either promote, or at least do not seriously impair, the system of freedom of expression.

A second major feature of the underlying legal structure consists of the rules for access to the means of communication. An abstract legal right to expression is of little practical use in the absence of the means for exercising that right. At the present time the monopoly or near-monopoly of the major media of communication by a small group representing similar economic, political and social interests has created a serious distortion in the system. This lack of access to the mass media is perhaps the major weakness in the existing system.

Full equality of access, for every individual and every group, is neither possible nor necessary. It is likely that the dominant forces in any society will always control a larger share of the means of communication. Indeed, complete equality could be achieved only at the price of complete governmental regulation. Fortunately the system can operate successfully as long as minority groups and viewpoints can make themselves heard to an appreciable extent. On the other hand, unlimited laissez faire is bound to produce distortion in a system as complex as ours has become. Clearly some action by the Government to restore a more equitable balance in the present system is essential.

To call on the Government for assistance in eliminating distortion in the system of freedom of expression presents something of a paradox. By its very nature the system must be largely laissez faire. Government interference with content is forbidden, and government regulation of traffic must be held to a minimum. The mere presence of elaborate government controls, whether heavy-handed or subtle, has a severely dampening effect. Nevertheless, the delicate task of using government machinery to promote more even access to the means of communication, while at the same time preventing the Government from controlling or influencing content, must be undertaken.

Existing legal rules governing access to the means of communication are sketchy in substance and largely undeveloped in theory. By and large the problem has been left to laissez-faire forces. Yet some legal principles have emerged. In 1937, in a case involving the efforts of Mayor Frank Hague to keep CIO organizers out of Jersey City, the Supreme Court ruled that streets, parks and similar public open spaces "have immemorially been held in trust for use of the public and, time out of mind, have been used for purposes of assembly, communicating thoughts between citizens, and discussing public questions." Schools and other public buildings are usually available for meetings and, whereas the courts have not yet held that the Government has an affirmative obligation to open them up for such purposes, once open to any group they must be furnished to all on a nondiscriminatory basis. The First Amendment was clearly intended to prohibit any restoration of the ancient English censorship laws, or any licensing or similar restriction of printing presses and other duplicating machinery.

The gravest distortions in the right of access to the means of expression have occurred in the field of radio and television communication, and it is here that most attention has been given to some redress of the balance. The progress made thus far, however, has been minimal. The Federal Communications Act requires a broadcasting station to give equal time to all candidates for political office, if it gives time to any, but this requirement has operated to shut off more communication than it has promoted. The act also provides that a station must "afford reasonable opportunity for discussion of conflicting views on issues of public importance," but the application of this "fairness doctrine" by the Federal Communications Commission has not produced any great amount of diversity.

In 1969, in the Red Lion Broadcasting case, the Supreme Court opened the constitutional door to more radical methods for achieving greater equality of access to radio and television facilities. Upholding the equal time and the fairness doctrines against the claim that they infringed the broadcaster's freedom of expression, the court laid down the basic principle: "It is the right of the viewers and listeners, not the right of the broadcasters, which is paramount." Under this doctrine our entire approach to the use of the broadcasting medium could be revolutionized. Instead of granting a monopoly to a single broadcaster for each open channel, the law could provide that the broadcaster must act as an agent of the public and grant access to all comers on equal terms. The ensuing problems of allocating time and paying the cost would be enormous, but there is no reason to suppose they could not be overcome.

The development of cable television furnishes the opportunity for a vast increase in the facilities available to individuals and groups seeking to use the broadcasting medium. Unless determined efforts are made to ensure this outcome, however, the chance could easily be lost. In any event some affirmative action by the community is clearly necessary if the present distortion in access to the most powerful medium of communication available is not to be perpetuated.

In the end achievement of more equal access to the means of communication will probably require a new constitutional approach. A primary cause of the present inequality is economic. Many individuals and groups simply do not have the financial resources to gain access to modern means of communication. The only answer to this would appear to be public financial support. Such a development would mean that the Government would in effect be subsidizing opposition to its own policies and actions. The beginnings of such a movement can already be discerned: in public support for legal-assistance offices, in the recently enacted Presidential Election Campaign Fund Act and in some public funding for free or independent schools. Solution of the access problem along these lines would require formula-tion of novel legal doctrines and procedures. It would pose in acute form the paradox of looking to the Government for aid while simultaneously warding off government control. Nevertheless, maintenance of an effective system of freedom of expression may ultimately depend on progress in this direction.

A third major area in the system of freedom of expression concerns the legal rules regarding access to information, often called "the right to know." This area embraces partly the right of a communicator to obtain information relevant to the matters about which he wants to communicate, but more important it includes the right of the general public to receive communications. In order for the system to perform its prescribed functions, every participant must have as complete access as possible to the raw materials out of which his impressions, beliefs, opinions and judgments are formed. Moreover, the right to know has a further significance in the operation of the system. Past experience suggests that the withholding of information from the public in periods of crisis creates anxieties and hostilities that are directed against the Government and in turn provoke repressive measures. Thus the entire system can be jeopardized by an excessive secrecy that impairs the right to know.

The First Amendment contains no express language that guarantees a right to know. Constitutional doctrine must therefore be derived by implication from the basic role of the First Amendment in supporting the system of free expression. The formulation of specific legal rules presents unusual difficulties. It is probably not possible to postulate an absolute right to know, available under all circumstances, and therefore some kind of balancing test must be used to define the boundaries of the right. Consequently it is not surprising to find that the legal foundations of the right to know have barely been laid.

The Supreme Court, in overturning a Federal statute that required persons receiving "communist political propaganda" from abroad to fill out a government form requesting its delivery, has expressly held that the First Amendment confers "the right to receive publications." In another case upholding the right of every person to read whatever literature he pleases, including pornography, in the privacy of his home, the court summed up the law by saying: "[It] is now well established that the Constitution protects the right to receive information and ideas." The Red Lion Broadcasting case also rests on the First Amendment right to listen and to hear. Yet these decisions have not advanced the constitutional doctrine very far. And in the Pentagon-papers case, where the central issue was the right of Congress and the public to see government documents of crucial concern in the making of foreign policy, the Supreme Court did not address itself to the problem.

Somewhat more progress has been made in this area through legislation. The Federal Freedom of Information Act and a variety of state acts provide statutory authority for the citizen to have greater access to government information and to observe government agencies at work. At the present time these laws are tentative and weak. Further development of this legislation, as well as implementation of the general constitutional right, are essential to a vigorous system of freedom of expression.

A fourth salient feature of the system of freedom of expression involves its application within private (nongovernmental) centers of power. The ordinary citizen is not only a member of the general community, where he must deal with the formal apparatus of the state. He is usually also a member of one or more specialized communities, such as a corporate enterprise, a labor union, a professional association or a farmers cooperative. Often he has little or no choice about joining such an organization. These unofficial bureaucracies may have a more direct impact on his daily life than the Government itself; they are in many respects private governments. To what extent should the system of freedom of expression apply in this critical area?

It will be noted immediately that additional complications arise when the system is introduced into the operation of private associations. A three-way set of rights and obligations—those of the individual, the association and the state—must be reconciled. The private association, which plays a vital role in a democratic society, is entitled to protection from undue interference from the state. Moreover, it has a relationship with its members that is somewhat different from the one that exists between the state and a citizen of the general community. For example, the right of a member to thwart the will of the association, or his right to criticize or antagonize fellow workers in the enterprise, presents special kinds of problems.

In addition there are differences in the basis of legal authority to protect freedom of expression within private centers of power. The First Amendment restricts only action of the government, Federal or state, not action of private individuals or groups. Hence the courts must look to sources of power in doctrines of private law, such as contract, tort or fiduciary relations, rather than to the Constitution. On the other hand, efforts by a court or by a legislature to guarantee free expression in a private association are subject to the limitation that they cannot infringe the First Amendment right of the association itself.

For all these reasons the establishment of legal rules to govern this area has been slow to materialize. Only the beginnings of a trend to enlarge the system of freedom of expression to the operations of private associations has appeared. Although the Supreme Court has not yet had occasion to rule on the issue, some lower courts have shown a willingness to protect members of a private association seeking to exercise a right of expression against retaliatory action by the association. In the Labor-Management Reporting and Disclosure Act of 1959, Congress has created substantial rights to freedom of expression for members of labor organizations. On another front the Supreme Court has held that, at least as to associations where membership is in effect compulsory, dues of objecting members cannot be used to finance political causes to which such members are opposed.

In the end, if a system of freedom of expression is to be truly meaningful, it will have to be adapted to the nongovernmental exercise of power as well as the governmental. Only associations that are purely private, in the sense that they have no substantial impact on public issues, can be allowed to remain outside the system.

The formulation of legal rules to govern the system of freedom of expression is not confined to the four areas I have described. There are a number of other important problems for which some solution must be found. It is necessary to reconcile the system of free expression with the system of personal privacy. Rules must be developed for determining the physical location at which the right to freedom of speech, assembly and petition may be exercised. The legal doctrine that prohibits the use of prior restraint in curbing expression, which was at issue in the Pentagon-papers case, plays an important role in supporting the system. The rights of persons who are employed by the Government, or who participate in our educational institutions as faculty, students or staff, raise special kinds of issues for the system. The Government itself has a right to expression, although this is subject to some limitations. Rules are needed to deal with particular areas, namely the rights of persons in "total institutions" (the military, prisons and mental hospitals), expression by business enterprises for purely commercial purposes, and the rights of children. Exploration of most of these areas has barely begun.

There remains the question of whether or not a system of freedom of expression is viable in a modern technological society. From one side it is argued that the system does not ensure sufficient stability—that it accentuates divisiveness, provides a cover for violence and leads to the collapse of law, order and authority. From another side it is contended that the system does not permit significant change—that it never really allows radical expression, is loaded in favor of the status quo and merely diverts public attention from the need for action. Others have urged that the system is based on outdated theories of pluralism and can never provide the moral or organizing force necessary to create a government capable of dealing with the problems of the modern world.

No one can deny the force of these various objections. Still, the question remains an open one. Certainly the system of freedom of expression cannot by itself provide stability in a world of change. Only if the economic, social and political arrangements of the society provide a sufficient degree of consensus can one expect the system to survive. Nor can it be said that the system by itself will lead to rapid change or change in the right direction. Not only has the reality never conformed to the model, but also the system itself is merely an instrument for effecting change, not a guaranty of success. Again, an energizing principle capable of solving the world's present dilemmas may have to come, at least in part, from other sources.

In short, the system of freedom of expression cannot alone save humanity. It may nonetheless help. It provides the most civilized method devised so far for solving social problems while protecting the integrity of the individual. The alternative can only be reliance on sheer force, and the loss of all freedoms.

THE AUTHORS
BIBLIOGRAPHIES
INDEX

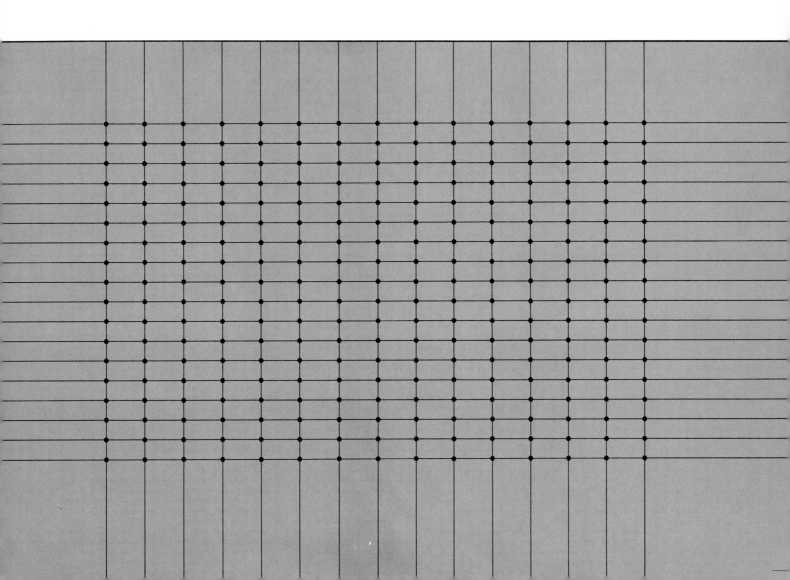

THE AUTHORS

JOHN R. PIERCE is professor of electrical engineering at the California Institute of Technology. He took up his work there a year ago after 35 years with the Bell Telephone Laboratories, where from 1965 to 1971 he was executive director for research in the communications sciences division and was responsible for research in radio, guided waves, electronics, acoustics, vision, mathematics, statistics, econometrics and behavioral science. His work on the traveling-wave tube led to its successful application in communication satellites; the work of Bell Laboratories on the Echo and Telstar satellites was based on his original suggestions. Pierce obtained his bachelor's, master's and doctor's degrees at Cal Tech in 1933, 1934 and 1936 respectively. He is a member of both the National Academy of Sciences and the National Academy of Engineering.

GUNTHER S. STENT is professor of molecular biology and of bacteriology at the University of California at Berkeley. Born in Germany, he came to the U.S. in 1940 and was graduated in 1945 from the University of Illinois, where he obtained his Ph.D. in 1948. He writes: "I have continued to work in the very same room to which I was assigned by the late Wendell Stanley on the opening of his Berkeley Virus Laboratory in 1952, except for sabbatical leaves in 1960 and 1969. My interest in molecular genetics began to wane with the breaking of the genetic code in 1961— a development that seemed sure to turn the field into an academic discipline as staid as the physical chemistry from which I had managed to escape in the 1940's. Like many of my friends, I then turned my attention to neurobiology, the last frontier (and, we hoped, a limitless one) of biology—not, however, without first composing a farewell message to my former trade in the form of the story-book *Molecular Genetics*. I am now working on the nervous system of the medicinal leech. For reasons that have never been explained, I was appointed Professor of Arts and Sciences at Berkeley during the 1967–1968 academic year. I used this appointment to write a notorious philosophical tract, *The Coming of the Golden Age*, in which I tried to show that the arts and sciences are now reaching their end. This turned out to be a self-fulfilling prophecy, in that the arts and sciences professorship survived my tenure by just one year and is now defunct."

EDWARD O. WILSON is professor of zoology at Harvard University. He was graduated from the University of Alabama in 1949, obtaining his master's degree there in 1950 and his Ph.D. from Harvard in 1955. "My original schizoid approach to biology," he writes, "in which I kept programs going in the seemingly unrelated fields of population biology and behavior, has now been healed through the happy discovery, by several researchers independently, that much of social behavior can be more deeply explained by recourse to theoretical population biology. My book *The Insect Societies* was published by Harvard University Press last year; in 1971 I also published *A Primer of Population Biology*, a short self-teaching textbook, with my colleague William H. Bossert. Earlier (1967) I coauthored *The Theory of Island Biogeography* with Robert H. MacArthur. My research continues to center on ants, with emphasis on their biogeography and social behavior."

ROMAN JAKOBSON is Samuel Hazzard Cross Professor Emeritus of Slavic Languages and Literatures and of General Linguistics at Harvard University and Institute Professor at the Massachusetts Institute of Technology. Born in Moscow, he received his master's degree from the University of Moscow in 1918 and his Ph.D. from the University of Prague in 1930. He came to the U.S. in 1941 and joined the Harvard faculty in 1949. Jakobson is a member of many linguistic societies and in 1956 was president of the Linguistic Society of America. Among the books of which he is author or coauthor is *Fundamentals of Language*.

E. H. GOMBRICH is professor of the history of the classical tradition at the University of London and director of the Warburg Institute there. He started work at the institute as a research assistant in 1936 after completing his education in Vienna (his birthplace) at the University of Vienna. He has also held appointments as professor of the history of art at University College London, professor of fine art at the universities of Oxford and Cambridge and visiting professor of fine art at Harvard University. His books include *The Story of Art*, *Art and Illusion*, *Norm and Form* and *In Search of Cultural History*. He was made a Knight Bachelor by Queen Elizabeth in July, 1972.

HENRI BUSIGNIES is senior vice-president and chief scientist of the International Telephone and Telegraph Corporation, a company with which he has been associated since 1928. He began as an engineer in the Paris laboratories two years after receiving his degree in electrical engineering at the University of Paris. Busignies invented the first automatic direction finder for aircraft, the moving-target-indicator radar employed at airports for traffic control and many other devices; he holds more than 140 patents in the fields of air navigation, radar and communication. He is a member of the National Academy of Engineering.

HIROSHI INOSE is professor of electronic engineering in the faculty of engineering of the University of Tokyo, where he obtained his *kogakushi* (bachelor of engineering) degree in 1948 and his *kogakuhakushi* (doctor of engineering) degree in 1955. He started work at the university's Institute of Industrial Science in 1953, spent a year and a half as an engineer with the Tokyo Shibaura Electric Company and then returned to the university, where he has remained except for interludes at the University of Pennsylvania and the University of Michigan.

ERNEST R. KRETZMER is with the Bell Telephone Laboratories, where he serves as director of the laboratory on data-communication technology and its applications. He received his bachelor's degree in electrical engineering at Worcester Polytechnic Institute in 1945 and his master's and doctor's degrees at the Massachusetts Institute of Technology in 1946 and 1949 respectively. He writes: "From M.I.T. went directly to Bell: research and development on various topics ranging from picture-signal encoding to data communication. Outside interests include music,

particularly choral, and education; I have served on the local school board for half a dozen years. Love nature, travel and the outdoors."

PETER C. GOLDMARK is president and director of research of Goldmark Communications Corporations, a subsidiary of Warner Communications, Inc. For 35 years until 1972 he was with the Columbia Broadcasting System, retiring as head of CBS Laboratories. Goldmark, who holds some 160 patents in sight and sound technology, is the inventor of the first practical color-television system and the long-playing record. Born in Budapest, he obtained his bachelor's degree and his Ph.D. at the Vienna Technical University between 1925 and 1931. His firm has a contract with the U.S. Department of Housing and Urban Development to study what he calls the "new rural society." The purpose of the study is to find ways of using communication technology to make rural areas more livable. Goldmark is an accomplished pianist and cellist.

GEORGE GERBNER is professor of communications at the Annenberg School of Communications of the University of Pennsylvania and dean of the school. He grew up in Hungary and was a student at the University of Budapest for a year before coming to the U.S. in 1939. Continuing his education, he obtained his bachelor's

degree at the University of California at Berkeley in 1943 and his Ph.D. from the University of Southern California in 1955. During World War II he was with the Office of Strategic Services, performing missions in North Africa, Italy, Yugoslavia and Austria. "Actually," he writes, "I landed in Yugoslavia by mistake; the plane dropped me some 50 miles short of the target area. Anyway, in May, 1946, my O.S.S. buddy and I rounded up the Hungarian pro-Nazi prime minister, his cabinet and general staff—some 60 people—who has fled west to escape the Russians." In his spare time Gerbner enjoys skiing, sailing and tennis.

THOMAS I. EMERSON is Lines Professor of Law at the Yale Law School, where he has been a member of the faculty since 1946. He was graduated from Yale College in 1928 and from the Yale Law School in 1931, returning to the university after practicing law in New York and serving as counsel for a number of Federal agencies. From 1937 to 1940 he was associate general counsel of the National Labor Relations Board. In 1940 he became special assistant to the attorney-general. During World War II he was deputy administrator for enforcement of the Office of Price Administration and general counsel of the Office of Economic Stabilization and the Office of War Mobilization and Reconversion.

BIBLIOGRAPHIES

Readers interested in further reading on the subjects covered by articles in this issue may find the lists below helpful.

COMMUNICATION

CYBERNETICS OR CONTROL AND COMMUNICATION IN THE ANIMAL AND THE MACHINE. Norbert Wiener. The Technology Press of Massachusetts Institute of Technology and John Wiley & Sons, Inc., 1948.

SYNTACTIC STRUCTURES. Noam Chomsky. Mouton & Co., 1957.

THE MATHEMATICAL THEORY OF COMMUNICATION. Claude E. Shannon and Warren Weaver. The University of Illinois Press, 1959.

SYMBOLS, SIGNALS AND NOISE: THE NATURE AND PROCESS OF COMMUNICATION. J. R. Pierce. Harper & Brothers, 1961.

SCIENCE, ART AND COMMUNICATION. J. R. Pierce. Clarkson N. Potter, Inc., 1968.

CELLULAR COMMUNICATION

STRUCTURALISM. Jean Piaget. Basic Books, Inc., 1970.

PAPERS IN CELLULAR NEUROPHYSIOLOGY. Edited by I. Cooke and M. Lipkin, Jr. Holt, Rinehart and Winston, 1972.

ANIMAL COMMUNICATION

MECHANISMS OF ANIMAL BEHAVIOR. P. R. Marler and W. J. Hamilton III. John Wiley & Sons, Inc., 1966.

ANIMAL COMMUNICATION: TECHNIQUES OF STUDY AND RESULTS OF RESEARCH. Edited by T. A. Sebeok. Indiana University Press, 1968.

SEX PHEROMONE SPECIFICITY: TAXONOMIC AND EVOLUTIONARY ASPECTS IN LEPIDOPTERA. Wendell L. Roelofs and Andre Comeau in *Science*, Vol. 165, No. 3891, pages 398–400; July 25, 1969.

THE INSECT SOCIETIES. Edward O. Wilson. The Belknap Press of Harvard University Press, 1971.

LANGUAGE IN CHIMPANZEE? David Premack in *Science*, Vol. 172, No. 3985, pages 808–822; May 21, 1971.

NON-VERBAL COMMUNICATION. Edited by R. A. Hinde. Cambridge University Press, 1972.

VERBAL COMMUNICATION

SELECTED WRITINGS OF EDWARD SAPIR IN LANGUAGE, CULTURE, AND PERSONALITY. Edited by David G. Mandelbaum. University of California Press, 1949.

LINGUISTICS AND POETICS. Roman Jakobson in *Style in Language*, edited by Thomas A. Sebeok. The Technology Press of Massachusetts Institute of Technology and John Wiley & Sons, Inc., 1960.

FORMAL PROPERTIES OF GRAMMARS. N. Chomsky in *Handbook of Mathematical Psychology*, edited by R. D. Luce, R. R. Bush and E. Galanter. John Wiley & Sons, Inc., 1963.

PROBLEMS IN GENERAL LINGUISTICS. Émile Benveniste, translated by Mary Elizabeth Meek. University of Miami Press, 1971.

SELECTED WRITINGS, VOL. I: PHONOLOGICAL STUDIES; VOL. II: WORD AND LANGUAGE. Roman Jakobson. Mouton & Co., 1971.

THE VISUAL IMAGE

PRINTS AND VISUAL COMMUNICATION. William M. Ivins, Jr. Harvard University Press, 1953.

ART AND ILLUSION: A STUDY IN THE PSYCHOLOGY OF PICTORIAL REPRESENTATION. Ernst H. Gombrich. Princeton University Press, 1956.

RELIGIOUS ART: FROM THE TWELFTH TO THE EIGHTEENTH CENTURY. Émile Mâle. Farrar, Straus & Giroux, Inc., 1958.

STUDIES IN ICONOLOGY. Erwin Panofsky. Harper & Row, Publishers, 1962.

SYMBOLIC IMAGES. Ernst H. Gombrich. Phaidon Press, 1971.

COMMUNICATION CHANNELS

ON HUMAN COMMUNICATION: A REVIEW, A SURVEY, AND A CRITICISM. Colin Cherry. The Technology Press of Massachusetts Institute of Technology and John Wiley & Sons, Inc., 1957.

SYMBOLS, SIGNALS AND NOISE: THE NATURE AND PROCESS OF COMMUNICATION. J. R. Pierce. Harper & Brothers, 1961.

REFERENCE DATA FOR RADIO ENGINEERS. Edited by Harold P. Westman. Howard W. Sams & Company, Inc., International Telephone and Telegraph Corporation, 1968.

THE APPLICATION OF SOCIAL AND ECONOMIC VALUES TO SPECTRUM MANAGEMENT. Report by the Committee on Telecommunications, National Academy of Engineering, June, 1970.

TRENDS AND FUTURE OF TELECOMMUNICATIONS. Henri Busignies in *Signal*, Vol. 26, No. 3, pages 16–19; November, 1971.

COMMUNICATION NETWORKS

ELECTRONS, WAVES AND MESSAGES. John R. Pierce. Hanover House, 1956.

No. 1 ELECTRONIC SWITCHING SYSTEM. *The Bell System Technical Journal*, Vol. 43, No. 5, Parts 1 and 2; September, 1964.

COMMUNICATION SYSTEM ENGINEERING HANDBOOK. Edited by Donald H. Hamsher. McGraw-Hill Book Company, 1967.

OUTLOOK TO PCM SWITCHING SYSTEMS AND THEIR CALCULATION BY TRAFFIC THEORY. H. Inose and T. Saito in *Proceedings of the 6th International Teletraffic Congress*, 1970.

COMMUNICATION TERMINALS

SYMBOLS, SIGNALS AND NOISE: THE NATURE AND PROCESS OF COMMUNICATION. J. R. Pierce. Harper & Brothers, 1961.

THE GROUND STATION TRANSMITTER AND RECEIVER. J. Schill and A. F. Perks in *Bell Laboratories Record*, Vol. 41, No. 4, pages 135–141; April, 1963.

THE ELUSIVE PROCESS OF SPEECH. P. B. Denes in *Bell Laboratories Record*, Vol. 44, No. 8, pages 254–259; September, 1966.

PRINCIPLES OF DATA COMMUNICATION. R. W. Lucky, J. Salz and E. J. Weldon, Jr. McGraw-Hill Book Company, 1968.

TELECOMMUNICATIONS AND THE COMPUTER. James Martin. Prentice-Hall, Inc., 1969.

A READING EYE FOR THE BLIND. J. Stephen Brugler and James A. Baer in *Optical Spectra*, Vol. 5, Issue 2, pages 18–22; February, 1971.

DIGITAL COMMUNICATIONS—A TUTORIAL. R. G. McKay in *Bell Laboratories Record*, Vol. 49, No. 9, pages 278–284; October, 1971.

COMMUNICATION AND THE COMMUNITY

TELEDIAGNOSIS: A NEW COMMUNITY HEALTH RESOURCE. Kenneth T. Bird in *Educational and Instructional Broadcasting*, February, 1969.

ADVANCES IN COMPUTER-BASED EDUCATION. D. Alpert and D. L. Bitzer in *Science*, Vol. 167, No. 3925, pages 1582–1590; March 20, 1970.

COMMUNICATIONS TECHNOLOGY FOR URBAN IMPROVEMENT. Report to the Department of Housing and Urban Development by the Committee on Telecommunications, National Academy of Engineering, June, 1971.

COMMUNICATION AND SOCIAL ENVIRONMENT

MASS COMMUNICATION: A SOCIOLOGICAL PERSPECTIVE. Charles R. Wright. Random House, 1959.

PEOPLE, SOCIETY, AND MASS COMMUNICATIONS. Edited by Lewis Anthony Dexter and David Manning White. The Free Press of Glencoe, 1964.

THEORIES OF MASS COMMUNICATION. Melvin L. De Fleur. David McKay Company, Inc., 1966.

CULTURAL INDICATORS: THE CASE OF VIOLENCE IN TELEVISION DRAMA. George Gerbner in *The Annals of the American Academy of Political and Social Science*, Vol. 388, pages 69–81; March, 1970.

THE PROCESS AND EFFECTS OF MASS COMMUNICATION. Edited by Wilbur Schramm and Donald F. Roberts. University of Illinois Press, 1971.

COMMUNICATION AND FREEDOM OF EXPRESSION

FREE SPEECH IN THE UNITED STATES. Zechariah Chafee, Jr. Harvard University Press, 1941.

FREEDOM OF SPEECH: THE SUPREME COURT AND JUDICIAL REVIEW. Martin Shapiro. Prentice-Hall, Inc., 1966.

THE SYSTEM OF FREEDOM OF EXPRESSION. Thomas I. Emerson. Random House, 1970.

A THEORY OF FREEDOM OF EXPRESSION. Thomas Scanlon in *Philosophy & Public Affairs*, Vol. 1, No. 2, pages 204–226; Winter, 1972.

INDEX